DOING BUSINESS WITH CRIMINALS

Legitimate companies occasionally find themselves doing business with criminals, wittingly or unwittingly. Past decades have witnessed a dramatic expansion in the array of criminal law and regulatory rules that govern such entanglements. These rules raise fundamental questions about commerce and society, such as: When can someone be excluded from day-to-day commercial interactions? Where is the boundary between legitimate surveillance of suspicious transactions and financial privacy? And, ultimately, what is the point of financial crime rules: Are they meant to exclude suspected criminals from the legitimate economy or help to gather intelligence on them?

This book is the first comprehensive account of how these dilemmas shape financial crime rules. Based on a sweeping overview of international experience, it tells a story that will be of interest to a wide audience ranging from the seasoned financial crime expert to the general reader.

Anton Moiseienko is a senior lecturer in law at the Australian National University. He has advised governments and parliaments on financial crime in Australia, Europe and North America. His previous book is *Corruption and Targeted Sanctions* (2019). He is also an associate fellow at the Royal United Services Institute, UK.

Doing Business with Criminals

BETWEEN EXCLUSION AND SURVEILLANCE

ANTON MOISEIENKO
Australian National University

CAMBRIDGE
UNIVERSITY PRESS

CAMBRIDGE
UNIVERSITY PRESS

Shaftesbury Road, Cambridge CB2 8EA, United Kingdom

One Liberty Plaza, 20th Floor, New York, NY 10006, USA

477 Williamstown Road, Port Melbourne, VIC 3207, Australia

314–321, 3rd Floor, Plot 3, Splendor Forum, Jasola District Centre, New Delhi – 110025, India

103 Penang Road, #05–06/07, Visioncrest Commercial, Singapore 238467

Cambridge University Press is part of Cambridge University Press & Assessment, a department of the University of Cambridge.

We share the University's mission to contribute to society through the pursuit of education, learning and research at the highest international levels of excellence.

www.cambridge.org
Information on this title: www.cambridge.org/9781009609876

DOI: 10.1017/9781009609845

When citing this work, please include a reference to the DOI 10.1017/9781009609845

First published 2025

A catalogue record for this publication is available from the British Library

A Cataloging-in-Publication data record for this book is available from the Library of Congress

ISBN 978-1-009-60987-6 Hardback
ISBN 978-1-009-60982-1 Paperback

Contents

Figures

Tables

Acknowledgements

I am grateful to my colleagues at the Australian National University (ANU) for the convivial and truly collegial environment within which this book was written. Special thanks are due to Will Bateman for his encouragement of this project, as well as to Tony Connolly and James Stellios for their unwavering support of my work, including through the College of Law's travel grant that made interviews in Europe possible.

Those whom I have interviewed for this book have been unfailingly generous with their time and insight. John Byrne and Valsamis Mitsilegas commented on parts of an earlier draft. I would like to thank Sharon McCann from Cambridge University Press for giving this book her vote of confidence and thank her, Claire Sissen, Ramya Selvaraj and Richard Walshe for their diligence in the production of the book. I am also grateful to Jake Fitzgerald for his superb research assistance.

During the preparation of the manuscript, I have benefitted from the International Fellowship at the University of Texas at Austin awarded by ANU's Australian Studies Institute. At Austin, my warm thanks go to Rhonda Evans of the Edward A. Clark Center for Australia and New Zealand Studies and Adam Klein of the Robert S. Strauss Center for International Security and Law for their hospitality, insight and the useful introductions made. Within the Australian Studies Institute, Fiona Preston was invaluable in arranging the fellowship. Henry Ergas and Gillian Bird showed tremendous hospitality during my fieldwork in Paris. In Basel, Gretta Fenner, who has tragically passed away since, was instrumental in arranging several illuminating interviews. Thomas Biersteker and Erica Moret helped me in Geneva. I am also grateful to Saskia Hufnagel and Colin King for their friendship and encouragement, which I have enjoyed in both London and Australia.

Many of the topics this book covers relate to the interests I developed during the four years that I spent at the Centre for Finance and Security at the Royal United Services Institute (RUSI), and I would like to thank the entire RUSI team, and Tom Keatinge in particular, for making that time as enjoyable and productive as it was. Finally, this book would not have been possible without the dedication and support of my parents, Olena and Sergiy, to whom goes my greatest gratitude.

Abbreviations

ABA	American Bar Association
ACAMS	Association of Certified Anti-Money Laundering Specialists
ACLU	American Civil Liberties Unition
AML	Anti-money laundering
AMLA	Anti-Money Laundering and Countering the Financing of Terrorism Authority (EU)
APG	Asia/Pacific Group on Money Laundering
AUSTRAC	Australian Financial Reports and Analysis Centre
BCLC	British Columbia Lottery Corporation (Canada)
CBDC	Central bank digital currency
CDD	Customer due diligence
CJEU	Court of Justice of the European Union
CPF	Counter-proliferation financing
CRI	Counter Ransomware Initiative
CTF	Counterterrorist financing
CTR	Cash transaction report
DeFi	Decentralised finance
DNFBP	Designated non-financial business or profession
EAG	Eurasian Group on Combating Money Laundering and Terrorist Financing
ECHR	European Convention on Human Rights
ECtHR	European Court of Human Rights
ESAAMLG	Eastern and Southern Africa Anti-Money Laundering Group
FATF	Financial Action Task Force
FBAR	Report of Foreign Bank and Financial Accounts
FCA	Financial Conduct Authority (UK)
FCPA	Foreign Corrupt Practices Act (US)
FinCEN	Financial Crimes Enforcement Network (US)
FIU	Financial Intelligence Unit
FSRB	FATF-style regional body

GTO	Geographic targeting order
ICJ	International Court of Justice
ICIJ	International Consortium of Investigative Journalists
ICRG	International Co-operation Review Group
IEEPA	International Emergency Economic Powers Act 1977 (US)
IFTI	International funds transfer instruction
IMF	International Monetary Fund
IRA	Irish Republican Army
IRS	Internal Revenue Service (US)
ISEWG	Intelligence Sharing Expert Working Group
ISIS	Islamic State of Iran and Syria
JCPOA	Joint Comprehensive Plan of Action
JMLIT	Joint Money Laundering Intelligence Taskforce (UK)
MER	Mutual evaluation report
MLA	Mutual legal assistance
MLD	Money Laundering Directive
NCA	National Crime Agency (UK)
OCC	Office of the Comptroller of the Currency
OECD	Organisation for Economic Cooperation and Development
OFAC	Office of Foreign Assets Control (US)
OFSI	Office of Financial Sanctions Implementation (UK)
PEP	Politically exposed person
RICO	Racketeer Influenced and Corrupt Organizations Act 1970 (US)
RUSI	Royal United Services Institute
SAMLA	Sanctions and Anti-Money Laundering Act 2018 (UK)
SAR	Suspicious activity report
SLAPP	Strategic lawsuit against public participation
SMR	Suspicious matter report
STR	Suspicious transaction report
TMNL	Transactie Monitoring Nederland
UKFIU	UK Financial Intelligence Unit
UNCAC	UN Convention Against Corruption
UNTOC	UN Convention against Transnational Organized Crime
UTR	Unusual transaction report
VASP	Virtual asset service provider

1

Business with Criminals

1.1 PRELUDE

The only time I ever bought a painting was in a town called Cooma in New South Wales, Australia, less than two hours' drive from the Australian National University in Canberra. This happened by accident as I had not planned on purchasing any artwork, let alone one by a convicted murderer.

I was visiting one of the town's attractions, a photography gallery tucked away in a former Methodist church. Its proprietor, Charles Davis, specialises in taking photos of Australian animals in the Snowy Mountains that surround Cooma. Kangaroos peering out from behind snow-covered branches of a tree; echidnas trudging on through the vast whiteness of improbably cold Australian winters; parrots standing out against the leaden sky in bursts of colour – all available for sale as prints, mugs and fridge magnets. All priced to reflect their creator's mastery and, save for one print of a wombat in the snow, judged by me to be too expensive a luxury.

A couple of blocks away is a prison, formally known as Cooma Correctional Centre. It was built in the 1950s specifically to house gay men convicted of sodomy under the law repealed in 1984. Next to it is a museum of New South Wales's prison system, another of Cooma's landmarks. The museum has the ambience of a cheap horror production from the 1970s, at once morbid and oddly upbeat. Its collection ranges from gallows used to execute upwards of fifty people, some of them for stealing bread, to the broken prison bars from the Long Bay prison in Sydney through which robber Russell 'Mad Dog' Cox escaped to freedom, all the way to trivia of prison life, such as a poster reading: 'Today's prison officer is a SUPERMAN with a sense of humour'.

Like any museum, this one features a shop. A sign announces that all products are made by inmates from a minimum-security prison next door, and they receive 75 per cent of the revenue. It was a Sunday, and Andrew, the museum manager, was manning the shop himself. We struck up a conversation, and as there was hardly anyone else in the building, Andrew took me on an hour-long tour of the museum collection. Formerly a prison official in the UK, he had left the prison system for a more tranquil museum career and began scouring Australian prisons for discarded clothes, tools, contraband items and other accoutrements of the life behind bars.

As the tour drew to a close, I felt it would be stingy to leave without buying anything at all. There was, however, nothing particularly to my liking in the assortment of rugby-themed mugs, bottle holders and wooden figurines. At last, I settled on a funky-looking abstract painting coming together with a small wooden easel for a reasonable price of $20. Like parrots in the photo gallery I had just visited, the painting was a burst of bright colours of a canvas.

'How interesting you should choose that one,' said Andrew. 'This was made by a Colombian drug mule'.

This removed the last traces of hesitation in my mind. Cravenly, I had felt queasy about buying a painting in a prison. The prospect of unknowingly purchasing the work of some twisted, sadistic mind did not appeal to me. By contrast, a Colombian drug mule sounded respectable. And, as I was starting to write a book provisionally entitled *Doing Business with Criminals*, one could not think of better decoration for my hitherto artless office.

The following day, I proudly demonstrated my acquisition to a colleague in the office. She was distinctly unimpressed by my prison tourism and, even more so, by the indefatigable museum manager Andrew's role in enabling it. Still, the colleague was intrigued by the painting and, as she turned it around, she noticed the author's signature on the back of the canvas. She then put it into Google – and, to my surprise, several articles lit up.

As it turned out, my new friend Andrew had been economical with the truth. The artist did hail from Latin America, albeit not from Colombia, and was no stranger to drugs. His real crime, though, was attempting to murder his wife by stabbing her so violently that the knife handle broke. She survived; he went to prison for several years; and then, on his release, attacked another woman in a similarly gruesome fashion. By way of justification he said, simply, that Satan had told him to do so.

In my usual spirit of generosity, I offered the painting as a gift to the colleague who, through her Google research skills, discovered this story. She declined. So did the professor of public law next door. Then, at a work meeting that same day, at last I found someone possessed of a more scientific mindset than the rest of us; a quivering, superstitious lot. 'It's just a panting', the braver colleague said as she graciously accepted it. 'It looks nice, and it's got a history. He might have been reformed by now anyway'. The painting is still at ANU's Law School and, once I got over Andrew's economy with the truth in selling me the painting – which, after all, is not unheard of in the murky world of art dealing – I mustered the magnanimity to leave him a glowing review on TripAdvisor.

1.2 INTRODUCTION

Whatever one thinks of the relationship between the artwork and its creator, this story offers a useful, if self-indulgent, introduction to the topic of doing business with criminals. In this instance, I did not make any direct payment to an inmate, although he ought to have received $15 out of the $20 I spent. But even if I had engaged with him directly, the law would in no way encroach on my doing so. Subject to prison rules that apply to current inmates, whether someone is a convicted criminal has no bearing on their ability to do business, buy or sell property or pay taxes.[1] Our criminal justice system pursues the dual goals of rehabilitation and deterrence, alongside multiple other similar if ill-defined objectives,[2] not indefinite exclusion from social interactions.

But multiple areas of the law do regulate transacting with criminals, including those who have never been found guilty. On the one hand, I can lawfully buy a house from a drug dealer, convicted or not. On the other hand, if I knew that the house represents the proceeds of drug trade, or were reckless or even negligent as to that being so, I would be a committing a money laundering offence under Australian federal law.[3] In theory, I could know that someone is a drug trafficker yet reason that his or her house has been lawfully acquired from funds wholly unconnected to the drug trade. That would be a fine line, and therefore not buying houses from drug traffickers is a good rule of thumb.

Most ordinary citizens are unlikely ever to have to think about this issue. Some businesses, especially financial institutions, have to do so all the time. Anti-money laundering (AML) regulation obliges them to ensure they have programmes in place to make sure they are not used to invest, move or spend proceeds of crime – an activity known as money laundering. And, of course, they are precisely the place one would go to in order to invest, move or spend such proceeds. Banks and other regulated businesses are therefore locked into a never-ending time- and resource-intensive effort to safeguard their services from criminals, convicted or not, known or unknown. Furthermore, unlike private individuals, they are subject to the

1 However, if a person who has committed an offence, whether or not convicted of it, has written a book or made a TV show about it, his or her income from it ('literary proceeds') can be liable to confiscation under federal and some state laws in Australia: Section 152 of the Proceeds of Crime Act 2002 (Cth). See also Jordan English, Sam Hickey and Simon Bronitt, *Federal Proceeds of Crime Law* (Thomson Reuters, 2023) 337–363.

2 For example, the purposes of federal sentencing in Australia under Section 3A of the Crimes (Sentencing Procedure) Act 1999 (Cth) include punishment, deterrence, protection of the community, rehabilitation, accountability, denunciation and recognition of harm.

3 See Division 14 in the Criminal Code (Cth), which sets out a range of money laundering offences that differ primarily by the amount involved and the defendant's state of mind (e.g. knowledge, recklessness or negligence as to the property being the proceeds of crime). Money laundering offences also exist at the state and territory levels in Australia.

obligation to make suspicious activity reports (SARs), also known as suspicious transaction reports (STRs) in some jurisdictions or suspicious matter reports (SMRs) in Australia.

Related to, but distinct from, AML is counterterrorist financing (CTF) regulation. As the term suggests, terrorist financing involves the provision of funds or other resources in support of terrorist activities. The paradigmatic example of terrorist financing is Osama bin Laden's financing of the 9/11 attacks, primarily done through tapping into Al Qaeda's resources and not, as the popular view holds, relying on family wealth.[4] Terrorist financing need not only involve overseas financiers knowingly funding acts of terror. Lasting controversy has surrounded the potential involvement in terrorist financing of perfectly legitimate actors acting under pressure or in pursuit of humanitarian aims, such as organisations or families paying ransom for hostages captured by terrorist groups; charities seeking to deliver life-saving aid to people within terrorist-held territories; or companies yielding to terrorist demands of a 'tax' to preserve their property. In those situations, the policy imperative of denying terrorists access to the resources they need clashes against the realities of coercion. In the meantime, the legal and reputational imperative of excluding terrorists from financial services may undermine the efforts to generate financial intelligence that can be useful in investigating terrorist activities.

In the context of AML/CTF measures, it is largely up to regulated businesses to ascertain whether their customer or counterparty might be laundering organised crime money or funding terrorism. Targeted financial sanctions, which present another key area of financial crime regulation, are different. Such sanctions involve a prohibition against anyone within the respective state's jurisdiction transacting with designated persons, individuals or companies, as well as the freezing of their assets. By using sanctions, governments manually control who should be treated as a bad actor to be isolated from the legitimate economy. By contrast with the AML/CTF regime,[5] which is characterised by a duality of purpose in terms of excluding known criminals from the economy and surveilling suspected criminals, sanctions are geared towards exclusion and the freezing of assets. This presents a similar but distinct range of challenges compared to AML/CTF.

Sanctions are perhaps best known as a means of addressing matters of high politics or international security, such as Iran's or North Korea's nuclear proliferation or Russia's invasion of Ukraine. However, they are also increasingly used to address money laundering, terrorist financing and other types of crime by designating persons suspected of involvement in it. This means that sanctions are both an area of

4 9/11 Commission, *Final Report of the National Commission on Terrorist Attacks upon the United States*, July 2004, 122.

5 'Regime' is understood here as a composite term comprising laws, institutions and practices. The word 'framework' is used in this book to denote the legal framework or, in other words, the corpus of AML rules, whether criminal, administrative or civil.

financial crime regulation in their own right and part and parcel of the response to other, more familiar financial crime threats.

The expansion of all these financial crime measures, as well as their reach into our commercial and personal lives, belies their novelty. The AML reporting regime started taking shape in the 1970s, and the laws criminalising money laundering only emerged in the 1980s. Until then, dealing with the proceeds of crime was not necessarily illegal and, notoriously, certain states promoted bank secrecy as their unique selling point without a concerted international pushback. As Peter Alldridge, a professor of criminal law at Queen Mary University of London, once put it in a lecture: 'Before the adoption of AML/CTF laws, you could turn up at a bank with a suitcase full of cash and say your name was Mickey Mouse. And the bank teller would reply, "Thank you for your custom, Mr Mouse."'

Likewise, as late as in the 1990s, there was no global consensus around the criminalisation of terrorist financing. This is not to suggest that bin Laden-style financing was considered legal, but simply that it would have been dealt with through general criminal law rules on complicity. However, those rules could place significant constraints on governments' ability to bring prosecutions against financiers-cum-accomplices. The outright criminalisation of terrorist financing dispenses with some of those technical obstacles, as well as creating the preconditions for establishing a broader CTF regime, such as extended record-keeping requirements for international wire transfers under the so-called travel rule.

Nowadays, if a transaction is suspicious, regulated businesses such as banks are obliged to report it to law enforcement authorities, via an agency known as a financial intelligence unit (FIU). In itself, this is a relatively benign affair. Hundreds of thousands of SARs are generated every year in major financial hubs, and few of them lead to the commencement of investigations. But the real risk for a customer is that, from a bank's perspective, the ongoing effort required to deal with suspicious customers is not worth the candle, with the result that it is cheaper to drop (or 'exit') the client relationship than keep worrying about record-keeping and reporting requirements. If this approach is taken to a whole swathe of customers, such as nationals of a particular high-risk country,[6] this can result in wholesale financial exclusion, often described as 'derisking'. Unsurprisingly, in some sectors of the economy, there is a particular disquiet about both the reporting obligations and the potential denial of access to services, especially in the legal profession.

Crucially, for any regulated business, the filing of a SAR does not eliminate the risk of liability for money laundering if it has the requisite *mens rea*, such as knowledge of the criminal origin of funds. Since the filing of a SAR indicates at least a suspicion of criminality, the safest course of action is to drop a customer once a SAR has been submitted. That sacrifices a potentially valuable source of further financial

[6] Although one could draw a distinction between 'high-risk' and 'higher-risk' countries, customers and so on, this book uses the term 'high-risk' for the sake of simplicity.

intelligence and is a prime example of the tension between exclusion and surveillance: one can either shut the criminals out of the financial system or use banks as the government's eyes and ears to spy on criminals, but not both at the same time. This also means that regulated businesses make decisions on a daily basis that sit uneasily with a broad, civic-minded conception of the presumption of innocence according to which state and private institutions should treat citizens as presumptively innocent in routine personal and commercial interactions.

It is not only financial crime regulation alone that gives rise to such encroachments on the presumption of innocence. Reputational pressure is an increasingly powerful incentive for businesses to self-police their choice of partners and customers. While financial surveillance, such as through the filing of SARs, remains a product of regulation, the exclusion of criminal actors from the legitimate economy is no longer solely government-driven. There has by now arguably emerged a moral and political principle that illicit actors should not benefit from interactions with the legitimate economy. Understanding the appeal of this principle, as well as the challenges it engenders, is vital to avoiding a caricatured portrayal of the existing financial crime regime as wholly misguided and based on knee-jerk reactions by politicians. It also explains the steady encroachment of such regulation upon other, previously sacrosanct principles: bank secrecy in the past and legal professional privilege and client confidentiality today.

1.2.1 *This Book's Project*

The principal aim of this book is to contribute to our current collective understanding of the legal and policy choices that need to be made as governments and parliaments attempt to regulate criminals' interactions with the legitimate economy. In essence, this is an exercise in ordering and clarifying our thinking about the objectives, incentives and challenges that manifest themselves across the sprawling, increasingly complicated domain of financial crime regulation.

This book's central argument is threefold.

First, there is a fundamental tension at the core of financial crime regulation. This is because financial crime regulation typically pursues two distinct objectives. The first of those is exclusion, or ensuring that known or suspected criminals do not benefit from financial interactions with the legitimate economy. The second is surveillance, or the gathering of financial intelligence about criminal activities to facilitate their investigation and prosecution. While those objectives are compatible up to a certain point, they become mutually exclusive if pursued aggressively. Our current regulatory frameworks do not commit wholeheartedly to either of these objectives: instead, they contain an admixture of elements that pull private-sector actors in two different directions.

However, there are also significant differences in how this dilemma manifests itself across various domains of financial crime regulation. For example, compared to AML regulation, where the tension is at its strongest, sanctions are almost entirely exclusion-oriented but present a distinct set of challenges associated with 'targeted' exclusion of identified individuals and groups. Terrorist financing features a combination of AML-style ambivalence and sanctions-style exclusion of designated terrorist groups.

Second, there is another layer of tensions arising from the dual objectives of exclusion and surveillance. Those objectives are not absolute, and the extent to which we as society pursue them is a function of two sets of conflicting values and principles. For exclusion, the notion of denying some of our fellow citizens access to commercial services they would otherwise be entitled to conflicts with the presumption of innocence, understood as a manifestation of civic trust that we owe each other rather than as merely a fair trial guarantee. For surveillance, the benefit of gathering financial intelligence on the activities of potential criminals conflicts with citizens' financial privacy. This, too, explains why financial crime regulation is never without reserve in its embrace of exclusion and surveillance.

So, underneath concrete policy choices lurk differing conceptions and intuitions as to the value of the integrity of the legitimate economy; the presumption of innocence; financial intelligence; and financial privacy. In practical terms, much of the thinking surrounding these issues is preoccupied with avoiding the unintended consequences of financial crime regulation, such as derisking, the displacement effect, defensive reporting and tick-box compliance. This is summarised in Figure 1.1.

Third, the contemporary financial crime regime is characterised by the *undirected deputisation* of the private sector with the carrying out of government policy.

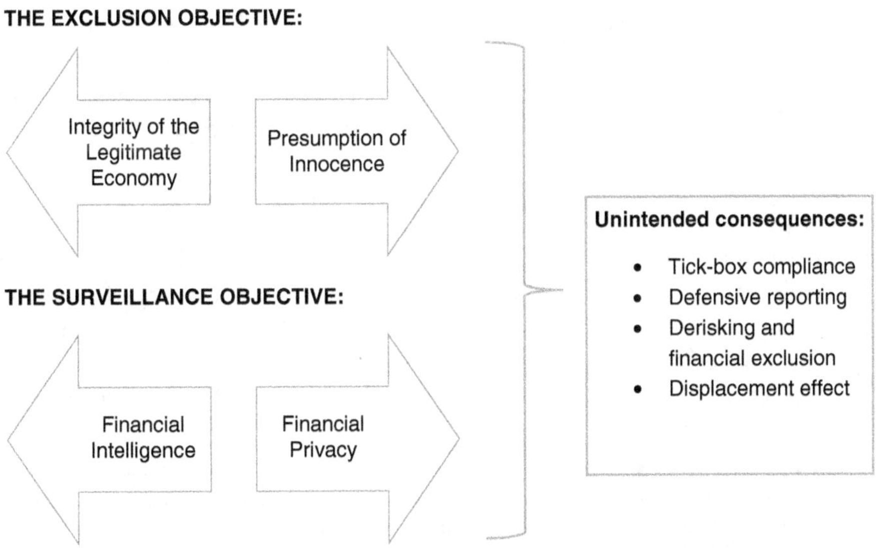

FIGURE 1.1 Key tensions of financial crime regulation

It is ultimately private-sector businesses who, acting within the framework of applicable financial crime rules, need to choose whether to deny their services to a particular customer or report his or her activities. One way to approach the task is to do as little as legally possible at the lowest available cost ('tick-box compliance'). Suppose, however, that a business wants to genuinely contribute to fighting financial crime. Then it has to confront the exceedingly difficult questions about the objectives behind the rules, other competing values and principles and unintended consequences.

Those are issues that few if any governments have entirely come to terms with. Even if a particular government has a fully fledged vision of how those tensions are to be resolved, the mechanisms for conveying that vision to the private sector, such as public–private partnerships, are in their infancy. Furthermore, their effectiveness relies entirely on private-sector goodwill. The incentives created by financial crime rules are too crude to give effect to government priorities in fighting financial crime. The key problem is therefore not so much that of deputising the private sector to interdict the proceeds of crime, but doing so without providing the details that are necessary to carry out the task in the most meaningful fashion. Those challenges manifest themselves across the board but are particularly acute in business sectors that prize client confidentiality and equal access, such as the legal profession.

The rest of the book demonstrates how the tensions identified earlier in this chapter shape the design of laws and regulations, affect the formulation and implementation of government policy and inform private-sector actions. For all their challenges and shortcomings, it is shortsighted to dismiss the financial crime regime as a product of flawed policymaking. In reality, they reflect a shift in public mores characterised by a growing societal pressure to eschew business dealings with criminal, or even controversial, counterparties.[7] The history of financial crime regulation is both a story of governments making rules and a story of them responding to the pressures that the public at large brings to bear on government and private-sector stakeholders.

1.2.2 *Contribution to Knowledge*

Financial crime law remains understudied. The paucity of financial crime-oriented academic courses and publications belies the scope and sophistication of the international and domestic regulatory regime. It hardly reflects the influence of specialised intergovernmental organisations, such as the Financial Action Task Force (FATF) or the Egmont Group of FIUs; the reams of AML/CTF regulations

7 The emergence of the exclusion objective, which is centred around the role of private industry in facilitating illicit business, can be compared to the crystallisation of a state-centred moral and policy norm that 'prohibit[s] countries from hosting money stolen by senior officials of another country': J. C. Sharman, *The Despot's Guide to Wealth Management: On the International Campaign against Grand Corruption* (Cornell University Press, 2017) 4.

and guidance published by domestic governments; the expansion in legal services related to proceeds of crime law, AML/CTF compliance and sanctions advice; and the existence of a multibillion-dollar private-sector compliance industry. Slowly, this is beginning to change, and there has been a steady trickle of high-quality monographs published in this space over the past decade – yet none that fills the gap that this book addresses.

Some publications provide a *tour d'horizon* of financial crime, serving as a useful overview laws, institutions and typologies. Those include Martin Navias's *Finance and Security*, Stephen Platt's *Criminal Capital* and Kris Hinterseer's somewhat dated *Criminal Finance,* as well as Guy Stessens's international law-oriented monograph *Money Laundering.*[8] Moreover, multiple handbooks published over the past decade supply sweeping, panoramic overviews of current financial crime concerns.[9] Building on that work, this book focuses on the higher-order principles and values that cut across the areas of financial crime regulation, thus taking the discussion a step beyond outlining the regulatory and institutional frameworks in place.

Some existing literature traverses a similar terrain. There is a strand of critical scholarship interrogating the objectives and assumptions behind contemporary AML/CTF regulation, represented in its most forceful form in Peter Alldridge's *Money Laundering Law* and his openly polemical *What Went Wrong with Money Laundering Law?*[10] Critiques that are not dissimilar, albeit more sympathetic to governments' efforts against financial crime, can be found in the work of J. C. Sharman, especially his book *The Money Laundry*, and Michael Levi and Peter Reuter.[11] Some authors provide a more explicitly economic analysis of AML/CTF measures that seeks to quantify its substantial costs and notoriously elusive benefits.[12]

[8] Martin Navias, *Finance and Security: Global Vulnerabilities, Threats, and Responses* (Hurst Publishers, 2020); Stephen Platt, *Criminal Capital: How the Finance Industry Facilitates Crime* (Palgrave Macmillan, 2015); Kris Hinterseer, *Criminal Finance: The Political Economy of Money Laundering in a Comparative Legal Context* (Kluwer Law International, 2002); Guy Stessens, *Money Laundering: A New International Law Enforcement Model* (Cambridge University Press, 2000).

[9] Doron Goldbarsht and Louis de Koker, *Financial Crime and the Law: Identifying and Mitigating Risk* (Springer, 2024); Doron Goldbarsht and Louis de Koker, *Financial Technology and the Law: Combating Financial Crime* (Springer, 2022); Colin King, Clive Walker and Jimmy Gurule (eds), *The Palgrave Handbook of Criminal and Terrorism Financing Law* (Palgrave Macmillan, 2018); Barry Rider, *Research Handbook on International Financial Crime* (Edward Elgar, 2016); Brigitte Unger and Daan van der Linde, *Research Handbook on Money Laundering* (Edward Elgar, 2013).

[10] Peter Alldridge, *Money Laundering Law: Forfeiture, Confiscation, Civil Recovery, Criminal Laundering and Taxation of the Proceeds of Crime* (Hart Publishing 2003); Peter Alldridge, *What Went Wrong with Money Laundering Law?* (Palgrave Macmillan, 2016).

[11] J. C. Sharman, *The Money Laundry* (Cornell University Press, 2011); Michael Levi and Peter Reuter, 'Money Laundering' in Michael Tonry (ed), *Crime and Justice: A Review of Research* (Volume 34, Chicago University Press, 2006).

[12] See, for example, Joras Ferwerda, 'Criminological Perspectives on Money Laundering: The Efficiency of Anti-Money Laundering Policies' in Valsamis Mitsilegas, Saskia Hufnagel and Anton Moiseienko (eds), *Research Handbook on Transnational Crime* (Edward Elgar, 2019) 112–121.

With only modest simplification, the current state of debate can be summarised thus: while most would agree that crime should not pay,[13] existing regulation fails to deliver on that objective, lacks a clear vision of how it can be achieved, and imposes significant burdens on those it applies to. From my experience of speaking to practitioners and government officials working in this area, many of them echo that assessment, so it cannot be dismissed as mere academic second-guessing by those removed from the grind of law enforcement activities. Indeed, one of the recent books highly critical of the extant regime, *Dirty Money* by Nicholas Gilmour and Tristram Hicks, was co-authored by a former head of proceeds of crime confiscation team at London's Metropolitan Police.[14]

There is much truth to this by-now conventional account of well-meaning yet ultimately misconfigured and occasionally unproductive government policies – domestically and internationally. Still, in my view, there is a vital piece of that story that remains missing. It relates to the tension between the two principal objectives of financial crime regulation, exclusion and surveillance, as well as the constant renegotiation of the principles and values underpinning our pursuit of those objectives. If that is correct, then the major limitations of the financial crime regime will endure. It would be simplistic to ascribe them solely to the FATF's or national governments' want of foresight, inertia or under-investment. All of those factors may play a role, to varying extents depending on the jurisdiction and context, but they form second-order concerns. Underneath them is a fundamental, intrinsic contradiction. We want to ensure that legitimate enterprises, such as banks, do not do business with, say, drug cartels, but we also want to deputise banks to collect intelligence on cartels' financial activities – all while living in a society where one is presumed innocent until proven guilty and financial privacy is respected.

And there's the rub: all those things are worth having. It would be easy to draw a caricature of the financial crime regime as an exercise in self-placating pursuit of objectives that, while sounding good, are ultimately unattainable or counterproductive. Exclusion of criminal actors is a particularly appealing target, which one might describe as a moralistic, puritanical preoccupation that merely displaces proceeds of crime to unregulated sectors of the economy and compromises our ability to gather valuable financial intelligence. As this book will demonstrate, there is a grain of truth in that, and the moral and political imperative of doing *no* business with criminals infuses policymaking and broader societal attitudes to an extent that can become problematic. Still, what gives rise to the truly fundamental challenges is not that this principle exists, but that its application needs to be moulded in light of multiple other, competing considerations.

[13] For instance, 'no disagreement whatsoever' with this precept was observed among the criminal justice practitioners interviewed in Colin King and Jennifer Hendry, *Civil Recovery of Criminal Property* (Oxford University Press, 2023) 102.

[14] Nicholas Gilmour and Tristram Hicks, *Dirty Money* (Bristol University Press, 2023).

In recognising this, this book aims to provide an account that is sympathetic towards the need for financial crime regulation yet clear-eyed about the problems it engenders.[15] While the challenges involved vary somewhat across money laundering, terrorist financing and sanctions evasion, they can be distilled to a similar set of tensions and trade-offs that play out differently depending on the specific criminal risks and political and economic environment. For simplicity, this book refers to all those different areas of crime – money laundering, terrorist financing and sanctions evasion – as financial crime, without purporting to set out any generally applicable definition of the concept.

As the astute reader will recognise, the subject matter of this book tracks the FATF's mandate, including terrorist financing-related and proliferation financing-related targeted financial sanctions. All of those forms of sanctions entail the overarching challenge of ensuring that private businesses identify whom they are dealing with; for example, whether an innocuous-looking Singaporean transport company is in fact a front for North Korea. This book does not deal with broader counter-proliferation financing measures, sometimes known as activity-based controls, that are aimed to deny nuclear proliferators access to the materials they require.[16] A thoughtful discussion of those issues would require straying into the domain of trade and export controls, as well as attempting a review of Western policies vis-à-vis two states presenting the greatest proliferation threat, namely Iran and North Korea, that other scholars are best placed to provide.[17]

The primary focus of this book is the regulation that governments impose on private-sector businesses, such as the obligations to undertake customer due diligence and file SARs. Such regulatory norms are themselves only one part of a broader spectrum of financial crime laws, including those that allow for the prosecution of money launderers or terrorist financiers and the confiscation of the proceeds and instrumentalities of crime, whether in criminal or in civil trials. While regulation is in the foreground of this book, those other domains of the law are also addressed as and when appropriate, especially to explore the extent to which private-sector compliance efforts genuinely support law enforcement activities, such as prosecutions and asset confiscations.

15 The ambition of this book could therefore be compared to Andrew Ashworth's attempt to identify 'the principled core of criminal law', except that the area of law I am concerned with – financial crime law – is best thought as a cross-cutting field that incorporates aspects of criminal law, financial regulation and international law. See Andrew Ashworth, 'Is the Criminal Law a Lost Cause?' (2000) 116 *LQR* 225; Andrew Ashworth, 'Towards a Theory of Criminal Legislation' (1989) 1 *Crim LR* 41.

16 For an explanation of the difference between targeted financial sanctions and activity-based proliferation financing controls, see Togzhan Kassenova and Bryan R. Early, 'Countering the Challenges of Proliferation Financing', *The Center for Policy Research*, July 2023.

17 See Richard Nephew, *The Art of Sanctions: A View from the Field* (Columbia University Press, 2017) and Stephan Haggard and Marcus Noland, *Hard Target: Sanctions, Inducements, and the Case of North Korea* (Stanford University Press, 2017).

In essence, then, the questions that this book addresses can be summarised as follows. First, how did the extant regulatory regime come about? In exploring this, it is useful to consider both the historical development of applicable rules and the evolving policy thinking behind them. Second, what objectives does it pursue and what challenges does it encounter? Since those objectives and challenges are not static, this question is inextricably linked to the historical development of the regime. It leads, in turn, to the third and final major issue that this book seeks to address: what are the objectives of the financial crime regime that can be realistically pursued today, and how can the tension between exclusion and surveillance be best managed?

1.2.3 *Methodology*

Most of the content here is based on my own analysis of applicable legal, policy and ethical considerations. The former is achieved through doctrinal, black-letter research: that is, the study of legislation and case law with a view to identifying and critiquing cross-cutting principles or approaches, resolving or at least highlighting inconsistencies, and evaluating the state of the law in light of its explicit or presumed objectives, as well as the broader social consequences. In brief, doctrinal legal research involves understanding what the law says and whether it makes sense. This can be described, with greater gravitas, as 'legal hermeneutics'.[18]

In its treatment of policy and ethical concerns, the book also speaks of broader extra-legal considerations that shape the development and implementation of the law: objectives (e.g. exclusion and surveillance), values (e.g. the integrity of the legitimate economy and the availability of financial intelligence about crime) and principles (e.g. the presumption of innocence and financial privacy). Those terms are not used in a technical legal or philosophical sense, and the arguments made here do not hinge on the precise difference between objectives, values and principles. The point is simply to demonstrate and analyse the tensions between various desirable qualities that financial crime regulation simultaneously pursues. For completeness, though, I would describe 'values' as desirable social states of affairs that laws are meant to promote or protect,[19] and 'principles' as broad policy or moral norms that inform the development and implementation of laws.[20] 'Objectives' are,

[18] See Ralf Poscher, 'Hermeneutics and Law' in Michael N. Forster and Kristin Gjesdal (eds), *The Cambridge Companion to Hermeneutics* (Cambridge University Press, 2018) 326.

[19] While not expressly articulated, this understanding of values is implicit in Jeremy Horder, *Ashworth's Principles of Criminal Law* (9th edn, Oxford University Press, 2019) 38–55, who divides the values of criminal law into 'intrinsic values', such as bodily autonomy, and 'public goods', such as maintenance of public health. See also Julian V. Roberts and Lucia Zedner (eds), *Principles and Values in Criminal Law and Criminal Justice: Essays in Honour of Andrew Ashworth* (Oxford University Press, 2012).

[20] A principle could be broadly understood as a standard that 'argues in one direction, but does not necessitate a particular decision'; for '[t]here may be other principles or policies arguing in the other direction': Ronald Dworkin, 'The Model of Rules' (1967) 35(1) *U Chicago LR* 14, 26.

in my view, a self-explanatory term and can be either explicit or, as is often the case in financial crime regulation, implicit.

In carrying out this study, I have benefitted from many interactions with policymakers, law enforcement officers, legal professionals and private-sector compliance experts over the past ten years. This includes events and meetings held, as well as hundreds of research interviews conducted, during my four-year employment at the Centre for Finance and Security at RUSI, a defence and security think tank in the UK. None of those interactions constitute a source of research data for this book, nor do I rely or on cite any information obtained through them. Nonetheless, they shaped my understanding of a wide array of financial crime issues and complemented the knowledge I gained through my earlier doctoral research at Queen Mary University of London, later published as the book *Corruption and Targeted Sanctions*. Finally, my ongoing research at ANU has stimulated further development in my views on the subject matter of *Doing Business with Criminals*. Such experiences have been essential in the gestation of this book.

While most aspects of the book could be adequately addressed through desk-based research and pre-existing knowledge, some of them benefitted from additional empirical research. To that end, fourteen semi-structured research interviews were conducted with sixteen select experts, listed in Annex 1 to this book. They covered, in the order of the number of interviews, the history of AML/CTF regulation; its plausible objectives; the impact of reputational and other non-legal pressures on businesses' decision to engage with controversial clients or counterparties; and the implications of AML/CTF regulation for the legal profession.

The primary purpose of the interviews was to glean insight from those with practical, first-hand experience of those involved in the development of AML/CTF rules in a particular area or working in it. While they cannot be treated as necessarily representative of the views in respective professions writ large, the degree of convergence they exhibit suggest that nor can they be taken to be outliers. Whenever specific factual claims were made in the interviews, those are only cited here if they can be triangulated using other, publicly available information.

Finally, this book is not beholden to any theoretical or ideological approach. It is likely that the twin objectives of exclusion and surveillance and the manifold dilemmas they engender can be parsed out in the light of various academic schools and traditions, such as law and economics (to discover the most economically efficient solutions) or regulatory theory (to identify regulatory approaches best suited to securing compliance among the regulated sectors). Those may be valuable directions for future study, but my project here is to highlight that hitherto underappreciated foundation for much of today's efforts against financial crime. To that end, this book adopts a common-sense, history-driven narrative that is free of any overt theoretical biases.

This is a fast-moving area, and the book reflects the state of affairs as known to me of the end of July 2024, with minor updates made during its production in

February 2025. That said, while laws, institutions and practices might change – and new court cases will inevitably arise – the fundamental tensions considered here are likely to remain relevant for quite some time.

1.2.4 *Audience*

This book is intended to appeal to a broad audience, including domestic and international policymakers, practicing lawyers, private-sector compliance experts, academics and even the general reader. On the one hand, this is an academic legal work, which dictates certain conventions in style and content. It explores legislation, court cases and policy documents in a degree of detail that may be prohibitive in a non-academic publication. On the other hand, its subject matter – crime and money! – holds some inherent appeal. The case study-based structure of each of the book's chapters is intended to bring to light the practical implications of the legal and policy choices considered here, as well as telling stories that are intrinsically interesting due to the difficult trade-offs they entail.

As such, it is hoped that *Doing Business with Criminals* can be of interest both to those with an existing expertise in financial crime law who are interested in a fresh view on the well-known challenges that beset it, and those who are looking for a reasonably wide-ranging introduction to the area. Furthermore, as Lord Sumption, formerly of the UK's Supreme Court, once said, law is mostly 'common sense with knobs on it'.[21] None of the legal issues discussed here will be beyond the grasp of the educated lay person, although some readers may be inclined to skim a page or two at some point.

1.2.5 *Structure*

Following this introductory chapter, Chapter 2 proceeds to tell the history of AML measures from their earliest days to today. In doing so, I seek not only to recount the chronology of laws and institutions but also to trace the origins of the main concepts that make up our current AML regime. One could describe this as an 'intellectual history' of AML laws, which is essential to understanding the purposes and limitations of the regime we currently have. Chapter 3 then examines how those purposes and limitations manifest themselves in several key policy dilemmas, such as that between exclusion and surveillance, that remain unresolved. The lack of clarity about how conflicting values and principles – including the presumption of innocence and financial privacy – should be balanced means that, at the core of the AML regime, there is always some uncertainty about what exactly it should be pursuing, and at what cost. Some potential solutions to those challenges are also discussed in that part of the book. Chapter 4 introduces terrorist financing, which is

[21] Emma Brockes, 'The Importance of Being Learned', *The Guardian*, 31 October 1999.

the other half of what gave rise to the modern AML/CTF framework, and targeted financial sanctions, including those related to terrorist financing and proliferation financing. They involve many of the same challenges as AML rules, with an addition of one further objective in the CTF context, namely that of denying terrorist actors the access to resources they need. In the imposition of sanctions, whether terrorism-related or otherwise, governments exercise manual control over who exactly should be excluded from the legitimate economy by explicitly identifying targeted individuals and companies. Such targeted exclusion gives rise to distinct law, policy and implementation challenges. Finally, Chapter 5 sums up the challenges in ensuring that the legitimate economy does not do business with criminals; lays out several principles for an effective AML/CTF regime; and proposes priority areas for meaningful implementation of targeted financial sanctions.

2

From Stolen Cattle to Football Clubs

The History of Anti-money Laundering

2.1 INTRODUCTION

The history of AML regulation is rarely if ever told in detail, with close attention paid to contemporaneous policy thinking and not merely recounting in broad strokes the chronology of laws and institutions. This history is of more than mere academic interest. There are multiple ways in which it can, and should, inform the debates of today. The themes emerging from a historical overview include the practical convenience of designating money laundering as a distinct offence; the concept of complicity as one of the central tenets behind the evolution of AML laws; the distinction between trivial and professional money laundering activities; the tension between financial surveillance and privacy; and the persistence of concerns about the unintended consequences of AML laws, which have been raised from the very start but only became seriously acknowledged with time.

This chapter begins by setting out the history of AML regulation, which spans many centuries and jurisdictions. The regime we have is best understood as a product of evolution, rather than intelligent design, stemming from intuitions about complicity in crime and the benefits of financial surveillance. Section 2.1 outlines the development of thinking about money laundering as a species of complicity in underlying crime. Section 2.2 covers the genesis of the two central tenets of the AML regime: reporting obligations, ranging from suspicious activity reporting to multiple other modes of reporting, and customer due diligence (CDD). Finally, Section 2.3 traces the genesis of the international AML regime, as relates both to substantive rules and its institutional architecture. In particular, it explores how and why FATF, an initially ad hoc grouping convened in Paris in 1989, became the primary vehicle for the development of international standards against money laundering. The conclusion brings together the lessons that this historical experience holds for understanding and tackling the financial crime challenges of today.

2.2 MONEY LAUNDERING AS COMPLICITY IN CRIME

For most practical intents and purposes, AML regulation is a product of the late 1980s and early 1990s, when key regulations and institutions that continue to shape the field first took form. But the conceptual underpinnings of those rules are of truly ancient pedigree. They have to do with two intertwined ideas: that of complicity in acquisitive crime, and that of responsibility for handling stolen goods, which itself is essentially a species of complicity.

Simply put, complicity rules determine whether someone other than the direct perpetrator is sufficiently closely connected to the commission of a crime to be culpable themselves. In the words of Lord Bingham, '[a]ny coherent criminal law must develop a theory of accessory liability which will embrace those whose responsibility merits conviction and punishment even though they are not the primary offenders'.[1] This intuition has found expression in the law since its earliest days, and it is there that the origins of what would one day become AML rules can be discerned.

2.2.1 *Bad Men and Stolen Cattle in the Twelfth Century and Beyond: Complicity and Handling Stolen Goods*

In their magisterial history of English law before the reign of Edward I, Sir Frederick Pollock and Frederic William Maitland wrote as follows:

> Anglo-Saxon law knows the *rǽd-bana* as well as the *dǽd-bana*, the slayer by rede as well as the slayer by deed. In Bracton's day [13th century] there was a common proverb that met this case. The man who has commanded or counselled a murder has committed no crime until there has been a murder; but when the murder is committed he is guilty of it. (…) This rule lived on into modern times, when it looked absurd enough and did much mischief. It was the outcome of strict medieval logic. If you convict the accessory while the principal is neither convicted nor outlawed, you beg a question that should not be begged. The law will be shamed if the principal is acquitted after the accessory has been hanged.[2]

The derivative nature of accessorial liability persists until today and gives rise to considerable difficulties. On the one hand, the very nature of complicity is that it involves assisting or encouraging someone in the commission of a crime. On the other hand, requiring the proof beyond reasonable doubt not only of the accused's complicity but also of the primary perpetrator's crime can lead to paradoxical results even where the abettor's moral culpability is beyond any doubt. This can lead to difficult, almost philosophical discussions of whether the culpability of

1 *R v Rahman* [2008] UKHL 45; [2009] 1 AC 5, para 7.

2 Frederick Pollock and Frederic William Maitland, *The History of English Law before the Time of Edward I* (Liberty Fund Incorporated, 2010) 533 (508 in the original edition).

the abettor's conduct should at all depend on whether the principal perpetrator consummates the crime.[3]

These issues have a direct bearing on the development of money laundering as a self-standing criminal offence. Its first conceptual progenitor is the notion of accessory after the fact, which emerged to denote those who 'receive, relieve, comfort or assist' the felon after the commission of a crime.[4] Under the Assizes of Clarendon, enacted by Henry II in 1166, 'the receivers of murderers, robbers and thieves incur the penalty which is ordained for murder, robbery and theft'.[5] In connection with theft, or indeed other acquisitive offences such as fraud, accessorial liability raised the question of whether fencing stolen property amounted to such ex-post assistance.

For centuries, the answer in English law was that it did not. In a slander trial from the early seventeenth century known as Dawson's case an accusation of having knowingly bought stolen cattle was not found be slanderous 'for receipt or sale of goods stolen is not felony, nor makes any accessory, unless it is joined with a receipt or abetment of the felon himself'.[6] Up until the end of the seventeenth century, scholarly discussions gravitated towards the conclusion that receipt[7] of stolen gods, even with the knowledge they were stolen, did not suffice for liability.[8] That changed with the enactment of a statutory provision in 1692 that read as follows:

> And forasmuch as thieves and robbers are much encouraged to commit such offences, because a great number of persons made it their trade and business to deal in the buying of stolen goods; be it therefore enacted by the authority aforesaid, That if any person or persons shall buy or receive any goods or chattel that shall be feloniously taken or stolen from any other person, knowing the same to be stolen, he or they shall be taken and deemed an accessary or accessaries to such felony after the fact, and shall incur the same punishment, as an accessary or accessaries to the felony after the felony committed.[9]

This law foreshadowed the developments that would unfold 300 years later. The basic structure of the receipt of stolen goods is the same as that of money laundering: both involve the handling of property obtained through some other, underlying crime. Even the policy rationale alluded to in this enactment from William and Mary's reign ('because a great number of persons made it their trade and business to deal in the buying of stolen goods') is, save for its brevity, not too dissimilar to the recitals later to be found in the EU's Money Laundering Directives (MLDs).

3 See AP Simester, *Fundamentals of Criminal Law: Responsibility, Culpability, and Wrongdoing* (Oxford University Press, 2021) 154–184.

4 Pollock and Maitland, *The History of English Law*, 534 (509 in the original 1895 edition).

5 Ibid.

6 80 Eng Rep 4 (1602) cited in Jerome Hall, *Theft, Law and Society* (2nd end, The Bobbs-Merrill Company Inc., 1952) 53.

7 Originally the preferred term, later supplanted by 'handling' in the UK.

8 Hall, *Theft, Law and Society*, 53.

9 3 & 4 W and M IV, c 9, cited in Hall, *Theft, Law and Society*, 54.

Still, receipt of stolen goods was not yet a distinct criminal offence. This entailed prosecutorial challenges identified earlier on in this section but also meant that the available punishment was exactly the same as that attaching to the underlying offence. Complicity, after all, is not a crime in its own right but merely a mode of participating in crime, such that an accessory to murder is guilty of murder.

Later on, the emergence of organised criminal syndicates laid bare the deficiencies of this complicity-oriented mode of tackling the receipt of stolen goods. With the source of stolen goods often being obscure, the requirement to prove the underlying offence beyond reasonable doubt began to pose insurmountable obstacles. One well-known fence extraordinaire was Jonathan Wild, who put together a prolific organised crime group in the eighteenth century. Wild's operatives stole goods and then returned them to owners for a fee under the pretence of Wild's running a network of 'thief takers' able to recover misappropriated property.[10]

These developments led to reforms that allowed prosecutions to proceed in the absence of the thief's conviction.[11] Still, they remained beset with technicalities. For example, a conviction for receipt of stolen goods was only available if the thief had committed felonious larceny, which depended on the amount involved. With time, that changed so that the receiver could be convicted of a felony if the thief had committed a felony and of a misdemeanour if the thief had committed one.[12] In a bid to redress those and other challenges borne of the derivative nature of accessory liability, receipt of stolen goods became a self-standing substantive crime in 1827.[13]

Such was the state of the Anglo-American criminal law by the turn of the twentieth century, when what we could now anachronistically describe as money laundering became prominent as a subject of expert and public discussion. As we have now seen, the legal doctrines necessary for the prosecution of such conduct were not wholly absent but were to be found in either complicity rules, with all the strictures that they entailed, or in the prohibition on handling stolen goods, which was only concerned with the proceeds of theft alone. It took multiple developments throughout the twentieth century, spanning the US and Europe, for that position to change.

2.2.2 *Bootlegging, Tax and Crime in the 1920s–1940s: Money Laundering as a Necessity*

In 1919, a group of prominent lawyers and businessmen in Chicago decided they had had enough of the city's failure to address rampant crime. Together, thirty-five of them formed an organisation aimed at documenting the extent, nature and effects of organised crime activities in Chicago, to be known as the Chicago Crime

[10] Stuart P. Green, 'Thieving and Receiving: Overcriminalizing the Possession of Stolen Property' (2011) 14(1) *New Crim LR* 35, 39.

[11] Hall, *Theft, Law and Society*, 55.

[12] For a detailed account, see Hall, *Theft, Law and Society*, 53–61.

[13] Larceny (England) Act, 7 & 8 Geo IV, c 29.

Commission. Much of the Commission's activity was premised on a set of strikingly modern precepts. One of those was seeking to undermine the profitability of organised crime. Its first president, the attorney Henry Barrett Chamberlin, was reported as saying: 'Crime is a business. It is an organized business and it must be fought with business methods'.[14] In practice, this meant prodding the state police to seize contraband goods, shut down illicit gambling outfits and otherwise disrupt the manifold rackets that beset Chicago.

Essential to the Commission's modus operandi was what we would now describe as 'naming and shaming': not so much of the gangsters themselves but rather of the law enforcement agencies that allowed them to operate unmolested, as well as – indirectly – private organisations engaged in business with the likes of Al Capone. In 1930, under the leadership of another well-regarded lawyer by the name of Frank J. Loesch, the Commission published its first-ever list of twenty-eight 'public enemies', including one Alphonse Capone, designated as public enemy number one.[15] Loesch requested the Department of Justice to publish its own official list of 'public enemies': an idea that has unmissable resonance with today's targeted financial sanctions.[16]

Membership of the Chicago Crime Commission included, among others, Colonel Robert R. McCormick, the owner of the *Chicago Tribune*.[17] The promulgation of its list of public enemies was well noted by the press and wider population, and soon presidents of major banks and insurance companies vowed to accept no business linked to any of those public enemies.[18] The promise might have been less courageous than it would appear at first sight: as detailed by the Internal Revenue Service (IRS), neither Al Capone nor his associates were in the habit of holding bank accounts in their own names.[19] Therefore, unless one tried also to identify accounts linked to Al Capone's affiliates,[20] foregoing his custom would hardly pose a major challenge to a bank executive.

14 Dennis E. Hoffman, *Scarface Al and the Crime Crusaders: Chicago's Private War against Capone* (Southern Illinois University Press, 1993) 19. See also Henry Barrett Chamberlin, 'Chicago Crime Commission: How the Business Men of Chicago Are Fighting Crime' (1920) 11(3) *J Am Inst Crim L & Criminology* 386, 397 ('Crime today is a gigantic system organized and protected, reaching into business and politics, and while still subject to indictment and prosecution, is largely immune from punishment').

15 'The Public Enemies', *Chicago Tribune* (16 April 1931), www.newspapers.com/article/chicago-tribune-the-public-enemies/18035881/. See also William Elliott Hazelgrove, *Al Capone and the 1933 World's Fair: The End of the Ganster Era in Chicago* (Rowman & Littlefield, 2017) Ch 24 (discussing the public notoriety attendant on the Chicago Crime Commission's designation).

16 'URGES NATIONAL THUG LIST; F.J. Loesch Suggests That Department of Justice Compile It', *The New York Times*, 8 October 1933.

17 Hazelgrove, *Al Capone and the 1933 World's Fair*, 16–18.

18 Ibid, 114–115.

19 See footnote 22.

20 A challenge that, as we shall see in Chapter 4, remains far from trivial even for the technology-equipped banks of today.

That promise was wholly unenforceable at the time. It was a product of financial institutions' good will and nascent public pressure, not legal obligation. It would take more than half a century for the first laws criminalising money laundering – meaning, broadly speaking, the use of the proceeds of crime – to emerge in the US, first in the context of drug trafficking only. As we shall see, isolated prosecutions based on the doctrines of complicity and conspiracy would be brought before then, but money laundering as a distinct criminal offence would be unknown to US law until 1986.

While money laundering laws therefore played no role in Capone's downfall, financial investigation – a concept that today is often used in conjunction with the term money laundering – was indispensable to it. In 1929, following Frank J. Loesch's intercession with President Coolidge pleading to bring the force of federal law enforcement to bear on Capone, the IRS launched an investigation into Capone's tax evasion from 1924 onwards.[21] In a confidential letter made public by the IRS many decades since, the agents involved described their difficulties thus:

> That Al Capone is shrewd, there is no doubt, which, together with his native Italian secretiveness, has made this case a most difficult one to handle. Al Capone never had a bank account and only on one occasion could it be found there he ever endorsed a check, all of his financial transactions being made in currency.[22]

The agents' work therefore involved a painstaking gathering of scraps of evidence that pointed to the extent of Al Capone's undeclared income. This relied heavily on witness testimony that Al Capone did in fact control the businesses that he legally had nothing to do with, as well as the inferences that could be drawn from that single check that Al Capone had carelessly endorsed, which indicated that he was paid from the profits of the gambling establishment concerned.[23] Other bits and pieces, such as the amount held in a bank account opened in his wife Mae's name, were likewise added to the total estimate of Al Capone's untaxed income.[24]

In 1931, Al Capone was convicted of three counts of wilfully attempting to evade and defeat income tax and two counts of failing to file tax returns.[25] The road to Al Capone's prosecution had been paved in 1927 with the US Supreme Court's decision in *US v Sullivan*, which established that the privilege against self-incrimination under the Fifth Amendment did not preclude income from criminal activities from being reportable under federal tax laws.[26]

From then on, potential prosecution for tax evasion created an additional incentive for well-off organised crime figures to either conceal their wealth or declare it

[21] Hazelgrove, *Al Capone and the 1933 World's Fair*, 32–33.

[22] Treasury Department, Internal Revenue Service, 'In re: Alphonse Capone', 8 July 1931, 2.

[23] Ibid, 5.

[24] Christina M. Smith, 'The Shifting Structure of Chicago's Organized Crime Network and the Women It Left Behind' (PhD Thesis, University of Massachusetts Amherst, September 2015) 119–120.

[25] *Capone v US*, 56 F.2d 927 (1931), cert denied, 286 US 553 (1932).

[26] *US v Sullivan* 274 US 259 (1927).

and come up with a fictitious account of its legitimate origins. A widespread but apocryphal story traces the term 'money laundering' to Al Capone's activities in anticipation of a tax indictment. According to that story, he realised the need to come up with a facially plausible explanation of the origins of his substantial wealth. In order to do so, the story goes, he set up a chain of launderettes around Chicago.[27] One of the advantages of doing so was that the revenue of a given launderette on a given day was close to impossible for an external observer to estimate. That generated plausible deniability as to the sources of Al Capone's wealth, at least insofar as it made it difficult to disprove the possibility of it being traceable back to legitimate business activity. The money was, in that sense, 'washed' – or laundered.

As others have rightly noted, for all its literary merit, the story is untrue.[28] There is no real evidence for it, and the IRS documents on the Al Capone affair make no mention of the launderette business. Furthermore, Al Capone's real problem was not the *source* of his wealth but its *amount*. Following the US Supreme Court's decision in *Sullivan*, being in possession of undeclared wealth – whatever its origins, licit or illicit – could give rise to criminal liability. Hence the focus of the IRS investigation was on scraping together, invoice by invoice, the amount of Al Capone's holdings, with no need to establish its provenance. Concealing the origins of his wealth would have done nothing to frustrate that inquiry.

While incorrect in a historical sense, the Al Capone launderette anecdote contains a grain of truth about the nature of (one form of) money laundering. Suppose that, with foresight, Al Capone had decided to declare all his criminally obtained wealth. Truthfully describing it as proceeds of racketeering, bootlegging and other criminal activities would not be feasible as doing so would amount to an admission. He would therefore have had to come up with a plausible cover story, supported by a trail of documents speaking to the legitimate origins of his wealth. That, in essence, would be money laundering: making dirty (criminal) money appear clean (legitimate). The launderette story encapsulates a truth about the obligation to declare criminal income creating a tangible incentive to engage in what we would now describe as money laundering.

There is little doubt that, since Al Capone, organised crime figures and groups had been involved in money laundering. However, the term itself was not in circulation until the 1970s, and little is known about the techniques they utilised or the prevalence of the phenomenon. What we do know is that the US government

[27] Martin Navias, *Finance and Security: Global Vulnerabilities, Threats and Responses* (Hurst & Company, 2019) 25; Brigitte Unger, 'Money Laundering Regulation: From Al Capone to Al Qaeda' in Brigitte Unger and Daan Van der Linde (eds), *Research Handbook on Money Laundering* (Edward Elgar Publishing, 2013) 19; Kris Hinterseer, *Criminal Finance: The Political Economy of Money Laundering in a Comparative Legal Context* (Kluwer Law International, 2002) 34.

[28] Christopher Stringham, 'The Origin of Money Laundering What Al Capone Has and Doesn't Have to Do with It', *LinkedIn*, 27 September 2023, www.linkedin.com/posts/christopher-stringham_i-have-often-seen-people-reference-a-myth-activity-7112783271964401664-G4_F/.

carried on with its newfound tactic of prosecuting major organised crime leaders for tax evasion: in addition to Al Capone's brother Ralph, other significant gangsters prosecuted for tax evasion include Jake 'Greasy Thumb' Guzik, Frank 'The Enforcer' Nitti, Irving Wexler ('Waxey Gordon') and Athur Flegenheimer ('Dutch Shultz'), of which only the latter one was acquitted.[29] From among the available appellate judgments in these cases, the one in the matter of the bootlegger Waxey Gordon is unique in offering some account of what we would now recognise as a simple yet effective money laundering technique of holding property in some else's name:

> Enormous sums, amounting to over $2,000,000 each year, were traced from [Gordon's] sales of Eureka beer into the hands of two persons, Cohen and Gurock, who deposited them in two banks under fictitious names which they continually changed. Since by far the greater part of the business was illicit, these efforts to conceal the money ought not, however, necessarily to be attributed to a plan to escape the income tax, though it fitted well enough with that purpose as well. It was important, and indeed necessary, to establish that Cohen and Gurock held the money for Wexler [Waxey Gordon's real name].[30]

Further details about Gordon's financial affairs are to be found in the memoirs, published posthumously, of Thomas Dewey, a then-young US district attorney who led Irving Wexler's prosecution and went on to become the Governor of New York and two-time Republican presidential candidate. As Dewey's write-up demonstrates, the conceptual simplicity of how Gordon concealed his wealth belies the organisational prowess necessary to arrange what was in effect a money mule network. Gordon's men were also actively engaged in the destruction of financial evidence, and Dewey describes the race between the Department of Justice to secure documents related to Godon's nominee-held bank accounts and the Gordon gang to destroy those records.[31] As with Capone, one of Gordon's key mistakes proved to be signing checks in his own name: according to Dewey, 'handwriting analysis [of the checks] did more than any other single factor to tie the whole case together'.[32]

That gives us a glimpse into that era's financial investigation techniques, low-tech and laborious.[33] Until the 1960s, the strength of US tax controls relied on cross-checking the information submitted by employees and employers, respectively, such that there was 'no independent source of data on self-employed persons such

[29] David Lusty, 'Taxing the Untouchables Who Profit from Organised Crime' (2003) 10(3) *J Financial Crime* 209, 209.

[30] *US v Wexler* 79 F.2d 529 (1935).

[31] Thomas E. Dewey, *Twenty against the Underworld* (Doubleday, 1974) 118–119.

[32] Ibid, 119–120.

[33] Contrast this with a much greater array of financial intelligence available today. See also George A. Manning, *Financial Investigation and Forensic Accounting* (3rd edn, CRC Press, 2011), especially chapters 15 (sources of information) and 19 (money laundering).

as storekeepers or professionals'.[34] As the deputy chief of the Organized Crime and Racketeering Section at the US Department of Justice Michael DeFeo wrote in 1990, '[o]nly in 1913 was the modern system of comprehensive taxation of income, profits and inherited wealth implemented', meaning that 'the institutional memory of [the US] government in the field of citizen financial reporting and controls' would have been very shallow at the time of the Gordon prosecution.[35]

By contrast with the Waxey Gordon case, other tax-related judgments from the era supply little information on the precise money laundering techniques that might have been utilised by the defendants.[36] Still, it is apparent that mobsters began not only to seek to hide their income, a la Capone and Gordon, but also to invent facially plausible stories of the origins of their wealth, just like the launderette legend would have Capone do.

Bootlegging also gave rise to the first major US prosecution of businessmen that found themselves financially entangled with an organised crime group: *US v Falcone*. In an appeal decided by the US Court of Appeals for the Second Circuit in 1940, the issue was whether the sellers of sugar, yeast and cans could be held responsible for the supply of those goods to bootleggers in the knowledge that they would be used for criminal purposes. Speaking for the unanimous court, Judge Learned Hand held that knowledge alone was not enough to attach criminal liability to such actions, although it did not specify what precise state of mind would be required:

> [I]n prosecutions for conspiracy or abetting, [the defendant's] attitude towards the forbidden undertaking must be more positive. It is not enough that he does not forego a normally lawful activity, of the fruits of which he knows that others will make an unlawful use; he must in some sense promote their venture himself, make it his own, have a stake in its outcome.[37]

It is easy to see how dramatically different this approach is from the expectations that we now place upon AML-regulated businesses. Three years later, in a case involving the supply of morphine by a wholesale drug manufacturer to a small-town physician who dispensed it in wanton amounts, the Supreme Court clarified that conspiracy charges in that context require that the defendant 'intends to further, promote and cooperate in [the crime]'.[38] As US attorney Richard Strafer highlighted, the rules set

[34] Michael A. DeFeo, 'Depriving International Narcotics Traffickers and Other Organized Criminals of Illegal Proceeds and Combatting Money Laundering' (1990) 18 *Denv J Int'l L & Pol'y* 405, 406.

[35] Ibid.

[36] The Al Capone case in the Court of Appeals for the Seventh Circuit revolved around whether the government had sufficiently particularised the charges of tax evasion: *Alphonse Capone v US* 56 F.2d 927 (1932). The case involving Ralph Capone primarily concerned the statute of limitations: *Ralph Capone v US* 51 F.2d 609 (1931). *Guzik v US* 54 F.2d 618 (1931) involved matters relating to the admissibility of certain types of the evidence of Guzik's income.

[37] *US v Falcone et al*, 109 F.2d 579, 581 (1940). See the discussion of this case and the ones that followed in G. Richard Strafer, 'Money Laundering: The Crime of the 90's' (1989) 27 *Am Crim LR* 149.

[38] *Direct Sales Co Ltd v US*, 63 S.Ct. 1265, 1271 (1943).

out in those early proto-money laundering cases were tailored to the specific kinds of commodities involved.[39]

If one were to apply the contemporary taxonomy to those cases, they can be described as involving the supply of the instrumentalities of crime, that is, property used to commit crime, rather than the handling of its proceeds. Be that as it may, this focus of the early prosecutions suggests that the issue of what happens to the fruits of crime, and how they are moved and spent, had not yet become the subject of sustained law enforcement or popular attention. Nevertheless, consistent with the vision behind the Chicago Crime Commission and other similar bodies springing up across the country, these earliest forays into the finances of crime presaged a growing interest in the business component of organised crime activities.

2.2.3 *Handing of Stolen Goods in the 1930s–1940s*

One essential part of the US criminal ecosystem during that era was the spread of the interstate transportation of stolen property. The acknowledgement of the problem prompted a flurry of legislative developments at the state level, as well as proposals for federal legislation. One of those proposals, debated extensively but ultimately defeated in Congress, was that of a 'Bill to prohibit the sending and receipt of the stolen property through interstate and foreign commerce', proposed by Fiorello La Guardia, later the Mayor of New York, in 1929.[40] The bill would have criminalised 'sending', 'transporting' or 'causing to be sent or transported' stolen property if the person engaged in such conduct either knew the property was stolen or, 'notwithstanding good reason to believe' that it was stolen, 'omit[ted] diligent inquiry to ascertain the fact'.[41] That, in both substance and form, would have been tantamount to the introduction of due diligence obligations.

The regulatory burden this would place on transport intermediaries, railways chief among them, was readily apparent. The American Railway Association therefore lobbied to have a proviso inserted in the bill that would exempt 'common carriers' from its reach.[42] The concept of a common carrier harkens back to medieval England where certain professions, such as blacksmiths, innkeepers and wharfingers, were required to provide their services to the public at large without discrimination:

> If a man takes upon him a public employment, he is bound to serve the public as far as the employment extends; and for refusal an action lies, as against a farrier refusing to shoe a horse.[43]

39 Strafer, 'Money Laundering', 152.

40 Bill H.R. 10287 (1928).

41 US House of Representatives, Committee on the Judiciary, *Sending and Receipt of Stolen Property in Foreign and Interstate Commerce*, Hearing, 70th Congress, April 1928.

42 Ibid, 31 (Statement of Alfred P. Thom Jr, General Solicitor of the Association of Railway Executives).

43 *Lane v Cotton* (1701) 1 *Ld Raym* 646, 654 per Holt CJ. See also the erudite discussion of the medieval origins of common carriage in *Stapley v Towing Masters Pty Ltd (t/as Dynamic Towing)* [2009] NSWCA 382, paras 74–93 per Campbell JA.

La Guardia's bill ultimately failed to pass,[44] but its focus on intermediaries facilitating the movement of stolen goods foreshadows the gatekeeper-oriented model of future AML laws. Like that bill, contemporary AML regulation is predicated on imposing due diligence obligations on key financial intermediaries, such as banks, other financial institutions, lawyers, accountants, real estate agents and so on. Another aspect of the current AML regime that the bill presaged is the recurrent debates as to what sectors should be covered: for instance, despite its well-known potential to facilitate trade-based money laundering, the transport sector – such as shipping lines or freight forwarders – remains free from AML obligations.[45]

This evolution from a mode of accessorial liability to a self-standing criminal offence charts out the trajectory of money laundering: a cognate concept that, likewise, took on a life of its own as a substantive offence due to practical difficulties inherent in complicity-based prosecutions. There are a number of lessons that this history holds for the crime of money laundering. One of those is the difference between the one-off receiver of stolen property and the professional fence, which the law of handling stolen goods has arguably never properly accounted for. This critique, first put forward by Jerome Hall in 1931, has since been developed further by Stuart Green, who distinguishes between two rationales for criminalising the handling of stolen goods: a backwards-looking rationale, which treats handling as a way of perpetuating the victim's deprivation of his or her property, and a forward-looking one, which views it as generating incentives for more theft.[46] The latter conception of the harms of handling stolen goods corresponds well to the activities of professional fences, which Hall sums up as follows:

> [T]he executives in this business of dealing in stolen goods are experienced men, frequently specialists in their chosen fields, able to evaluate merchandise expertly and to compete generally on the basis of their special skills. Indeed, many criminal receivers reenter legitimate business, despite the police phrase 'once a fence – always a fence'.[47]

There is little doubt that this description of fencing is both accurate and enduring. One only need talk to a local police officer in any developed country to come across examples of, say, car parts stolen in rural England being tracked down in Indonesia a month later,[48] or of phones stolen in Manchester to be mass-shipped to Shenzhen, China.[49] Hall's passage also bears all the hallmarks of the twenty-first

44 Hall, *Theft, Law and Society*, 230.

45 Anton Moiseienko, Alexandria Reid and Isabella Chase, 'Improving Governance and Tackling Crime in Free-Trade Zones', *RUSI Occasional Paper*, October 2020, 45.

46 Green, 'Thieving and Receiving', 37.

47 Hall, *Theft, Law and Society*, 157.

48 Author's conversation with a former law enforcement officer, 30 March 2024.

49 Louise Eccles, 'How Your Stolen iPhone Ends Up in One Chinese City Market', *The Sunday Times*, 16 June 2024.

century discourse on professional money launderers who specialise in the provision of money laundering services to organised crime groups.[50] The intuition that professional fences (or, later, money launderers) are central to the business of organised crime has been essential to the targeting of law enforcement activities. By contrast, the occasional fence is by definition a less central, if still worthwhile, law enforcement target. The same can be said of 'self-laundering': the offence of money laundering that is technically committed when (say) a bank robber invests the proceeds of the robbery that he or she himself perpetrated.[51]

If thought of as a tool of disrupting organised crime activities, not all money laundering prosecutions are created equal – and the difficulty of accounting for that reality has plagued later efforts to ascertain the effectiveness of the AML regime worldwide. By the 1940s, however, the finances of organised crime were only beginning to come into focus as a priority area for law enforcement intervention. That line of thinking became more prominent in the following decade with the establishment of a US Senate committee investigating organised crime activities in the country.

2.2.4 *Kefauver Committee in 1950: Focus on Organised Crime Finances*

In 1950, the US Senate formed the Special Committee to Investigate Crime in Interstate Commerce, better known as the Kefauver Committee by the name of its chairman, Estes Kefauver. The Kefauver Committee gained public prominence by issuing subpoenas to leading mobsters, so that they were compelled to testify before the Committee on pain of contempt charges, and televising the hearings.[52] (Not everyone turned up, and not everyone who turned up participated meaningfully; the Committee cited several witnesses for contempt, some of whom were convicted and sentenced to jail time.)[53]

Financial techniques used by organised crime groups were central to the Kefauver Committee's proceedings. They fell into two broad categories. The first of those was the investment of proceeds of crime into legitimate businesses, which created opportunities for both generating lawful income and commingling it with criminal gains.[54] The Committee's investigation documented no fewer than seventy separate

50 See, e.g., FATF, *Professional Money Laundering*, July 2018.

51 See Chapter 3.

52 One of Kefauver's other well-known senatorial pursuits was chairing the US Senate Antitrust and Monopoly Subcommittee, which investigated, among other things, the claims of false advertising engaged in by the medical industry. See Patrick Radden Keefe, *Empire of Pain: The Secret History of the Sackler Dynasty* (Doubleday, 2021).

53 See US Senate Historical Office, 'Notable Senate Investigations: Special Committee on Organized Crime in Interstate Commerce', undated, www.senate.gov/about/resources/pdf/kefauver-committee-full-citations.pdf?ref=news-justin.

54 Estes Kefauver, *Crime in America* (Doubleday, 1951) 137–140.

types of businesses that had been infiltrated by organised crime, from advertising to haberdashery to, fittingly, 'washing machines'.[55] The company that drew Kefauver's ire more than any other was Continental Press,[56] a mob-controlled radio news service that broadcast horse racing results to illegal bookmakers across the country and was described by Kefauver as 'public enemy number one' in his book taking stock of the Committee's hearings.[57]

The second major method of concealing one's criminal income was the falsification of tax returns and receipts:

> It is apparent that many, if not all, of the returns submitted for the gamblers and gangsters are fraudulent, and that the Government is losing huge sums in tax revenue from the illegal ventures run by them. (…) [The gangster and boxer's] Mickey Cohen's return showed a gross income for 1949 of $14,845. In 1947, according to his tax lawyer, Sackman, he built a lavish and costly home. The greater part of this money was 'borrowed' without security. He has also 'borrowed' in similar fashion over $50,000 a year since 1947. These so-called borrowings are not reported as income.[58]

As foreshadowed by this reference to a tax lawyer, during his hearings Kefauver encountered a phenomenon that was here to stay in the world of economic crime, namely the hiring of professional lawyers and accountants by organised crime groups. One of the witnesses appearing before the Committee was Alvin E. Giesey, a veteran of two World Wars ('wearing a diamond-studded emblem of a veterans' organization'), a former IRS agent and a public accountant retained by an organised crime figure whom he himself, in his earlier career, had helped convict of tax evasion.[59] In that new capacity, in addition to tax advice as such, he acted as a corporate secretary to a restaurant and a real estate firm associated with organised crime figures.[60] At one point in the hearings, the following exchange occurred between the Committee's chief counsel, Rudolph Halley, and Giesey:

Q. Were you at all concerned about the possibility that you might be found to be aiding and abetting an illegal enterprise?
A. No, sir. I was not engaged in the gambling end.
Q. You were doing the accounting for the gambling end?
A. That is right.

55 Ibid, 138.

56 Not to be confused with today's wholly innocuous, Canada-based Continental Newspapers.

57 Kefauver, *Crime in America*, 35–52.

58 United States Senate's Special Committee to Investigate Organized Crime in Interstate Commerce ('Kefauver Committee'), 'Third Interim Report of the Special Committee to Investigate Organized Crime in Interstate Commerce', 1951, 32.

59 Kefauver, *Crime in America*, 202.

60 Ibid.

Q. You certainly would be aiding and abetting in it.
A. Well, that's a legal question I admit I hadn't thought of.[61]

Implicit in this dialogue is the question of responsibilities that professional advisers bear when dealing with potential criminals. It would take decades before AML regulation would provide a reasonably comprehensive set of answers. However, Halley's reference to aiding and abetting is noteworthy. As we have seen, the law of complicity could already form the basis for prosecuting professional money launderers, but by 1950 the only 'money laundering'-related prosecutions were those brought against people selling commodities to others in the knowledge that they would be misused for criminal purposes. Despite the pointed exchange at the hearings, Alvin E. Giesey was never charged with complicity in any crime.

From among the Kefauver Committee's recommendations, a number pertained to strengthening tax enforcement in connection with illicit income.[62] Still, for all its focus on the finances of organised crime, the Committee did not contemplate the development of a distinct AML regime separate from tax enforcement. It took the problem of foreign bank secrecy to give the impetus to the development of the first money laundering-related reporting obligations, as well as acknowledge money laundering as a transnational problem that it is widely seen as today.

2.3 ANTI-MONEY LAUNDERING REGULATION: REPORTING AND DUE DILIGENCE

A recognisably modern AML regime began to take shape in the 1970s and 1980s. This happened in two waves. The first one was the emergence of what some have described as 'preventative' AML measures, that is, CDD and various reporting obligations, in the 1970s.[63] The second wave was the criminalisation of money laundering and development of the proceeds of crime law in the 1980s: the 'enforcement' or 'repressive' side of AML laws. The rise of both these areas of AML laws were largely, but not exclusively, a product of US domestic developments, with a side serving of early Swiss regulatory efforts.

61 Ibid, 203.

62 Kefauver Committee, 'Final Report', 1951, 13–16. Those are the twenty-two recommendations originally made in the Committee's third interim report and restated in its final report, in addition to twelve new recommendations added in the final report. From the twenty-two original recommendations, taxation was the focal point of Recommendation 5 (for the IRS to enforce tax laws 'against the gamblers, gangsters, and racketeers who are continually flouting them', and for the violation of the requirement to keep adequate books and records to be made a felony); Recommendation 6 (for the casinos to be required to maintain 'daily records of money won and lost' and file them with the IRS); Recommendation 7 (for expenses incurred in the conduct of illegal gambling to be non-tax-deductible); and Recommendation 9 (to require 'any person who has been engaged in an illegitimate business netting in excess $2,500 a year for any of five years previously, to file a net-worth statement of all his assets, along with his income-tax returns').

63 Michael Levi and Peter Reuter, 'Money Laundering' in Michael Tonry (ed), *Crime and Justice: A Review of Research* (Volume 34, Chicago University Press, 2006) 333.

2.3.1 *US Bank Secrecy Act 1970: Reporting Requirements*

The first such key development was the enactment of the Bank Secrecy Act 1970, which retains its relevance as a cornerstone of US AML rules up until now: hence the frequently used term 'BSA/AML compliance'. The Act's principal contribution is the establishment of significant reporting obligations, first imposed on financial institutions and then expanded more broadly to other businesses. Since its adoption, the Bank Secrecy Act has required three categories of reports:

- currency transaction reports (CTRs) for all cash transactions above a certain threshold;
- reports of international transportation of currency or monetary instruments (CMIRs) for moving cash or monetary instruments above a certain threshold; and
- reports of foreign bank and financial accounts (FBAR) to be filed by US citizens with bank or other financial accounts overseas.[64]

The threshold for reporting was left for the Treasury to determine, which it did via regulations promulgated in 1972, which set the CTR threshold at US$10,000 (never since revised) and the CMIR threshold at US$5,000,[65] later brought to US$10,000.[66] Despite multiple amendments since,[67] all of those forms of reporting continue to be required in the US,[68] alongside the wire transfer reporting requirements introduced in 1992.[69]

The genesis of the Bank Secrecy Act lies only in part with organised crime-related concerns. In 1967, the President's Commission on Law Enforcement and Administration of Justice set up by Lyndon Johnson produced a major 300-page report on the state of organised crime in the US but made no finance-related recommendations.[70] What drew attention to the financial side of crime was the obstacle

64 US General Accountability Office, *Bank Secrecy Act: Treasury Can Improve Implementation of the Act*, 1986, 9.

65 37 CFR 6819, 6913 (5 April 1972).

66 31 CFR 1010.340(a).

67 The best overview of the history of CTRs is found in Jim Richards, 'Currency Transaction Reports – Past, Present, and Possible Future', 18 October 2023, https://antimoneylaundering.wtf/f/currency-transaction-reports—past-present-and-possible-future. For further detail, see Jonathan Rusch, 'Hue and Cry in the Counting-House: Some Observations on the Bank Secrecy Act' (1988) 37(2) *Catholic University LR* 465.

68 For CTRs, 31 USC § 5313 (provision introduced by the Bank Secrecy Act), implemented by 31 CFR § 1010.311 (regulation made by FinCEN). For CMIRs, 31 USC § 5316 and 31 CFR § 1010.340. For FBARs, 31 USC § 5314 and 31 CFR 1010.350.

69 Annunzio-Wylie Anti-Money Laundering Act, Pub. L. No. 102-550, § 1515, 106 Stat. 3672, 4058 (1992) discussed in Courtney J. Linn, 'Redefining the Bank Secrecy Act: Currency Reporting and the Crime of Structuring' (2010) 50(2) *Santa Clara LR* 407, 420. These requirements are contained in 31 CFR 103.33(e)–(f).

70 The closest it got to the issue was observing that 'gambling and other illegal goods and services' was generating twice as much revenue for organised crime as all other crime combined: President's Commission on Law Enforcement and Administration of Justice, *The Challenge of Crime in a Free*

that foreign bank secrecy increasingly proved to be across US efforts against a swathe of problems including tax evasion, organised crime, insider dealing and securities manipulation. As early as in the 1960s, Meyer Lansky, popularly known as the mob's accountant, set up bank accounts in Switzerland, Panama and other jurisdictions that came to be associated with 'offshore' financial activity.[71] The growing unease about foreign nations' bank secrecy harkened back to the suspicions during the 1940s that Swiss bank secrecy was being used to hold Nazi assets in the US via US branches of Swiss banks.[72]

This problem landed on the desk of the US Senate Committee on Banking and Currency, chaired by Senator William Proxmire. In 1970, the Committee convened hearings on foreign bank secrecy to gather expert testimony and explore Senator Proxmire's proposed bill to tackle the problem.[73] The bill consisted of multiple components, including the prohibition on US broker-dealers carrying out trades on behalf of foreign banks without knowing the identity of the ultimate customer; the filing of CTRs; and the retention of photocopies of certain documents, such as checks.

During the hearings, the overlap between financial obfuscation techniques used by organised crime and tax evaders became abundantly clear. Those techniques were somewhat more sophisticated than those encountered by the Kefauver Committee. For example, Assistant Attorney General Will Wilson spoke of the following case before the Banking and Currency Committee:

> We know that foreign banks are used to 'clean' dirty money. Here is an example of how it works – a racket controlled domestic corporation borrows $200,000 from a foreign bank. The loan is collateralized by the same $200,000 which never leaves the bank. We refer to this as a 'plug' loan. The corporation then loans $200,000 of illegally obtained funds to one of its officials, describing the foreign bank loan as the source of this money. Everyone benefits – the corporation deducts the interest on its foreign bank loan from its tax returns; the racketeer official deducts the interest he pays the corporation; more significant, he justifies possession of $200,000 and

Society, 1967, 32. The point about the Commission's lack of focus on finance was made in Mark Turkington, 'The Effectiveness of Private Sector Engagement in International Financial Crime Countermeasures' (PhD thesis, La Trobe Law School, February 2019) 37.

71 Some suggest that Lansky's money laundering via offshore banking was relatively unsophisticated in that he only secreted funds in Swiss bank accounts and never brought them back to the US, using the scheme 'as an elaborate version of cash under the bed': Robert Lacey, *Meyer Lansky: The Thinking Man's Gangster* (Apostrophe Books Ltd, 2015) Ch 17.

72 C. Todd Jones, 'Compulsion over Comity: The United States' Assault on Foreign Bank Secrecy' (1992) 12(3) *Northwestern J Int'l L & Bus* 454. Nor would those concerns be allayed by the Allied Powers' tortured experience of tracking overseas German holdings in countries beyond Switzerland after World War II: William Z. Slany, *U.S. and Allied Efforts to Recover and Restore Gold and Other Assets Stolen or Hidden by Germany during World War II: Preliminary Study*, 1997.

73 S. 3678, 91st Congress (1970). The Committee also considered similar a similar bill tabled in the House of Representatives: H.R. 15073, with part of the discussion revolving around the differences between the two bills.

> defeats efforts to prove a net worth tax case.[74] The foreign bank receives interest on money which it retains. The domestic money, illegally obtained, surfaces as clean money to be used in further illegal activities or penetrate legitimate business.[75]

Both the scheme described and the language used (making 'dirty' money 'clean') demonstrate that money laundering had become a phenomenon familiar to law enforcement agencies by 1970. There is also evidence of the term being current in popular press as early as in 1967.[76] Of greatest interest, though, is the discussion during the hearings of the Committee's proposed solutions to the foreign bank secrecy problem and the background to them.

The CTR reporting idea was not unprecedented.[77] It had first surfaced in regulations adopted by the Acting Secretary of the Treasury pursuant to the Trading with the Enemy Act 1917 in May 1945. Section 5(b) of the Act, which is still in force as amended, vests the US president with broad powers to, among other things, 'regulate (…) any transactions in foreign exchange, transfers of credit or payments between, by, through, or to any banking institution (…) by any person, or with respect to any property, subject to the jurisdiction of the United States'.[78] Based on a delegation of this presidential authority, a regulation promulgated in May 1945 provided as follows:

> Commencing with transactions occurring in the month of June, 1945, every financial institution in the United States shall file monthly reports on Form TCR-1 concerning each deposit or withdrawal, or other payment or transfer, effected by, through, or to such financial institution which involves United States currency in amounts or denominations which, in the judgment of the financial institution exceed those commensurate with the legitimate and customary conduct of the business, industry, or profession of the person or organization concerned. The fact that a transaction involves $1,000 or more of United States currency in denominations of $50 or higher, or involves $10,000 or more of United States currency in any denominations shall be deemed to necessitate the filing of a report on Form TCR-1 unless in the judgment of the financial institution the transaction is commensurate with the legitimate and customary conduct of the business, industry, or profession of the person or organization concerned.[79]

74 This refers to the government's ability to prove the taxpayer's taxable income by reference to his or her overall net worth in the absence of appropriately documented and itemised sources of such wealth. See Leslie Mills, 'The Net Worth Approach in Determining Income' (1955) 41(7) *Virginia LR* 927. Footnote not in the original quote.

75 US Senate Committee on Banking and Currency, Subcommittee on Financial Institutions, *Foreign Bank Secrecy* (US Government Printing Office, 1970) 58.

76 Richard Oulahan and William Lambert, 'The Scandal in the Bahamas', *Life Magazine*, 3 February 1967; Sylvan Fox, 'Few Loan Sharks Are Hooked by New and Stricter Laws', *The New York Times*, 29 January 1968. One author notes that the earliest use of the term 'money laundering' dates back to the 1910s but refers to the US Treasury's short-lived plan to clean ('launder') soiled banknotes instead of removing them from circulation: Stefano Siggia, 'The US Treasury's Money Laundering Machine' (2024) 74(4) *History Today*.

77 Richards, 'Currency Transaction Reports'.

78 Trading with the Enemy Act 1917 (US), 40 Stat. 411.

79 31 CFR § 102.1 (1949), 10 FR 6556.

Discernible in this dense language are the requirements to report unusual transactions ('exceed[ing] those commensurate with the legitimate and customary conduct of the business') and transactions exceeding a specified monetary threshold. The proviso that a report need not be made if the transaction is, in the judgment of the financial institution, 'commensurate' with the ordinary course of business suggests that the primary rationale behind the rule was precisely to collect information on presumptively unusual – and, thus, potentially suspicious – transactions rather than build a database of transactions of certain value.

This regulation marks the beginning of threshold-based and unusual transaction reporting. The latter form of reporting has since fell into disuse in common law countries in favour of a similar but distinct concept of *suspicious* transaction reporting,[80] although it continues to be utilised in certain civil law jurisdictions, notably in the Netherlands.[81] While the US government did not state at the time why those controls were being introduced in 1945, the time of Victory in Europe was when one could expect the Nazis to escalate their efforts to dissipate their funds overseas to go into hiding.[82] One might perceive a parallel here to the intensification of US anti-financial crime efforts in the aftermath of the invasion of Iraq in 2003 to deny the deposed Saddam Hussein's loyalists the funds that might otherwise have been available to them.[83]

Between 1945 and 1970, the currency reporting regime had undergone several changes. In 1952, the reporting obligation was amended to cover (a) transactions of US$2,500 or more in denominations of $100 or higher; (b) transactions of US$10,000 or more in any denomination; and (c) transactions of any amount 'which in the judgment of the financial institution exceed those commensurate with the customary conduct of the business, industry or profession of the person or organization concerned'.[84] Here, too, one sees a mixture of unusual transaction reports (UTRs) and threshold-based reports that is premised on certain amounts of transactions, or even the denomination of banknotes involved, being treated as a heuristic for being unusual or suspicious.

80 Save that the British Columbia Lottery Corporation (BCLC), the gambling regulator in the Canadian province of British Columbia, requires licenced gaming service providers to submit unusual transaction reports to it. The BCLC then decides whether those reports give rise to a suspicion of financial crime and therefore merit filing a suspicious transaction report (STR) to Canada's financial intelligence unit, FINTRAC. See Peter M. German QC, *Dirty Money: An Independent Review of Money Laundering in Lower Mainland Casinos Conducted for the Attorney General of British Columbia*, 31 March 2018, paras 359–365.

81 OECD, *Implementing the OECD Anti-Bribery Convention – Phase 4 Report: Netherlands*, 2021, paras 30–31.

82 See, e.g., Neil Barofsky, *Report of the Independent Ombudsperson and Independent Advisor to Credit Suisse*, 15 February 2023, 35 (referring to Nazi escape routes, known as 'ratlines', and suspicions of Swiss banks' involvement in their financial facilitation).

83 Juan Zarate, *Treasury's War: The Unleashing of a New Era of Financial Warfare* (PublicAffairs, 2013) 198–199.

84 17 CFR 1822, 2306.

The practical effect of these obligations seems to have been limited. In his testimony before the Banking and Currency Committee in 1970, Assistant Attorney General Wilson said UTRs under the Trading with the Enemy Act had not been useful due to banks' differing interpretations of what 'unusual' meant, as well as because of the obligation being limited to cash transactions alone, as distinct from, for example, wire transfers.[85] By contrast, in a subsequent Supreme Court case involving a legal challenge by the California Bankers Association to what became the Bank Secrecy Act, Justice Rehnquist, writing for the Court's majority, referred to the Treasury Secretary's statement in 1959 acknowledging the 'great value' of such reports.[86]

One noteworthy aspect of the Banking and Currency Committee's hearings was its adumbration of the by-now familiar concerns about the unintended consequences of the proposed legislation. Carl W. Desch, Senior Vice President at First National City Bank (now Citibank), cautioned that he and his fellow executives were 'gravely concerned by the possible impact of the bill on the international position of the dollar'[87]; a concern that has been repeated often since then, especially in connection with economic sanctions.[88] Another worry was the compliance burden and its cost: for instance, Coleman McGehee of First & Merchants Bank in Virginia, suggested that 'the [Treasury] Secretary should be authorized to reimburse the designated financial institutions for expenses incurred by them' in complying with the reporting requirements of the bill.[89]

Notwithstanding those notes of caution, the Bank Secrecy Act was adopted in 1970 and, for all practical effects and purposes, instituted the contemporary reporting regime. The first provision of the Act, entitled 'The Statement of Purpose', read as follows:

> It is the purpose of this [Act] to require certain reports or records where they have a high degree of usefulness in criminal, tax, or regulatory investigations or proceedings.[90]

This provision was amended by the Patriot Act following 9/11, which inserted the words 'or in the conduct of intelligence or counterintelligence activities, including analysis, to protect against international terrorism'.[91] This statement of purpose, in both its original and amended forms, highlights the focus of the Bank Secrecy Act

[85] US Senate Committee on Banking and Currency, Subcommittee on Financial Institutions, *Foreign Bank Secrecy* (US Government Printing Office, 1970) 66.

[86] *California Bankers Ass'n v Shultz*, 416 US 21, 38 (1974).

[87] *Foreign Bank Secrecy*, 188.

[88] See, e.g., Agathe Demarais, *Backfire: How Sanctions Reshape the World against U.S. Interests* (Columbia University Press, 2022).

[89] *Foreign Bank Secrecy*, 229.

[90] 31 USC § 5311.

[91] Section 385 of Uniting and Strengthening America by Providing Appropriate Tools Required to Intercept and Obstruct Terrorism (USA PATRIOT) Act of 2001.

on the supply of actionable intelligence to law enforcement agencies[92]; an objective that, as we shall see, has become adulterated with other considerations as time went on.

Despite the enactment of the Bank Secrecy Act, the reporting requirements under it were widely neglected until the mid 1980s. In 1979, a regulation published by the Treasury referred to the fact that '[a]lthough commercial banks alone are estimated to have processed in excess of 30 billion transaction in 1979, only about 120,000 reports were filed, less than one for every 200,000 transactions'.[93] That same year, the Government Accountability Office issued a report highly critical of the Treasury's modest enforcement efforts.[94]

The banking industry's paltry compliance record came into the open in the late 1970s and early 1980s.[95] The first harbinger of greater focus on it was the indictment in 1977 of Chemical Bank, the country's sixth largest bank charged with laundering money for Italian American mafia. Specifically, Chemical Bank 'failed to report more than $8.5 million in more than 500 cash transactions, some of which included individual cash exchanges ranging from $10,000 to $250,000'.[96] The bank and two of its officers pleaded guilty within the next two months: in the case of the officers, the offence was that not of disclosing the taxable income received as a commission for their money laundering services from the mobsters.[97] Robert Mazur, a one-time undercover IRS agent, has rightly described the enforcement action against Chemical Bank 'a groundbreaking case in its time' yet involving a fine that amounted to little more than 'a slap on the wrist and the cost of doing business'.[98]

This was followed by the indictment in 1982 and guilty plea in 1984 of the Great American Bank of Dade County for failures to file CTRs, which resulted from an eighteen-month multi-agency investigation into drug-related money laundering in Miami known as 'Operation Greenback'.[99] The origins of the operation stemmed from the realisation that, unlike other areas of the country, Miami had experienced a surfeit of cash as a result of the influx of drug proceeds.[100] Then, in 1985, the Bank

[92] John J. Byrne, 'The Bank Secrecy Act: Do Reporting Requirements Really Assist the Government' (1993) 44(3) *Ala LR* 801, 801; Jim Richards, 'White Paper: 50 Years of the Bank Secrecy Act', *Verafin*, 2020, 2.

[93] 45 FR 37818, 37819, as observed in Richards, 'Currency Transaction Reports'.

[94] *Treasury Can Improve Implementation of the Act*, 15.

[95] For an excellent historical account, see Paul Camacho, '50 Years of BSA: From Dormancy to Zeal' (2020) 19(4) *ACAMS Today* 40.

[96] President's Commission on Organized Crime, *The Cash Connection: Organized Crime, Financial Institutions and Money Laundering*, 1984, 48.

[97] Ibid; Arnold H. Lubasch, 'Chemical Bank to Pay $222,500 Fine', *New York Times*, 15 April 1977.

[98] Robert Mazur, *The Infiltrator: Undercover in the World of Drug Barons and Dirty Banks* (Corgi Books, 2015) Ch 1.

[99] 'Bank Pleads Guilty in $94 Million Money Laundering Scheme', *UPI Archives*, 17 April 1984, www.upi.com/Archives/1984/04/17/Bank-pleads-guilty-in-94-million-money-laundering-scheme/8235451026000/.

[100] 'Miami Bank Indicted on Charges of Laundering Illicit Drug Money', *New York Times*, 14 December 1982.

of Boston was prosecuted for organising, and not reporting, bulk shipments of cash to Switzerland on behalf of its customers.[101] The Bank of Boston pleaded guilty to criminal violations of the Bank Secrecy Act, and its president was compelled to testify before Congress.[102]

A notable feature of these banking debacles is that they involved not merely non-compliance with reporting requirements, but wilful facilitation of serious financial offending, even if only at the local branch level. This had drawn the US government's attention to the role of the banking industry in facilitating crime. In 1983, President Ronald Reagan established the President's Commission on Organized Crime, a twelve-member-strong advisory body vested with the task of providing evidence-based analysis of organised crime and responses thereto in the US.[103] The Chairman of the Commission was Judge Irving Kaufman, best known for sentencing to death the Soviet spies Julius and Ethel Rosenberg, but also with experience of presiding over mob trials.[104]

The Commission's first report, published in 1984, was devoted to money laundering and entitled *The Cash Connection*, a play on the newly uncovered drug distribution scheme involving pizza parlours known as the 'pizza connection' whose proceeds were laundered through the Bank of Boston.[105] The overall tenor of the report was to highlight the extent to which segments of the private sector had become wilfully complicit in the laundering of drug money. For example, in its account of Operation Greenback, the President's Commission wrote as follows:

> The targets identified to date include attorneys, accountants, money brokers, money couriers, bankers, and banks involved in facilitating the flow of drug money through financial institutions and across U.S. borders to foreign countries. Operation Greenback has documented $2.6 billion in U.S. currency that has been laundered through 16 narcotics organizations. There have been 164 arrests, 211 indictments, 63 convictions, $38.5 million in seized currency, $7.5 million in seized property, and $117 million in IRS jeopardy and termination assessments.[106]

The Cash Connection's analysis, conclusions and recommendations were pivotal for further development of the US's AML regime. First, it recommended the criminalisation of money laundering as a self-standing offence designed to capture

[101] For a detailed account of the allegations, see Rep. Lungren's statements in Dan Lungren (CA), 'Money Laundering', *Congressional Record* (1986) 1982–1985.

[102] First National Bank of Boston, CR 85 52-MA (D. Mass Feb 7, 1985). See also US Congress, *The First National Bank of Boston: Hearings before the Subcommittee on Financial Institutions Supervision, Regulation and Insurance of the Committee on Banking Finance and Urban Affairs*, 99th Congress 99–118, 1985.

[103] Executive Order 12435: President's Commission on Organized Crime, 48 FR 34723 (28 July 1983).

[104] Martin J. Siegel, *Judgment and Mercy: The Turbulent Life and Times of the Judge Who Condemned the Rosenbergs* (Cornell University, 2023) 161–167.

[105] Interview with a US lawyer specialising in AML/CTF (A), 14 November 2023.

[106] *The Cash Connection*, 26.

such instances of complicity as those that came to light in the Commission's inquiry. Second, while not explicitly recommending the establishment of a mandatory suspicious activity reporting regime, the Commission's zeroed in on then-existing obstacles to banks' ability to proactively report suspicious activities, including potential civil and criminal liability under the Right to Financial Privacy Act 1978.[107] The Right to Financial Privacy Act itself had been Congress's response to two Supreme Court cases holding that individuals enjoyed no constitutional protection from search and seizure vis-à-vis law enforcement agencies' subpoenas of their financial information from banks, attorneys or tax advisors.[108] In view of those challenges, the Commission proposed, among other things, the following legislative amendment, subsequently adopted as part of the Money Laundering Control Act 1986:

> Nothing in [the Right to Financial Privacy Act 1978] shall preclude any financial institution, or any officer, employee, or agent of a financial institution, from notifying a Government authority that such institution, or officer, employee, or agent has information which it believes may be relevant to a possible violation of any statute or regulation, and thereafter disclosing such information to that Government authority, regardless of whether a subpoena, summons, search warrant, or formal written request has been issued under the provisions of this chapter.[109]

These changes are emblematic of the renegotiation of the boundaries between AML-related financial surveillance and financial privacy that has been ongoing ever since. The Commission also touched upon the issue of what we would describe today as CDD, but without identifying it as a discrete area of focus. In describing Chemical Bank's groundbreaking prosecution under the Bank Secrecy Act, the Commission noted that, in response to these developments, the bank implemented a 'know your customer' policy that 'advises employees that it is the policy of Chemical Bank "to do business only with individuals, businesses, and other entities whose reputations are sound"'.[110] Although no suggestion was made by the Commission that all banks should follow suit in instituting such a policy, it drafted voluntary guidelines that it suggested financial institutions might wish to adopt. The Commission's guidelines included training bank employees in identifying typical traits of money laundering transactions, including a set of eight characteristics, such as:

> A person whose individual or corporate accounts show virtually no normal business-related banking activities and who uses those accounts primarily as a temporary repository for funds ultimately transferred to foreign bank accounts.[111]

[107] Ibid, 30.

[108] *US v Miller*, 425 US 435 (1976) (involving bank records); *Fisher v US*, 425 US 391 (1976) (involving records prepared by an accountant and held by an attorney). See Electronic Privacy Information Center, 'Right to Financial Privacy Act', undated, https://epic.org/the-right-to-financial-privacy-act/.

[109] Codified as 12 USC § 3403(c). See also *The Cash Connection*, 75.

[110] *The Cash Connection*, 49.

[111] Ibid, 54.

The notion of exercising vigilance to identify unusual activity patterns presupposes a certain understanding of what a given customer's normal activity would look like, which is the essence of CDD. While the Commission stopped short of articulating any due diligence-related requirements, its tentative foray into this topic signifies the emergence of CDD as another key form of financial crime controls. Which, as it happens, by that point had already become the focus of attention nowhere else but in Switzerland, the epicentre of many of a money laundering scandal that impelled US AML efforts. This is where, for the first time in our historical excursus, we need to shift our focus from the US to Europe to continue the story of how we got to the current AML regime.

2.3.2 *Swiss Due Diligence Agreement 1977: Customer Due Diligence*

In its money laundering report, the President's Commission on Organized Crime referred expressly to the need to lead by example in shutting the finances of organised crime from the legitimate financial sector:

> In calling upon our own private sector to turn away the mob's money, we draw upon the strength of our system of free enterprise because there is little reason to expect foreign governments to act if we cannot also secure the assistance of our own financial community.[112]

It is ironic that one of the countries of greatest concern to the US government at the moment was itself experimenting with introducing AML rules and has a plausible claim to becoming the first jurisdiction with formalised CDD rules: even if, as discussed below, their reach and import remained modest at first.

The origins of the concept of CDD reach back to a scandal that erupted in the Swiss banking sector in 1977. It involved a branch of Credit Suisse, the country's oldest bank, in the town of Chiasso, 'within suit-carrying distance' of the Italian border.[113] It transpired that the management of the branch had set up a company in Liechtenstein as an intermediary to enable Italian clients to open accounts with Credit Suisse with their identities obscured.[114] The total amount invested with Credit Suisse in this manner reached US$800 million, or US$4 billion in today's money.[115] The 8 per cent return the Chiasso branch of Credit Suisse was offering exceeded other available Swiss bank offerings at the time, and the investments it

[112] Ibid, 26.

[113] Michael Getler, 'Credit Suisse Scandal Casts Shadow over Swiss Banks', *The Washington Post*, 21 May 1977, www.washingtonpost.com/archive/business/1977/05/22/credit-suisse-scandal-casts-shadow-over-swiss-banks/3a5e8c74-0ea8-422b-beb1-f0f2e7b59344/.

[114] John M. Geddes, 'Swiss Banks Riding Out Scandal', *The New York Times*, 5 June 1979.

[115] '8% Returns and a Major Scandal at the Credit Bank in Switzerland', *The New York Times*, 2 May 1977. The currency value conversion is based on the information provided by the Federal Reserve Bank of Minneapolis at www.minneapolisfed.org/about-us/monetary-policy/inflation-calculator.

administered had features of a Ponzi scheme: that is, the funds of newly signed up investors were used to pay earlier investors.[116] The money was also invested in a coterie of Italian businesses. As the Italian economy contracted in the 1970s, the returns from those businesses dried up and the influx of new investors slowed down, such that the operation run from Credit Suisse's Chiasso branch realised a loss of US$700 million and forced the story into the open.[117]

The 'Chiasso case' promptly led to the conclusion of a Due Diligence Agreement[118] between the Swiss government, acting via the Swiss National Bank, and Swiss banks. As the title suggests, the Due Diligence Agreement required Swiss banks to identify who their customers were and where their money came from. For instance, Article 3 provided as follows:

> The banks undertake not to open bank accounts and securities deposits, not to effect fiduciary investments and not to provide safe-deposit facilities unless they have ascertained with such care as, according to circumstances, can reasonably be expected who the beneficial owner of the funds to be credited or to be invested or who the renter of the safe deposit box is.[119]

The obligation to ascertain the beneficial owner of the funds can be described as a proto-due diligence obligation. Unless the person concerned is a known criminal, someone's identity alone is insufficient to determine whether he or she is utilising a bank account for criminal purposes. This is why contemporary CDD involves establishing a baseline of expected normal activity against which the client's transactions could be judged.

This laissez-faire approach began morphing into a more well-defined set of practices in 1991 with the adoption by the Swiss Federal Banking Commission of indicators of suspicious activities, followed by the promulgation of a similar document by the Swiss Bankers Association in 1992.[120] Still, as detailed in Thomas Grant's interviews with Swiss bank compliance officers in the mid 1990s, the identification and investigation of suspicion remained driven by the relationship manager's gut feelings rather than any structured risk assessment process:

> If, for example, a pair of young men, holding Tunisian passports, enter the offices of Pictet with a valise containing ten million Swiss francs in small and medium bills, their request to open an account will not be granted without rigorous inquiry.[121]

116 Ibid.

117 Victor Lusinchi, 'Chiasso Bank's Ex-Head Takes Blame for Scandal', *The New York Times*, 29 May 1979.

118 Vereinbarung über die Standesregeln zur Sorgfaltspflicht der Banken (VSB).

119 Available in an unofficial English translation at www.swissbanking.ch/_Resources/Persistent/1/5/c/4/15c432fb98b85a9d53befc88b57fc95004996036/vsb_1977-en.pdf.

120 Thomas D. Grant, 'Toward a Swiss Solution for an American Problem: An Alternative Approach for Banks in the War on Drugs' (1995) 14 *Ann Rev Banking L* 225, 246–247.

121 Ibid, 248.

Despite the rudimentary nature of the checks to be performed, the Due Diligence Agreement presupposed that they would help banks identify criminal misuse and, on that basis, required them to forego certain business opportunities:

> The banks undertake not to transact any business if it is known to them or if it should be known to them in exercising reasonable care that the funds are entrusted to them for purposes that are considered to be improper within the meaning of this agreement.[122]

Improper purposes were defined to include acts punishable or calling for extradition under Swiss law, evasion of foreign capital controls and domestic or foreign tax evasion.[123] The undertaking to accept no improper business was complemented by the commitment to break off existing customer relationships 'if, in the course of business, suspicion should arise that the information obtained on the beneficial owner is not correct or that the customer performs acts through the bank which, within the meaning of this agreement, are improper'.[124]

The Due Diligence Agreement was underpinned by the establishment of an Arbitration Committee based in Zurich with the power to adjudicate alleged breaches and issue fines of up to 10 million Swiss francs, equivalent to approximately US$10 million in today's money. Since 2007, the Committee has been publishing summaries of its 'leading cases' online.[125] The incidence and amounts of financial penalties being levied has increased with time. For instance, while only 18 out of 113 violations identified between 2006 and 2011 led to a financial penalty of over 100,000 Swiss francs, 22 out of 52 violations adjudicated between 2011 and 2016 involved such penalties, including one in the amount of over 1 million Swiss francs.[126]

The historical record of the considerations that led Switzerland to adopt this model in response to the Chiasso scandal is incomplete but enables an educated guess. Archival research conducted by Stavros Gadinis and Colby Mangels of the University of California at Berkeley refers to the contemporaneous minutes of the meetings of the Swiss National Bank's board of directors that recorded Fritz Leutwiler, later president of the Bank for International Settlements, as saying as follows:

> There are bank clients with noticeably doubtful, yes even criminal backgrounds, and therefore should not have been accepted, nevertheless they were accepted, and there exists related money in Swiss banks.[127]

[122] Article 4 of the Due Diligence Agreement.

[123] Articles 2, 8 and 9 of the Due Diligence Agreement.

[124] Article 12 of the Due Diligence Agreement.

[125] Available at Swiss Banking, 'Combating Money Laundering', undated, www.swissbanking.ch/en/topics/regulation-and-compliance/the-fight-against-money-laundering.

[126] Georg Friedli and Dominik Eichenberger, 'Praxis der Aufsichtskommission zur Sorgfaltspflicht der Banken für die Jahre 2011 bis 2016', 29 June 2017, 5.

[127] Stavros Gadinis and Colby Mangels, 'Collaborative Gatekeepers' (2016) 73(2) *Washington & Lee LR* 797, 854, footnote 204.

Despite being primarily a tax affair the Chiasso scandal served as a catalyst for long-overdue action addressing the broader risks of criminal exploitation of the Swiss banking system, led by the Swiss National Bank's vice-chairman Leo Schürmann.[128] The storied history of financial scandals involving Switzerland might render one instinctually suspicious of suggestions that the Swiss government was undertaking a good-faith effort to clean up its financial system, but the sincerity of the intention matters less than the fact that Switzerland was forced to acknowledge the problem.

International pressures on Swiss bank secrecy were multiplying throughout the 1970s, ranging from US Congressional hearings that led to the Bank Secrecy Act 1970 to the awkward questions of locating and disposing of the Swiss-based bank accounts of foreign rulers in the aftermath of regime change. For instance, the issue arose in connection with the wealth of Iran's deposed Shah, Mohammad Reza Pahlavi, in the wake of the Iranian revolution of 1979.[129] The Swiss government's ability to respond to international criticism, including by helping foreign states recover the wealth of their rulers in the wake of regime change, was compromised by the near-total lack of visibility into whose money was being stored in Switzerland. The adoption of due diligence rules presented a modest concession to the dual imperatives of strengthening the Swiss regulatory regime to fend off foreign criticism and enabling Switzerland own's government to better understand whose funds Swiss banks did or did not keep.

The Due Diligence Agreement fell short of completely transforming the Swiss banking industry. In 1990, the Swiss sociology professor Jean Ziegler published a best-selling book *The Swiss Whitewash* in which he alleged that Switzerland had remained a favoured haven for organised crime, including Pablo Escobar's Medellin drug cartel, and foreign dictators, such as Ferdinand Marcos of the Philippines and Mobutu Sese Seko of Zaire (now, the Democratic Republic of the Congo).[130] Long-running cross-border attempts to recover Marcos's and Mobutu's loot attest to the validity of Ziegler's general assessment of the feeble state of Swiss defences against financial crime,[131] irrespective of the fairness of his characterisation of specific individuals or institutions, which led to a spate of libel lawsuits. The proactive involvement of Swiss banks in facilitating industrial-scale tax evasion by foreign citizens would continue to prove a recurrent source of embarrassment for decades since the Due Diligence Agreement was concluded, as demonstrated by the UBS whistleblower Bradley Birkenfeld's disclosures in 2007.[132]

128 Ibid, 852.

129 Interview with a Swiss banking expert, 17 January 2024.

130 Jean Ziegler, *Swiss Whitewash: Drugs, Dirty Money, and Laundering by the Swiss Banks* (Arcade Publishing, 1992).

131 See David Chaikin and J. C. Sharman, *Corruption and Money Laundering: A Symbiotic Relationship* (Palgrave Macmillan, 2009) 153–186.

132 US Senate Permanent Subcommittee on Investigations, *Tax Haven Banks and U.S. Tax Compliance*, Hearing of the Permanent Subcommittee on Investigations, 110th Congress, July 2008.

On the other hand, Switzerland retained its willingness to roll out legal reforms in response to major scandals, including laws informally known as Lex Duvalier and Lex Ben Ali after the respective Haitian and Tunisian dictators.[133] Over time, these changes have resulted in Switzerland becoming one of the easier jurisdictions to recover the proceeds of corruption from, although doubts remain as to the strengths of its preventative AML controls that would preclude dirty money from being invested in Switzerland to begin with.[134]

There are multiple clues suggesting that the Due Diligence Agreement was meant to be a modest concession to the need for regulation rather than a concerted effort to relegate Swiss bank secrecy to a thing of the past. For one thing, as already mentioned, the agreement itself created no reporting obligations. Self-standing obligations under Swiss law required the disclosure of certain banking information upon a law enforcement agency's valid request, but that stopped far short of a modern-style reporting obligation.

There are also other features of the Due Diligence Agreement that look inadequate from a contemporary perspective. For instance, the Due Diligence Agreement allowed Swiss banks to provide services to unknown customers introduced by foreign law firms or trustees provided only that such an intermediary furnished 'a written statement to the effect that the owner is known to him and that no improper transactions within the meaning of this agreement are involved'.[135] That provision alone was sufficient to entirely undermine the efficacy of the Due Diligence Agreement, and in 1991 the Swiss Banking Commission dispensed with it by only allowing allowance on a lawyer's or notary's due diligence if they certify that the funds were held for one of four narrowly defined purposes.[136]

Fundamentally, though, the impact of the Due Diligence Agreement lay in formalising the concept of CDD, as well as linking it directly to the bank's decision whether to onboard a client or continue an existing client relationship. The focus on due diligence for the purpose of deciding whether a customer is acceptable to onboard or retain, is emblematic of what can be described as an 'exclusionary' paradigm: a vision of financial crime regulation as being concerned with the exclusion of proceeds of crime from the legitimate economy. This can be contrasted with the 'surveillance' paradigm manifested in the US's early introduction of threshold-based and

133 Federal Act on the Restitution of Assets illicitly obtained by Politically Exposed Persons of 1 October 2010 ('Lex Duvalier') and Federal Act on the Freezing and the Restitution of Illicit Assets held by Foreign Politically Exposed Persons of 18 December 2015 ('Lex Ben Ali').

134 JC Sharman, *The Despot's Guide to Wealth Management: On the International Campaign against Grand Corruption* (Cornell University Press, 2017) 88. ('In terms of international regulatory politics, Switzerland has been most accommodating to poor and weak developing countries seeking the return of looted assets, but most defiant when it came to the demands of the United States and European Union seeking information on their citizens' Swiss bank accounts.')

135 Article 5 of the Due Diligence Agreement.

136 Grant, 'Toward a Swiss Solution for an American Problem', 244.

unusual transaction reporting. As we shall see, that exclusion-oriented vision of AML controls later reemerged in US and international efforts against financial crime.

The Swiss origins of the concept of due diligence imparted to it a degree of credibility that might have otherwise proved more difficult to achieve. Before long, the Council of Europe lent its support to the idea. In 1980, it adopted a non-binding recommendation calling upon member states to consider the introduction of 'identity checks on customers' in circumstances including (a) the opening of a bank account; (b) the renting of a safe deposit; (c) cash transactions above a certain threshold; and (d) inter-bank transfers above a certain threshold.[137] Beyond identity checks, an unusual form of currency controls found in the Council of Europe's Recommendation concerned 'set[ting] up machinery enabling banks, either by systematic comparison or by spot-checks, to refer to the list of banknotes used in connection with criminal offences when notes are paid in'. Its rationale becomes evident the moment one realises the Recommendation as a whole was proposed by Italy as a response to criminal activities, such as bank robberies and kidnappings, carried out by the left-wing extremist groups Brigate Rosse in Italy and Rote Armee Faktion in Germany.[138]

Like the Swiss Due Diligence Agreement, the Recommendation was a manifestation of the nascent policy consensus that banks should play a role in the detection of crime, although the precise contours of that obligation were only beginning to be elaborated. As discussed later, it took the establishment of the FATF in 1989 to provide an impetus for the greater crystallisation of due diligence rules.

2.3.3 *US Money Laundering Control Act 1986: Money Laundering as a Crime*

Before the establishment of the FATF, though, the next milestone in the development of the AML regime was the criminalisation of drug-related money laundering in 1986 in the US – and the UK following suit the same year. The vehicle for this change in the US was the Money Laundering Control Act 1986, which enacted into law many of the recommendations from *The Cash Connection* report.

The most important reform was the designation of drug-related money laundering as a self-standing criminal offence. Strictly speaking, money laundering could already be prosecuted, and had been successfully prosecuted, prior to the Act's adoption. One commentator has rightly described prosecutions for complicity as the 'first generation' of criminal law responses to money laundering.[139] This could be broken down further, since those prosecutions came in waves. The first such wave,

[137] Council of Europe, Recommendation No. R (80)10 *On Measures against the Transfer and the Safekeeping of Funds of Criminal Origin*, 1980.

[138] Michael Levi, 'Combatting the Financing of Terrorism: A History and Assessment of the Control of "Threat Finance"' (2010) 50(4) *Brit J Criminology* 650, 651.

[139] Guy Stessens, *Money Laundering: A New International Law Enforcement Model* (Cambridge University Press, 2000) 96–97.

discussed previously, involved prosecuting the knowing supply of commodities that would be used for criminal purposes. The second wave came with the revival of money laundering prosecutions from the mid 1970s onwards, this time focused on the activities of those who would today be described as 'professional enablers'.

The first reported US criminal trial featuring the phrase 'money laundering' took place in 1975 and involved Talmadge G. Rauhoff, a businessman who had designed a commercial arrangement for the clandestine payment of bribes to the Illinois Secretary of State Paul Powell.[140] Powell was notorious for his rapacity and, upon his death in a hotel room, US$150,000 in cash was discovered in shoeboxes beside him.[141] This prompted the state treasurer, Adlai Stevenson III, to quip that '[Powell's] shoeboxes will be hard to fill'.[142]

Rauhoff was convicted of mail fraud, bribery and tax violations. Some of those pertained to substantive violations of the underlying statute, such as certain mail fraud charges stemming from the mailing of checks in pursuance of the bribery scheme.[143] The judge described Rauhoff's involvement as essential to the scheme because it 'related to acceptance of the proceeds of the scheme, and facilitated concealment of the scheme'.[144] Other charges were brought on the basis of Rauhoff's conspiracy to violate the applicable statutes.[145] This demonstrates how, in common with many other categories of criminal conduct, money laundering can be tackled by means of various criminal laws.

This was followed by a spate of drug-related money laundering prosecutions, a linkage that would prove to be crucial to the evolution of AML laws. In 1971, President Richard Nixon declared in a message to Congress that drug abuse was 'America's public enemy number one', and it was 'necessary to wage a new, all-out offensive' against it.[146] That involved, among other things, going after the cartels' money. The inaugural drug-related case involving money laundering was that of *US v Barnes* in 1979 but, as Strafer observes, the defendants' money laundering merely formed one part of a plethora of their drug trafficking activities.[147] The first drug-related instance of money laundering being the sole basis for conspiracy charges

140 *US v Talmadge G. Rauhoff*, 525 F.2d 1170 (7th Cir 1975).

141 Jim Richards, 'Talmadge G. Rauhoff ... The First Reported Money Launderer?', 7 July 2023, https://antimoneylaundering.wtf/f/talmadge-g-rauhoff-the-first-reported-money-launderer. Other cases he discusses include *US v Papa*, 533 F.2d 815 (2d Cir 1976); *US v Metz*, 608 F.2d 147 (5th Cir 1979); *US v $4,255,625.39 in US Currency*, SDFL 551 (Supp. 314 1982).

142 Richards, 'Talmadge G. Rauhoff'.

143 For background on the use of mail fraud and wire fraud charges in US bribery cases, see Peter Henning and Lee Radek, *The Prosecution and Defense of Public Corruption: The Law and Legal Strategies* (Oxford University Press, 2011) 143–165.

144 *US v Talmadge G. Rauhoff*, 525 F.2d 1170, 1176 (7th Cir 1975).

145 Ibid.

146 Richard Nixon, 'Remarks about an Intensified Program for Drug Abuse Prevention and Control', 17 June 1971.

147 *US v Barnes et al*, 604 F.2d 121 (1979), discussed in Strafer, 'Money Laundering', 153.

was *US v Orozco-Prada*, which concerned four defendants who laundered US$150 million in drug proceeds via a coffee import company.[148] In *Orozco-Prada*, the Court of Appeals for the Second Circuit confirmed that the provision of money laundering services could be treated as taking part in the conspiracy to sell drugs so long as 'there was a sufficient link between [the money launderer's] operations and the underlying drug transactions'.[149]

The court did not elaborate on the precise meaning of that requirement, and in a subsequent case of *US v Della Espriella*, the Court of Appeals for the Ninth Circuit treated money laundering as inherently linked to the predicate offence.[150] *Della Espriella* is notable in that it also involved an attempt to prosecute the deliberate structuring of transactions into the deposit of cheques under US$10,000 each to avoid the filing of CTRs on the basis that such behaviour involved a conspiracy to violate the CTR provisions of the Bank Secrecy Act. The court overturned the defendants' conviction for structuring since no provision of the Bank Secrecy Act rendered it criminal.[151]

The question of proper law enforcement response to drug-related money laundering became the subject of hearings before the US Senate Subcommittee on Financial Institutions Supervision, Regulation, and Insurance in 1986. The hearings featured a raft of law enforcement officers, all of whom were asked whether money laundering ought to be a separate criminal offence. Subject to only several exceptions, the answer was a unanimous 'yes', qualified by the concern that such an offence should not 'proscribe inadvertent conduct or unwitting participants'.[152]

One particularly interesting answer was provided by Richard Wassenaar, Assistant Commissioner for Criminal Investigation at the IRS, who said he had been involved in the investigation of 800 money laundering cases between 1981 and 1986:

> I think it should [be a separate crime], absolutely. You know, an analogy might be that if there were no Federal crime for armed robbery of a bank, then you force the investigators and the prosecutors to use perhaps a violation of failure to register a weapon, when the real crime is robbing the bank.[153]

148 *US v Orozco-Prada*, 732 F.2d 1076 (2d Cir 1979). See also 'Importer Found Guilty of "Laundering" Drug Money', *The New York Times*, 24 May 1983.

149 *US v Orozco-Prada*, 732 F.2d 1076, 1081 (2d Cir 1979).

150 *US v Dela Espriella*, 781 F.2d 1432 (9th Cir 1986).

151 Ibid.

152 US Senate Subcommittee on Financial Institutions Supervision, Regulation, and Insurance, *Tax Evasion, Drug Trafficking, and Money Laundering as They Involve Financial Institutions* (US Government Printing Office, 1986) 634 (James R. Dudine, Chief, Special Activities Section, Federal Deposit Insurance Corporation); 638 (Robert E. Serino, Deputy Chief Counsel (Operations), Comptroller of the Currency); 787 (Stephen S. Trott, Assistant Attorney General, Criminal Division, Department of Justice); 888 (Matha R. Seger, member of the board of governors, Federal Reserve Board); 970 (James D. Harmon, former Executive Director, President's Commission on Organized Crime). The quotation is from Serino's statement.

153 *Tax Evasion*, 127.

This argument encapsulates the idea that criminal prosecutions should fairly capture the essence of the wrongful conduct, often described by English academic criminal lawyers as the 'fair labelling' principle.[154] One could easily appreciate Wassenaar's bank robbery analogy in relation to the use of mail and wire fraud charges to prosecute money laundering, as in *Rauhoff*. It is less obvious that fair labelling concerns, as opposed to practicalities of prosecution, could explain why money laundering ought not to be viewed as a form of complicity in the predicate offence. A slightly different argument was put forward by Stephen Trott, Assistant Attorney General at the Justice Department, who referred to the likely efficacy of a criminal prohibition against money laundering in disrupting criminal operations, comparing it to the adoption of the Racketeer Influenced and Corrupt Organizations Act (RICO) in 1970.[155]

Among the few sceptical voices was that of the American Bar Association (ABA). Samuel Buffone, appearing on the ABA's behalf, objected to the proposed offence on the basis of the difficulties it would create 'for any attorney who received a fee from a client with any indication that the fee may have been derived from illegal conduct'.[156] Still, not all of the ABA's concerns were lawyer-centric. In a fuller statement submitted to the ABA, it outlined the broader civic implications of excluding those with proceeds of crime to spend from day-to-day commercial interactions:

> [T]he actus reus and mens rea components of the crime are so minimal that a likely result will be to bring within its reach criminal lawyers, merchants, and others who merely provide criminal defendants with goods and services. A grocer who sells a can of tuna fish to a person under indictment for being a member of a RICO organization, for example, would appear to risk committing the offense defined by the first part of new § 2322. In this sense, a 'status' crime is created, whereby any person with a reputation for being connected to organized crime may be effectively isolated from completing ordinary, day-to-day, financial transactions because the other party will fear incurring 'receipt of criminal proceeds' liability.[157]

The American Civil Liberties Unition (ACLU), which also opposed the criminalisation of money laundering, made substantially the same argument. In a not too subtle attempt to make matters relatable for Congress members, the ACLU's list of everyday interactions that would be affected included the receipt of campaign contributions:

[154] James Chalmers and Fiona Leverick, 'Fair Labelling in Criminal Law' (2008) 71(2) *MLR* 217 (tracing the evolution of the principle from the writings of Andrew Ashworth in the 1980s).

[155] *Tax Evasion*, 127, 787–788.

[156] Ibid, 972 (Samuel J. Buffone, White Collar Crime Committee, American Bar Association).

[157] Jeffrey Glekel and Lawrence B. Pedowitz, 'Statement on Behalf of the American Bar Association Concerning Money Laundering Legislation', Subcommittee on Financial Institutions Supervision, Regulation and Insurance, 14 May 1986, 1129.

> A car salesman, a brokerage firm, a real estate company, or politician who engaged in any transaction with anyone in circumstances where they 'should have known' that the money received was indirectly derived from illegal activity would also be guilty of money laundering.[158]

Up until then, it was only gun dealers who had to exercise care in their choice of customers. The Federal Firearms Act of 1938 prohibited dealers from selling firearms 'knowing or having reasonable cause to believe' that the customers was convicted of a crime of violence, under indictment for such a crime or a fugitive from justice.[159] The proposed criminalisation of money laundering was dramatically novel in its focus not on providing a criminal with what they need to commit further crimes, but on the use of criminally obtained money.

The arguments of those opposing this unprecedented measure held some sway, and the Money Laundering Control Act as enacted contained a less far-reaching money laundering offence than initially envisaged. The original bill would have criminalised engaging in financial transactions either (a) with an intent to promote unlawful activity, similar to the provision of resources for crime as in *Falcone* and *Direct Sales* in the 1940s, or (b) 'with knowledge or reason to know that such monetary instruments represent income derived, directly or indirectly, from any unlawful activity, or the proceeds of such income'.[160] The version ultimately adopted retained that approach but dispensed with the 'reason to know' wording, which would have imposed liability based on an extraneous objective standard even when the accused did not know the property was the proceeds of crime.[161] The many implications of rendering money laundering a self-standing criminal offence are discussed later in Chapter 3.

Another issue aired in the 1986 hearings was the need for the criminalisation of structuring, that is, the intentional splitting of transactions so as to avoid the US$10,000 reporting threshold. Structuring is also commonly known as 'smurfing', in a nod to the industrious blue-skinned dwarves created by the Belgian comic artist Peyo.[162] Following a number of appellate judgments holding that structuring was not an offence under the Bank Secrecy Act,[163] the criminalisation of structuring was included among the package of provisions that subsequently became the Money Laundering Control Act.[164] Like with the crime of money laundering, the extent of support for this legal reform expressed at the hearings was overwhelming.

158 *Tax Evasion*, 127, 1226, Testimony of Jerry J. Berman, Chief Legislative Counsel, ACLU.

159 Sections 2(d)–(e) of the Federal Firearms Act of 1938 (US), Pub. L. 75-785 (1938).

160 H.R. 1367, 99th Congress.

161 18 USC § 1956.

162 Michael Levi, 'Money Laundering and Its Regulation' (2002) 582(2) *Annals Am Acad Pol & Soc Sci* 181, 185.

163 See the discussion in Linn, 'Redefining the Bank Secrecy Act', 436–440.

164 The proposal received particularly warm praise from Francis A. Keating II, Assistant Secretary (Enforcement and Operations), US Treasury in *Tax Evasion*, 641.

The members of the committee were especially impressed with the testimony of one of the witnesses, a convicted 'smurf' Herb Friedberg, who shocked them with his account of regularly depositing US$9,000 in cash with the same bank tellers with no questions asked.[165] Like the offence of money laundering, the criminalisation of structuring was largely uncontroversial despite its capacity to catch the activities of otherwise blameless bank customers seeking to evade reporting requirements for privacy reasons, without any proceeds of crime being involved.

2.3.4 *US Reforms in 1988–1992: Geographic Targeting Orders and Suspicious Activity Reports*

The development of US AML laws was far from over, and during the years that followed two key reporting mechanisms were introduced. One of them, the geographic targeting orders (GTO), has remained a US idiosyncrasy, albeit with the potential of being implemented elsewhere, whereas the other one, the suspicious activity report (SAR),[166] has become a pillar of the global response to money laundering. Even prior to these reforms, the Treasury Department had circulated a letter to the CEOs of US financial institutions suggesting it was 'critical that suspicious transactions be reported to the Criminal Investigation Division at your local office of the Internal Revenue Service'.[167]

GTOs were introduced as a means of authorising the Treasury to require the reporting of additional information by 'any domestic financial institution or non-financial trade or business or group of domestic financial institutions or nonfinancial trades or businesses in a geographic area' provided that the Treasury finds 'that reasonable grounds exist for concluding that additional recordkeeping and reporting requirements are necessary to carry out the purposes of [fighting financial crime]'.[168] The concept of GTOs was first proposed in 1985 as part of a bill put forward by congressman Esteban Torres, who described it as a way to tailor reporting requirements to 'geographic areas where there is a recognised high volume of money laundering activities, such as are prevalent in Miami and (…) Los Angeles'.[169] The idea behind this was to ensure that potentially burdensome reporting requirements were not unnecessarily extended to all areas in the US, including those facing

165 *Tax Evasion*, 79–109.

166 Generally speaking, SARs are synonymous to STRs and suspicious matter reports (SMRs), which are all terms used in different jurisdictions to describe the same concept. However, some jurisdictions, such as South Africa, use both SARs and STRs, the former referring specifically to suspicious activity that does not involve the carrying out of a financial transaction: FATF, *Anti-Money Laundering and Counter-Terrorist Financing Measures: South Africa Mutual Evaluation Report*, October 2021, 54.

167 Department of the Treasury, Letter, 1 May 1985, available in *Tax Evasion*, 398.

168 31 USC § 5326.

169 US Senate Subcommittee on Financial Institutions Supervision, Regulation, and Insurance, *Money Laundering Control Act of 1986 and the Regulations Implementing the Bank Secrecy Act* (US Government Printing Office, 1986) 7.

lesser money laundering risks.[170] GTOs were ultimately enacted into law in 1988, and, as of the time of this writing, multiple GTOs were in place across the US requiring title insurance companies to report certain non-financed purchases of residential real estate.[171]

It took longer for SAR reporting to be instituted in law. The origins of SARs are in banking regulation. In 1971, the Office of the Comptroller of the Currency (OCC) – the US banking regulator – issued a requirement for bank employees to report to the OCC's regional branch, the FBI and the DOJ '[a]ny known or suspected theft, embezzlement, check-kiting operation, misappropriation or other defalcation involving bank personnel or bank funds in any amount' as well as '[a]ny state of facts growing out of the affairs of the bank known or suspected to involve criminal violation of any other section of the United States Code'.[172] Criminal Referral Forms were not consistently filed, and the information provided was often of poor quality.[173]

By the early 1980s, the OCC came to the conclusion that the requirement was widely disregarded because of lack of certainty as to whether a certain activity was reportable, as well as perceived litigation risks due to breaching clients' privacy.[174] The same concern was reflected in *The Cash Connection* report: as mentioned previously, its first legislative recommendation was to amend the Right to Financial Privacy Act to expressly allow the proactive reporting of suspicious activities by financial institutions in the absence of a law enforcement request or referral.[175] The OCC published the final rule on the new Criminal Referral Form in 1989.[176] These regulations still did not provide for any 'safe harbour', or immunity from lawsuits based on the making of the report – and, therefore, did not fully address the concerns that had been articulated up until then.[177]

This changed with the Annunzio-Wiley Anti-Money Laundering Act of 1992, which introduced SAR reporting into US law.[178] The Act's provisions on SARs authorised the Treasury to require their reporting; shielded financial institutions

[170] Ibid, 32.

[171] For an example, see FinCEN, 'Geographic Targeting Order', 19 April 2024, www.fincen.gov/sites/default/files/shared/RRE-GTOs-Phase-18-Order.pdf. For a summary of GTOs in place as of April 2024, see Jim Richards, LinkedIn, 17 April 2024, www.linkedin.com/posts/richards1_fincen-gtos-january-2016-through-april-activity-7186510622069526528-H5Wt?.

[172] Codified at 36 FR 17012-13. This and some of the following information about the history of SARs was generously shared by Jim Richards, Principal and Founder of RegTech Consulting LLC, in an email of 6 June 2024.

[173] Interview with a US lawyer specialising in AML/CTF (A), 14 November 2023.

[174] An account of the deliberations of the DOJ-led working group convened to consider these issues in 1984 is available at 54 FR 25839 (20 June 1989).

[175] *The Cash Connection*, 59.

[176] Codified at 54 CFR 25839.

[177] Interview with a US lawyer specialising in AML/CTF (A), 14 November 2023; email from Jim Richards of 6 June 2024.

[178] 12 USC § 3403(c).

from any liability for such reporting and prohibited the disclosure of the fact that a SAR has been filed or its content (popularly known as a tipping-off prohibition).[179] One of the alternative proposals, which was considered but rejected at the time, was to limit safe harbour from liability to instances of 'good-faith' SAR reporting by the banks.[180] Although the prohibition of tipping off should prevent the subject of a SAR from knowing that the report has been filed, the fear was that the 'good-faith' proviso could nonetheless expose banks to risks of litigation in connection with the submission of SARs.[181] The prescience of this concern was demonstrated when, in June 2024, the Russian businessman Alisher Usmanov sued the German subsidiary of UBS for allegedly filing SARs in relation to Usmanov to the German FIU.[182]

Like the Money Laundering Control Act before it, the Annunzio-Wiley Act contained a smorgasbord of provisions aimed to bolster the US's response to money laundering. These provisions were Congress's response to the embarrassment of large-scale money laundering facilitated by the Bank of Credit and Commerce International (BCCI).[183] BCCI had been set up by a Pakistani businessman with support from wealthy Abu Dhabi families and had presented itself as the bank for the Third World with a moral mission to support developing countries. In reality, it catered to drug cartels and dictators, such as Iraq's Saddam Hussein and Panama's Manuel Noriega, as well as engaging in fraud to disguise unsound loans extended to its founder's friends.[184] BCCI's collapse was precipitated by the IRS agent Robert Mazur's undercover work with the Medellin drug cartel, whose representatives alerted him to the money laundering opportunities available at BCCI, later followed by very constructive meetings with BCCI executives eager to assist.[185] The culmination of the operation was the arrest of a number of BCCI's officers in Tampa, Florida while attending a fake wedding staged between Robert Mazur and Kathy Ertz, another undercover agent.[186]

BCCI pleaded guilty to US federal charges in 1990, and then later to New York state charges in 1991, following an investigation led by the US District Attorney

179 Section 1517 of the Annunzio-Wylie Anti-Money Laundering Act (US), Title XV, Pub. L. 102-550, 102nd Congress, 1992. The Treasury's Regulations are found in 12 CFR § 21.11 et seq.

180 Interview with a US lawyer specialising in AML/CTF (A), 14 November 2023.

181 Ibid.

182 'Russian Oligarch Sues UBS over "Unlawful" Money Laundering Alerts', *Swiss Info*, 18 June 2024, www.swissinfo.ch/eng/banking-fintech/russian-oligarch-sues-ubs-over-unlawful-money-laundering-alerts/81027942. A somewhat similar case is an attempt by an Indonesian family to sue an Australian bank for allegedly *not* filing a SAR in a timely fashion: *Marundrury v Commonwealth Bank of Australia (No 2)* [2022] FCA 916; *Marundrury v Commonwealth Bank of Australia* [2021] FCA 1379.

183 Matthew S. Morgan, 'Money Laundering: The American Law and Its Global Influence' (1997) 3(3) *Law & Bus Rev Americas* 24, 41.

184 See Peter Truell and Larry Gurvin, *BCCI: The Inside Story of the World's Most Corrupt Financial Empire* (Bloomsbury, 1992).

185 Robert Mazur, *The Infiltrator: Undercover in the World of Drug Barons and Dirty Banks* (Corgi Books, 2015).

186 Ibid.

Robert Morgenthau.[187] The reforms provided for by the Annunzio-Wiley Act were one part of the fallout from BCCI's collapse. It also involved the preparation of a report by the US Senate Foreign Relations Committee focused on BCCI's entanglements in drug-related money laundering,[188] as well as Lord Bingham's report on the quality of UK bank supervision that contributed to the unravelling of BCCI.[189]

Ensuing litigation was varied, multi-jurisdictional and prolific, including individual criminal prosecutions[190]; Panama's unsuccessful RICO claims against BCCI and its US subsidiary, First American, for laundering Noriega's drug trafficking proceeds[191]; the forfeiture of US$1.2 billion to the US government[192]; employment claims by BCCI's former staff unable to find work because of the bank's tarnished reputation[193]; and even long-running litigation brought by BCCI's liquidators, Deloitte, who sued the Bank of England for malfeasance in public office, ultimately discontinued in 2006.[194] Of all these elements of the denouement of BCCI's affair, Lord Bingham's review of banking supervision in the UK is notable for its brief acknowledgement of the evolving international expectations around money laundering, which had begun to take shape in the late 1980s. This takes us to the next stage in the development of AML rules: their internationalisation.

2.4 INTERNATIONAL STANDARDS: THE BASEL COMMITTEE, FATF AND EU

The efforts against money laundering assumed an international dimension in the late 1980s. This incremental internationalisation has ultimately turned AML regulation into an area of global concern, and a major source of business expenditure, that it is today. There are multiple notable features of how this process unfolded, not least that the FATF's 'soft law' standards have become its focal point, rather than the UN's legally binding (and global) treaties – as well as initial preoccupation with drug trafficking, which later ceded ground to a broader concern with organised crime. First of all, however, it is important to acknowledge that, by the 1980s, anxieties about the financial footprint of drug trafficking had developed organically

[187] David Johnston, 'B.C.C.I. Agrees to Plead Guilty and Will Forfeit $550 Million', *New York Times*, 20 December 1991.

[188] Senator John Kerry and Senator Hank Brown, 'The BCCI Affair', December 1992.

[189] The Right Honourable Lord Justice Bingham, 'Inquiry into the Supervision of the Bank of Commerce and Credit International', October 1992.

[190] *US v Awan*, 966 F.2d 1415 (11th Cir 1992). See also Sharon Walsh, 'Clifford, Altman Settle BCCI Case: Partners to Forfeit $5 Million, Keep Nearly $15 Million', *The Washington Post*, 4 February 1998.

[191] *Panama v BCCI Holdings (Luxembourg) S.A.*, 119 F.3d 935 (11th Cir 1997).

[192] *US v BCCI Holdings* 69 F. Supp. 2d 36 (DDC 1999).

[193] *Malik v BCCI* [1998] AC 20; [1997] ICR 606.

[194] Simon Bowers, 'BCCI Scandal: Long Legal Wrangling over Collapsed Bank', *The Guardian*, 18 May 2012.

across much of (at least) the common law world, and so one could no longer consider the crusade against it to be a peculiarly American obsession.

2.4.1 *Domestic Efforts against Drug Money: Beyond the US*

By the turn of the decade, the shift in the emphasis of drug control measures towards tackling drug-related financial flows became observable on both sides of the Atlantic. In 1981, the House of Lords – then still the UK's apex court – issued a unanimous decision in *R v Cuthbertson*, in which Lord Denning held 'with considerable regret' that neither the Misuse of Drugs Act 1971 nor the common law authorised the forfeiture of drug proceeds.[195] This led to the establishment by the Howard League for Penal reform of a committee chaired by Sir Derek Hodgson, whose final report made forty-nine recommendations across the entire spectrum of confiscation law.[196] In a short chapter on the international aspects of confiscating the proceeds of crime, the Hodgson Committee made an implicit case in favour of the reporting obligations that were then absent in English law:

> Detecting movement of 'dirty money' out of the United Kingdom has become much more difficult since the abolition of exchange control. By comparison even quite small currency dealings are monitored in the United States. Under the Federal Bank Secrecy Act of 1970 individuals must report movements over $5000. They must also report any foreign bank accounts. Currency exchanges over $10,000 must be notified by banks. There are the predictable problems of delated and inadequate compliance and the shortage of staff to analyse the information, but a small study by the Comptroller-General's report in 1981 showed that of thirty-one cases where forfeiture or confiscation of drug proceeds were involved, four had made use of currency or bank reports.[197]

The Hodgson Committee's report was made with widespread approval and led to the enactment of the Drug Trafficking Offenders Act 1986, which introduced the offence of assisting another to retain the benefit of drug trafficking.[198] Prior to that, similar to the US, the offence of handling stolen goods provided a limited means of prosecuting money laundering-like conduct. One example was the prosecution of the individuals involved in the Brink's-Mat robbery: the theft of gold bullion, diamonds and cash worth £23 million from a secure warehouse in Heathrow in 1983.[199]

[195] [1981] AC 470, discussed in Peter Alldridge, *What Went Wrong with Money Laundering Law?* (Palgrave Macmillan, 2016) 10.

[196] Howard League for Penal Reform, *Profits of Crime and Their Recovery: Report of a Committee Chaired by Sir Derek Hodgson* (Heinemann, 1984) 150–156. For a concise discussion, see Colin King and Jennifer Hendry, *Civil Recovery of Criminal Property* (Oxford University Press, 2023) 10–11.

[197] *Profits of Crime*, 141.

[198] Section 24.

[199] Nicholas Clark, 'The Impact of Recent Money Laundering Legislation on Financial Intermediaries' (1996) 14(3) *Dickinson J Int'l L* 467, 473.

Those convicted included a fifty-year-old solicitor from Surrey whose role was first to set up bank accounts in Switzerland and Liechtenstein and then invest the proceeds of the robbery in UK real estate.[200] The limitations of such prosecutions included their ability to only be brought in relation to the handling of goods (rather than, say, money) obtained through theft (rather than, say, drug trafficking).

There appears to have been no substantial controversy over the adoption of the Hodgson Committee's recommendations. Shortly before the introduction of the Drug Trafficking Offenders Act 1986, Lord Denning, who penned the *Cuthbertson* judgment, spoke as follows in the House of Lords:

> My Lords, is it not the case that the huge proceeds of bank robberies and airport robberies are spirited abroad almost at once and that, to use an expressive Americanism, they are laundered through the banks so as to make them apparently clean and are then brought back by the rogues and put into the hands of apparently innocent people? Is it not time that legislation was introduced to freeze those proceeds, to prevent the rogues from making use of them and to confiscate them?[201]

Very similar developments had been afoot in Australia. In 1977, the Royal Commission into Drug Trafficking was set up under the chairmanship of Philip Woodward, a judge of the Supreme Court of New South Wales. The inquiry's principal findings pertained to the organised nature of drug trafficking in Australia, and among its chief recommendations was the need for greater utilisation of financial investigations. Only several years later, in 1981, another inquiry into drug trafficking followed, led by Justice Donald Stewart, specifically to investigate the activities of a particular organised crime group led by one Terry Clark. Despite being supported by forensic accountants, the Stewart Commission faced major difficulties in tracing the Clark syndicate's use of drug proceeds, attributed by the Commission to 'the fact that considerable amounts of money were transferred overseas by the syndicate using couriers to take cash in suitcases, usually to Singapore'.[202]

Multiple academics have criticised these developments, in all of the countries concerned, on the grounds that policymakers, as well as the public at large, had succumbed to sensationalist narratives about crime and money. Desmond Manderson has argued that the Australian discourse on drugs became fixated on the proverbial 'Mr Big' as the justification for increasingly repressive policies.[203] Similarly, Peter Alldridge has written that, for all the invocations of offshore bank accounts and

[200] 'Michael Relton', *Public Interest Investigations Powerbase*, https://powerbase.info/index.php/Michael_Relton.

[201] HL Deb 21 May 1986, Vol 475, Col 295.

[202] Philip Woodward, *Royal Commission of Inquiry into Drug Trafficking Report*, February 1983, 145.

[203] Desmond Manderson, *From Mr. Sin to Mr. Big: A History of Australian Drug Laws* (Oxford University Press, 1993) 181–187. See also Anne Imobersteg Harvey, *Anti-Money Laundering and Counter-Terrorism Financing Law and Policy: Showcasing Australia* (Brill, 2019) 1 (citing Arie Freiberg's description of a 'moral panic' resulting from the Woodward Commission).

sophisticated money laundering schemes, most money laundering is unimaginative, dull and quotidian, contrary to the picture of it that policymakers and law enforcement agencies paint.[204]

These critiques contain a fair observation on the stylistic choices of major policy documents and inquiries, which emphasise high-profile cases over mundane ones. For instance, *The Cash Connection* report by the US Presidential Commission on Organized Crime opened with a quote from Michele Sindona, an Italian banker and freemason who had laundered money for the Sicilian mafia and provided banking services to the Vatican.[205] Still, there is nothing illegitimate about these presentational choices; nor do they negate the reality of money laundering that those vivid illustrations seek to exemplify. The organic emergence of the concern with drug money across substantial swathes of the Western world bespeaks of the very real nature of the problem, as confirmed by many decades' worth of evidence from multiple jurisdictions and inquiries.

In Australia, the findings emerging in the late 1980s contributed to a chain of events that led, among other things, to the enactment of legislation requiring all international funds transfers to or from Australia to be reported to the Australian Financial Reports and Analysis Centre (AUSTRAC).[206] Donald Stewart went on to become the founding chairman of Australia's National Crime Authority, which in 1991 published a report on money laundering highlighting that 'the proceeds of crime are regularly transferred overseas'.[207] At the same time, AUSTRAC officials learned from the US experience that wire transfers were regularly used by Mexican drug cartels to launder their proceeds and therefore recommended that such transactions be reportable in Australia.[208] However, the first explicit recommendation that an international fund transfer reporting regime be established stemmed from the tax context: namely, a report by a committee set up by the House of Representatives to investigate non-compliance with Australian withholding tax obligations.[209] The reporting of international fund transfer instructions (IFTIs) thus became yet another option for transmitting information from the regulated sectors to the government, alongside SARs, UTRs, GTOs and CTRs.[210] By that time in 1991, however, the first

[204] Alldridge, *What Went Wrong with Money Laundering Law?*, 4.

[205] *The Cash Connection*, 7.

[206] Section 3 of the Financial Transaction Reports Act 1988 (Cth). For fuller history of the 1992 amendments, see Neil Jensen, 'International Fund Transfer Instructions: Australia at the Leading Edge of Financial Transaction Reporting' (1993) 4(2) *J Law Info Sci* 304.

[207] National Crime Authority, *Taken to the Cleaners: Money Laundering in Australia*, 1991.

[208] Interview with an Australian AML/CTF expert (A), 14 June 2024; interview with an Australian AML/CTF expert (B), 1 July 2024.

[209] Standing Committee on Finance and Public Administration, House of Representatives (Australia), *Follow the Yellow Brick Road – The Final Report of an Efficiency Audit of the Australian Taxation Office: Profit Shifting*, March 1991, paras 5.27–5.30.

[210] For an account of Westpac's high-prolife failure to file IFTIs and the resulting AUSTRAC enforcement action in 2019, see Nathan Lynch, *The Lucky Laundry* (Harper Collins Publishers, 2022) 151–173.

set of international AML standards had already taken shape, with a focus on SAR reporting, as discussed in Section 2.4.3.

2.4.2 *Basel Committee for Banking Supervision: Regulatory Response*

It would no doubt be possible to muster countless other examples of governments taking notice of the problem of drug-related money laundering. The need for a coordinated international approach was palpable. As early as in 1986, at a Senate hearing in the run-up to the adoption of the Money Laundering Control Act, Congressman George Wortley of New York suggested that the topic of money laundering should be brought before the Bank for International Settlements.[211] Wortley's choice of the proposed venue for the development of international AML standards is noteworthy. As an organisation of central banks, set up originally for the purpose of managing the payment of post-World War I reparations and then expanded as a platform for discussions of financial regulation and monetary policy,[212] the Bank for International Settlements may not have been the first forum that comes to mind for criminal justice-oriented conversations. However, since 1974, the Bank for International Settlements has hosted the Basel Committee on Banking Supervision, whose task is to formulate best practices in banking regulation and supervision.[213] The identification by the US government of these two institutions as key to the formulation of international AML measures evinces a shift to viewing AML as a matter at the intersection of criminal justice and financial regulation.

Up until then, the US had not had much success with internationalising its approach to cross-border economic crime. Since 1977, successive US governments had struggled to secure global support for the criminalisation of foreign bribery, introduced by the Foreign Corrupt Practices Act 1977 (FCPA).[214] The FCPA was a response to embarrassing revelations that US corporations had bankrolled foreign leaders, including the Japanese prime minister Kakuei Tanaka and Dutch crown prince Bernhard, which emerged from one of the spin-offs of the Watergate investigations.[215] The group of non-aligned states professed disinterest in the topic on the basis that the real scandal was the behaviour of transnational corporations in exploiting the natural resources of developing countries. With the failure of abortive negotiations for an international convention against foreign bribery within the

[211] *Tax Evasion*, 657.

[212] For a detailed account of its origins, see Manley O. Hudson, 'The Bank for International Settlements' (1930) 24(3) *AJIL* 561. For a description of its more recent focus, see Carola Westermeier, 'The Bank of International Settlements as a Think Tank for Financial Policy-Making' (2018) 37(2) *Pol & Soc* 170.

[213] Charles Goodhart, *The Basel Committee on Banking Supervision: A History of the Early Years 1974–1997* (Cambridge University Press, 2011).

[214] See Anton Moiseienko, *Corruption and Targeted Sanctions: The Law and Policy of Anti-Corruption Entry Bans* (Brill, 2019) 95–109. For a more theoretical perspective on foreign bribery, see Branislav Hock, *Extraterritoriality and International Bribery: A Collective Action Perspective* (Routledge, 2019).

[215] Mike Koehler, 'The Story of the Foreign Corrupt Practices Act' (2012) 73 *Ohio State LJ* 929, 934–935.

UN framework, the US government began shifting its attention to other multilateral fora, especially those bringing together like-minded industrial countries.[216]

This reorientation of US economic crime diplomacy informed its approach to money laundering.[217] However, the issue was also sufficiently different from foreign bribery. States shared a common interest in the fight against drug trafficking to a greater extent than they ever did in the fight against corruption, an issue too laden with good governance connotations to be free from controversy.[218] In 1988, the UN General Assembly adopted the Convention against Illicit Traffic in Narcotic Drugs and Psychotropic Substances, which included a provision on the confiscation of proceeds of drug trafficking.[219]

Still, unsurprisingly, the US government continued to explore technocratic, finance-oriented avenues for action. In December of the same year, the Basel Committee on Banking Supervision published its first set of principles on the *Prevention of Criminal Use of the Banking System for the Purpose of Money-Laundering*. In explaining its involvement in the newly emerging domain of fighting money laundering, the Committee alluded to a mixture of moral, reputational and practical considerations stemming from banks' involvement in money laundering:

> Public confidence in banks, and hence their stability, can be undermined by adverse publicity as a result of inadvertent association by banks with criminals. In addition, banks may lay themselves open to direct losses from fraud, either through negligence in screening undesirable customers or where the integrity of their own officers has been undermined through association with criminals. For these reasons the members of the Basle Committee consider that banking supervisors have a general role to encourage ethical standards of professional conduct among banks and other financial institution.[220]

2.4.3 *The FATF Recommendations: Adoption*

The following year, the first meeting took place in Paris of the FATF, an intergovernmental grouping intended specifically to address the problem of drug-related

[216] The broader history of UN involvement in crime control is detailed in Jarrett Blaustein, Tom Chodor and Nathan W. Pino, *Unraveling the Crime-Development Nexus* (Rowman & Littlefield, 2022) 76–123.

[217] See John Cusack, 'The Early History of the Financial Action Task Force: What We Can Learn from the Founders and What This Means for the Fight against Financial Crime', *Financial Crime News*, December 2023, https://thefinancialcrimenews.com/wp-content/uploads/2023/12/AML-History-incl-FATF-41223-by-FCN.pdf.

[218] For insightful analysis of the nexus between early AML measures and responses to drug trafficking, see Valsamis Mitsilegas, *Money Laundering Counter-Measures in the European Union: A New Paradigm of Security Governance versus Fundamental Legal Principles* (Kluwer Law International, 2003) 40–44.

[219] Article 5.

[220] Basel Committee on Banking Supervision, *Prevention of Criminal Use of the Banking System for the Purpose of Money-Laundering*, December 1988, para 4.

money laundering. Mark Pieth, a Swiss law professor and then-diplomat, provides a colourful account of the negotiations that gave birth to the FATF. In his recollection, the French president Francois Mitterrand was eager to convene a major international summit to inaugurate the Arche de la Défence, a distinctive building conceived as a modern counterpart to the better-known Arc de Triomphe, dedicated to peacetime achievements rather than martial triumphs. Michel Camdessus, the ex-governor of the Banque de France who had just become the managing director of the International Monetary Fund (IMF), proposed 'tax havens' as the topic of the summit, and the US administration agreed but suggested that the focus be specifically on drug-related money laundering.[221] This is how the FATF came into being, and Pieth describes its first meeting thus:

> Seated around the table were the G7 countries and a series of financial centres of which one did not really know whether they were here to discuss or to be accused of participating in money laundering (like Luxembourg or Switzerland, my own country: I was part of a team of three – together with Alexis Lautenberg, the diplomat, and Daniel Zuberbühler, the director of the Secretariat of the Swiss Bank Supervisory Authority – myself representing the Swiss Office of Justice). Amongst the original group of twelve participant countries everyone threw their hobby horse into the discussion: the United States suggested cash controls, the UK notification of suspicious transactions, and the Swiss wanted their newly invented concept of identification of customers to be internationalized. Overall, the elements were stitched together in the so-called '40 Recommendations' and frankly – at the time (in 1989) – no one believed they would survive the next three months. Now, in 2012 the same basic concepts have just been updated for the fourth time.[222]

The sense of spontaneity that Pieth reflects in this passage needs to be understood in its proper context. The FATF's inaugural gathering had been predated by over a decade of 'follow-the-money' style thinking about organised crime both in the US and in Europe. None of the ideas mentioned above was entirely novel, but they had never been brought together in a coherent set of standards. The participants in the meeting were therefore not conjuring up ideas from a clean slate, but bringing together approaches that had been trialled, sometimes tentatively and with modest success, across their jurisdictions.

Among the least tried-and-tested of those ideas was suspicious activity reporting, which, as discussed previously, had been gestating in the US in the rather truncated format of Criminal Referral Forms. The FATF's first-ever annual report noted disagreement among the delegations as to whether suspicious activity reporting by banks

221 Mark Pieth, 'Finance and the "Shadow Economy"' in Fritz Heimann and Mark Pieth, *Confronting Corruption: Past Concerns, Present Challenges, and Future Strategies* (Oxford University Press, 2018) 124–125.

222 Ibid.

ought to be required or merely permitted.[223] A permissive, rather than mandatory, model was therefore incorporated in the first edition of the Recommendations.[224]

The fact that, according to Pieth, the UK proposed SARs to the FATF is a historical curiosity because the UK was not much father advanced, if at all, than the US in that respect. The closest the UK had come to implementing such a system was by authorising, but not requiring, the disclosure of 'a suspicion or belief that any money or other property is or is derived from terrorist funds' under the Prevention of Terrorism (Temporary Provisions) Act 1989.[225] The same approach of voluntary reporting, informally and without any legal basis at all, was taken by banks in the UK to proceeds of other, non-terrorism-related crimes. A leading scholar of economic crime Michael Levi wrote as follows in 1991:

> Police and customs officers vary in their opinions on how much filtering they want the financial institutions to engage in: some realise that they could become overwhelmed by 'aggressive compliance', particularly given tight personnel budgets which constrain the processing of the data. Presently, over 3,000 voluntary disclosures are made annually by banks and building societies, which strains agency processing capacity.[226]

The concern about over-reporting expressed by UK law enforcement agencies in those early days of non-mandatory reporting is strikingly prescient of the challenges of 'defensive reporting' that, with time, manifested themselves. In any event, mandatory SAR reporting was instituted in the UK in 1993.[227]

Whether the FATF Recommendations ever became a truly coherent body of standards remains open to question. Coherence demands that the Recommendations be harmonious in their pursuit of a central objective or set of objectives, but those objectives have been strikingly vague throughout the group's history. The FATF's first annual report spoke in general terms of 'fighting' drug-related money laundering, as well as a number of concrete steps that could be taken to that end, including understanding the scale and nature of the problem, introducing CDD, requiring financial and other institutions to cooperate with law enforcement agencies, and so on.[228] What it omitted to provide was any particular vision of what success would look like: Would it be the exclusion of drug money from the financial system? The ability to surveil its flows? Something else?

223 Financial Action Task Force, 'Report', 1990, 20.

224 FATF, *The Forty Recommendations of the Financial Action Task Force on Money Laundering*, 1990, Recommendation 16.

225 Section 12.

226 Michael Levi, 'Pecunia Non Olet: Cleansing the Money-Launderers from the Temple' (1991) 16(3) *Crime, Law and Social Change* 217, 298.

227 Sections 29 and 30 of the Criminal Justice Act 1993 (UK), amending the Criminal Justice Act 1988. See also Michael Levi, *The Legal and Institutional Infrastructure of Anti-Money Laundering in the UK: A Report for the Cullen Commission*, 2020, 1–2.

228 FATF, 'Report', 1990, 7.

The FATF never grappled with those questions entirely satisfactorily. In the introduction to the second edition of the Recommendations, published in 1996, the FATF stated explicitly that its 'policies aim to prevent such proceeds [of crime] from being utilised in future criminal activities and from affecting legitimate economic activities'.[229] This wording seems to suggest that the FATF's objective was to prevent the proceeds of crime from being put to any use, whether in the criminal or legitimate economy, but is silent as to what exactly it entails. At the same time, the FATF's mandate since its founding has referred to 'protect[ing] financial systems and the broader economy from threats of money laundering and the financing of terrorism and proliferation, thereby strengthening financial sector integrity and contributing to safety and security'.[230]

Peter Alldridge rightly highlights the vagueness of the 'financial integrity' language: an extraordinary lack of clarity given the ubiquitous invocation of financial integrity by the FATF, EU, IMF and other organisations active in the AML field.[231] In a narrow sense, which is the one that Alldridge proffers, 'integrity' here may mean compliance with AML rules, which does not answer the question of why those rules are necessary in the first place, or what objectives they pursue.[232] However, the history of AML legislation points to another possible conception of integrity: namely, avoiding the witting or unwitting complicity in money laundering. In this context, complicity can be understood as not merely a legal doctrine, but a broader moral judgment on a bank's facilitating of money laundering. There is little doubt that scandals such as the BCCI's fall evoked a general public perception that the businesses involved were lacking integrity in that broader sense.

Furthermore, as Mark Pieth's account of the Swiss participation in the FATF's inaugural meeting demonstrates, with time the same charges of complicity became to be levelled against entire countries, not only individuals and companies.[233] The sense that international financial centres, or 'tax havens', were complicit in the misery that befell other countries proved to be essential to the FATF's evolution, and marked a departure from the preoccupation with drug trafficking as the sole predicate offence. By the late 1980s, the cliché of a potentate from a developing country enjoying ill-gotten gains elsewhere had started to take shape. For instance, Jean-Claude Duvalier of Haiti 'enjoyed a comfortable period in exile in France, unmolested by local authorities'.[234] The trend continued in the 1990s.

229 FATF, *The Forty Recommendations of the Financial Action Task Force on Money Laundering*, 1996, 2.

230 FATF, 'Mandate of the FATF', undated, available at www.fatf-gafi.org/en/the-fatf/mandate-of-the-fatf.html#accordion-ffdocfcabc-item-a5fb5ae357.

231 Alldridge, *What Went Wrong with Money Laundering Law?*, 35–36.

232 Ibid.

233 Raymond Baker, *Capitalism's Achilles Heel: Dirty Money and How to Renew the Free-Market System* (John Wiley & Sons, 2005) 209; Alexander Cooley and John Heathershaw, *Dictators without Borders: Power and Money in Central Asia* (Yale University Press, 2017) 222–231.

234 Sharman, *The Despot's Guide to Wealth Management*, 102–103.

Transparency International was founded by former World Bank employees in 1993,[235] and the *Financial Times* famously called 1995 the 'year of corruption'.[236] With the globalisation of finance and communications, wealth amassed through corruption flooded into developed countries from developing ones. In the British journalist Oliver Bullough's metaphor:

> [I]magine an oil tanker. If it has just one huge tank, then the oil can slosh backwards and forwards in ever greater waves, until it destabilises the vessel, which overturns and sinks. At the Bretton Woods conference, the oil was divided between smaller tanks, one for each country. The liquid could slosh back and forth within its little compartments, but would be unable to achieve enough momentum to damage the integrity of the vessel.[237]

In the case of corruption, what particularly damaged global governance was the ability to steal from one country while secreting the proceeds in another one, therefore removing any incentive for corrupt local rulers to improve the living conditions at home.[238] The growing global awareness of this problem also led to increased attention paid to the role of the jurisdictions facilitating such abuse. Michael Reisman, an eminent international lawyer at Yale Law School, proposed to treat such involvement as a mode of participating in what he described as the crime of 'indigenous spoliation':

> Because the spoliations cannot be accomplished without havens abroad, the exercise of the banking jurisdiction of another state in such a way as to conceal funds is effectively part of the delict. It violates the international legal rights of the deprived states and may itself constitute an international legal wrong.[239]

The international legal wrong proposed by Reisman has never materialised: there is, to this day, no effective recourse that international law would provide against a 'tax haven' to a state whose public funds have been unlawfully secreted into that jurisdiction.[240] Nor are states in the grip of dictatorial regimes likely to pursue remedies for their own rulers' corruption. Thus, the only case ever brought at the

[235] Peter Eigen, *Das Netz der Korruption: Wie eine weltweite Bewegung gegen Bestechung kämpft* (Campus Verlag, 2003) 28–36.

[236] Vito Tanzi, 'Corruption around the World: Causes, Consequences, Scope, and Cures' (1998) 45 *IMF Staff Papers* 559, 561–562.

[237] Oliver Bullough, 'The Real Goldfinger: The London Banker Who Broke the World', *The Guardian*, 7 September 2018. See also Oliver Bullough, *Moneyland: Why Thieves and Crooks Now Rule the World* (Profile Books, 2018).

[238] For multiple examples of the same point, see Baker, *Capitalism's Achilles Heel*; Raymond Fisman and Edward Manuel, *Economic Gangsters: Corruption, Violence and Poverty of Nations* (Princeton University Press, 2008).

[239] W. Michael Reisman, 'Harnessing International Law to Restrain and Recapture Indigenous Spoliations' (1989) 83(1) *AJIL* 56, 58.

[240] Anton Moiseienko, 'Does International Law Prohibit the Facilitation of Money Laundering?' (2023) 36(1) *Leiden J Int'l L* 109.

International Court of Justice (ICJ) by a state victim of large-scale corruption against a state that hosted its proceeds involved not a request for assistance, but an attempt to thwart the investigation. In 2016, Equatorial Guinea filed claims against France arguing that the French prosecution of its vice-president, Theodorin Obiang, for corruption-related money laundering was in breach of his official immunities, and that his real estate in Paris had been transferred to Equatorial Guinea's embassy and was therefore inviolable.[241] The investigation had come about following extensive advocacy by local non-profit organisations, including Transparency International France and Sherpa. Equatorial Guinea's claims in the ICJ failed, Obiang was convicted *in absentia* by a Paris court, and his French property was confiscated.[242] As of this writing, Equatorial Guinea is pursuing a second set of claims in the ICJ aimed to recover from France the confiscated proceeds of Obiang's corruption.[243]

In the absence of other robust mechanisms for tackling the problem of countries that set up store as destinations for the proceeds of overseas crimes, the FATF has instantiated an essentially regulatory response to it. This response, in the form of mutual evaluation reviews (MERs), has been central to the FATF's success and, despite the fact not being widely known, has served as a template for other peer review mechanisms, especially that of the OECD Anti-Bribery Convention, often described as the 'gold standard' of treaty implementation mechanisms.[244] (In reality, the review mechanism under the OECD Anti-Bribery Convention is less impactful than the FATF process because it is not underpinned by any tangible economic consequences of non-compliance. Hence only twenty-five out of forty-six states parties to the Convention have successfully prosecuted a foreign bribery case![245])

2.4.4 *The FATF Recommendations: Mutual Evaluation*

Besides the promulgation of its first set of Recommendations, another key project of the FATF's early years was the establishment of a mechanism for enforcing the new standards. Enforcement has always been the Achilles's heel of international norm-making, and the implementation of AML rules was bound to present a

[241] *Immunities and Criminal Proceedings (Equatorial Guinea v France)*, Application Instituting the Proceedings, 13 June 2016.

[242] *Immunities and Criminal Proceedings (Equatorial Guinea v France)*, Judgment of 11 December 2020, [2020] ICJ Rep 300; *Immunities and Criminal Proceedings (Equatorial Guinea v France)*, Provisional Measures, Judgement of 7 December 2016, [2016] ICJ Rep 1148.

[243] *Request Relating to the Return of Property Confiscated in Criminal Proceedings (Equatorial Guinea v France)*, Application Instituting the Proceedings, 29 September 2022.

[244] See, e.g., Seunghyun Nam, 'Domestic Impact of the Management Process under the OECD Anti-Bribery Convention' (2018) 39(4) *U Pa J Int'l L* 955, 958. See also Mathis Lohaus, *Towards a Global Consensus against Corruption: International Agreements as Products of Diffusion and Signals of Commitment* (Routledge, 2019).

[245] OECD Working Group on Bribery, '2021 Enforcement of the OECD Anti-Bribery Convention: Investigations, Proceedings, and Sanctions', 20 December 2022.

challenge given the financial incentive for states to attract foreign business, legitimate or otherwise. The FATF's ingenious solution was to provide for a system of peer review where each participating jurisdiction[246] would be regularly assessed by others, with the resulting report being publicly available to 'name and shame' laggard countries.

The real strength of that system lies not so much in the censorious power of a poor MER, but in the practical consequences attendant on it. The determination that a particular jurisdiction is falling short of the FATF's Recommendations is likely to lead regulators in other countries to require heightened due diligence in handling business emanating from those 'high-risk' jurisdictions. This entails additional costs and causes friction that poses a disincentive to engage with businesses from the countries viewed unfavourably by the FATF.[247] In essence, compliance with the FATF Recommendations is underwritten by regulators in major international financial centres, such as the US and the UK, taking the FATF seriously. The effect is particularly pronounced in the case of jurisdictions formally placed on the FATF's 'grey-list' (technically, jurisdictions under increased monitoring) or 'black-list' (technically, high-risk jurisdictions subject to a call for action).[248] Multiple empirical studies document the deleterious effect of grey-listing, let alone black-listing, on the levels of foreign direct investment in a country or its banks' ability to secure correspondent banking relationships necessary to conduct financial transactions internationally.[249]

The influence of the FATF system has almost certainly exceeded its framers' expectations. As the host of the FATF's founding summit, France had to gamely subject itself to the first-ever mutual evaluation, conducted by three experts in 1992. According to Mark Pieth's recollection shared in an interview, they produced their twenty-page report in a pub based on three days of monitoring.[250] (The rhetorical question that Pieth asked was whether the FATF's MERs of today, running into hundreds of pages, were substantially better!).

For all of the innovation of the FATF's early monitoring efforts, one crucial limitation was their focus on 'technical compliance' alone, or the country's implementation of the FATF standards into its domestic legislation. A spotless record of technical compliance could coexist with a complete failure to enforce those rules in practice, which meant that the FATF's evaluation efforts only took account of a

[246] The FATF's preferred term is 'jurisdiction', rather than 'country' or 'state', so as to conduct separate MERs on jurisdictions such as Hong Kong or Macao.

[247] Julia C. Morse, *The Bankers' Blacklist: Unofficial Market Enforcement and the Global Fight against Illicit Financing* (Cornell University Press, 2022).

[248] FATF, 'Black and Grey Lists', www.fatf-gafi.org/en/countries/black-and-grey-lists.html.

[249] Louis de Koker, John Howell and Nicholas Morris, 'Economic Consequences of Greylisting by the Financial Action Task Force' (2023) 11(5) *Risks* 81; Matthew Collin, Samantha Cook and Kimmo Soramaki, 'The Impact of Anti-Money Laundering Regulation on Payment Flows: Evidence from SWIFT Data', *Center for Global Development Working Paper No* 445, 2016.

[250] Interview with Mark Pieth, Basel, 15 January 2024.

narrow slice of the country's capacity to fight money laundering. That changed in 2013 with the adoption of a new FATF methodology, which requires assessing the effectiveness of implementation alongside technical compliance,[251] subsequently amended in 2022 and 2024.[252]

This concern with the effectiveness of implementation added renewed urgency to the question of the objectives behind the FATF's Recommendations, that is, what they are supposed to be effective at. The approach the FATF has opted for is to define a 'hierarchy of outcomes': countries are assessed against a set of eleven immediate outcomes, which are assumed to translate into the achievement of three intermediate outcomes, which in turn are assumed to translate into the achievement of a single overarching objective.[253] That overarching objective is swathed in metaphor:

> Financial systems and the broader economy are protected from the threats of money laundering and the financing of terrorism and proliferation, thereby strengthening financial sector integrity and contributing to safety and security.[254]

The language of money laundering and other financial crimes posing a 'threat' or 'risk' to regulated businesses has become well accepted in a compliance industry now steeped in threat assessments and risk assessments. That terminology makes sense given the potential regulatory and reputational consequences of inadvertently (let alone knowingly) facilitating such activities. However, unless one is being somewhat loose with the language, the more natural way to think of the issue at a systemic level is in terms of ensuring that the financial system does not facilitate crime, rather than protecting it from the threats posed by money laundering. The point is of practical, and not merely semantic, importance. Note, in particular, the elision of the preoccupation with reporting and information-gathering that characterised early US AML measures. That focus re-emerges in the second of the FATF's three intermediate outcomes:

> Proceeds of crime and funds in support of terrorism are prevented from entering the financial and other sectors or are detected and reported by these sectors.[255]

Those are the two objectives – described in this book in shorthand as 'exclusion' and 'surveillance', respectively – that are capable of accounting for the entirety of the AML regulatory regime. As discussed in Chapter 3, the key question that the FATF's dual objectives give rise to is whether exclusion or surveillance is to be prioritised, and how far those objectives are to be pursued in light of other contrasting values or

[251] FATF, *Methodology for Assessing Technical Compliance with the FATF Recommendations and the Effectiveness of AML/CTF Systems*, February 2013.

[252] FATF, *Methodology for Assessing Technical Compliance with the FATF Recommendations and the Effectiveness of AML/CFT/CPF Systems*, updated July 2024.

[253] Ibid, 20–21.

[254] Ibid, 20.

[255] Ibid.

principles, such as the presumption of innocence or financial privacy. The FATF's methodology provides no answer to those difficult questions, and they are appropriately left for national governments to resolve; which, less appropriately, governments rarely do.

The FATF's other intermediate outcomes relate to, first, 'policy, coordination and cooperation' being in place to mitigate money laundering and terrorist financing and, second, the ultimate law enforcement objectives that the AML/CTF framework is meant to serve:

> Money laundering threats are detected and disrupted, and criminals are sanctioned and deprived of illicit proceeds. Terrorist financing threats are detected and disrupted, terrorists are deprived of resources, and those who finance terrorism are sanctioned, thereby contributing to the prevention of terrorist acts.[256]

These are perfectly sensible objectives for any country's law enforcement agencies to pursue. The challenge they present is that they describe the outcomes of a country's entire law enforcement system, which means that their achievement depends on broader contextual factors, such as the capacity of the judiciary to process financial crime cases without undue delay.

In any event, the FATF does not directly assess the achievement of either the overarching objective or the intermediary ones. Instead, its mutual evaluation process is limited to the assessment of eleven immediate outcomes, which range from the requirement for money laundering and terrorist financing risks to be well understood (Immediate Outcome 1) to the requirement that financial intelligence is 'appropriately used' by competent authorities (Immediate Outcome 6).

The practicalities of the FATF's assessment have not been free from controversy. The main abiding concern has been that well-resourced states are able to 'game the system' to satisfy the FATF's requirements without necessarily achieving meaningful progress in fighting money laundering or terrorist financing. One example is the UK, which for several years was the best-ranked FATF-assessed jurisdiction – before ceding that position to France – while its own National Crime Agency (NCA) consistently estimated that somewhere between tens and hundreds of billions of pounds had been laundered through the UK annually.[257]

A yet more striking illustration is Russia, whose 2019 MER put it among the top five FATF-rated nations, ahead of Australia and Singapore.[258] Russia is one of the very few countries, alongside Israel, the Netherlands and Spain, to have been assessed as 'highly effective' (the FATF's highest rating) under Immediate

[256] Ibid, 21.

[257] NCA, *National Strategic Assessment of Serious and Organised Crime 2023*, 2023, 34–37; NCA, *National Strategic Assessment of Serious and Organised Crime 2017*, June 2017, para 41; NCA, *National Strategic Assessment of Serious and Organised Crime 2015*, June 2015, para 69.

[258] See FATF, 'Consolidated Assessment Ratings', undated, available at www.fatf-gafi.org/en/publications/Mutualevaluations/Assessment-ratings.html.

Outcome 6, or the use of financial investigations.[259] All of this happened against the backdrop of large-scale money laundering scandals, known as 'laundromats', involving the outflow of questionable and outright criminal funds from Russia.[260] The FATF has also rated Russia as 'highly effective' in investigating and prosecuting terrorist financing, despite a significant proportion of Russia's CTF measures pertaining to the so-called extremists designated as such by the Kremlin, among them religious minorities and, since 2022, the now-dead Alexei Navalny and his aides.[261] Although the FATF suspended Russia's membership in the aftermath of its full-scale invasion of Ukraine in February 2022,[262] it never publicly commented on the counterintuitive results of the 2019 MER, which serve as a reminder of well-organised agencies' capacity to charm FATF assessor teams into writing their evaluations based upon highly curated information.

This might convey an impression of the FATF as a technical body whose preoccupation with following its methodology obscures the broader social or political realities. But this is not the case either. For some time, the FATF has been struggling to combine the technical nature of its MERs with the political process that ratifies the results of each MER.[263] For instance, under the FATF rules, certain MER results – such as a rating of 'low effectiveness' for six out of nine Immediate Outcomes – automatically result in a reference to the FATF's International Co-operation Review Group (ICRG), which can then lead to grey-listing or black-listing.[264] However, because each MER needs to be approved by consensus at an FATF plenary session, this merely creates incentives for 'horse-trading' at the stage of the MER being discussed. That, too, detracts from the FATF's credibility and its capacity to address serious financial crime threats.

The evident disconnect between some FATF assessments and countries' actual capacity to tackle money laundering has given rise to several reform proposals, such as: adjusting the requirements or assessment process to reflect a country's financial footprint (so that the same set of requirements no longer applies to, say, the US and Vanuatu)[265]; adjusting the weighting afforded to various Immediate

259 FATF, EAG and the Council of Europe, *Anti-Money Laundering and Counter-Terrorist Financing Measures – Russian Federation: Mutual Evaluation Report*, December 2019, 14.

260 See, e.g., Organised Crime and Corruption Reporting Project, *The Secret Caretaker*, 3 April 2016.

261 See Maria Kravchenko, 'Inventing Extremists: The Impact of Russian Anti-Extremism Policies on Freedom of Religion or Belief', *US Commission on International Religious Freedom*, January 2018; 'Russia Adds Putin Critic Navalny to List of "Terrorists and Extremists"', *Reuters*, 25 January 2022.

262 FATF, 'FATF Statement on the Russian Federation', 24 February 2023.

263 Tom Keatinge, 'Between a Rock and a Hard Place: The Financial Action Task Force Faces an Iranian Crunch', *RUSI Commentary*, 6 February 2020.

264 FATF, 'High-Risk and Other Monitored Jurisdictions', undated, available at www.fatf-gafi.org/en/publications/High-risk-and-other-monitored-jurisdictions/.

265 David Lewis, 'Remarks at the RUSI Meeting on the Financial Action Task Force Strategic Review', FATF, 18 November 2019, www.fatf-gafi.org/en/publications/Fatfgeneral/Rusi-fatf-strategic-review.html ('Should evaluations continue to treat all countries identically, regardless of risk and of the capacity of countries to implement the FATF Standards?'). For a useful overview of how the FATF

Outcomes (so that, say, a mere understanding of financial crime risks is not treated as equally important to investigating and prosecuting financial crime)[266]; and integrating civil society perspectives into the assessment process to minimise governments' control over the information to which FATF assessor teams are exposed.[267]

Despite the FATF's review of its own effectiveness launched in 2021, no definitive results came out of it,[268] and none of these suggestions have been adopted yet. The only significant recent change that has occurred to the FATF's MER process is the introduction of thematic, 'horizontal' reviews that assess multiple countries' performance in a particular area, such as beneficial ownership transparency, in addition to the regular comprehensive examinations of a particular country across all FATF Recommendations. The first such horizontal review was published in July 2024 and contained damning observations on the failure by Australia, China and the US to regulate relevant non-financial businesses.[269] The need for such reviews reflects the multiple avenues of the FATF's expansion, in terms of both its membership and the subject matter that its Recommendations cover, that has characterised its development since 1989, as discussed in Section 2.4.5.

2.4.5 *The FATF Recommendations: Expansion*

As the threat of money laundering garnered ever greater attention, the FATF continued to expand in four principal ways. First, it expanded its membership in a bid to ensure the FATF's worldwide credibility and move it beyond its origins as a club of wealthy Western nations. The selection of new invitees is motivated by a combination of economic and geopolitical concerns: on the one hand, the FATF is seeking to secure the buy-in of jurisdictions with an outsized financial footprint; and, on the other hand, it is also eager to bring in countries with significant political clout. For instance, Russia joined in 2003; China in 2007; and Indonesia, the world's largest

Recommendations have affected small jurisdictions with an outsized financial footprint, that is, traditional 'offshore' jurisdiction, see Dominic Thomas-James, *Offshore Financial Centres and the Law* (Routledge, 2022).

266 Tom Keatinge, Anton Moiseienko, Florence Keen, David Artingstall and Helena Wood, 'No Rest for the Wicked Driving Change in the UK's Post-FATF Evaluation AML Regime', *RUSI Whitehall Report*, February 2019, 6.

267 Stephen Reimer, 'Suppression Laundering: Using FATF as a Fig Leaf to Target Civil Society', *RUSI Policy Brief*, 13 June 2024, https://rusi.org/explore-our-research/publications/policy-briefs/suppression-laundering-using-fatf-fig-leaf-target-civil-society.

268 Lewis, 'Remarks at the RUSI Meeting'; FATF, 'FATF Ministers Commit to Take Decisive Action against Money Laundering, Terrorist and Proliferation Financing', 21 April 2022.

269 FATF, *Horizontal Review of Gatekeepers' Technical Compliance Related to Corruption*, July 2024. For contemporaneous analysis, see Paul O'Donoghue, 'UPDATED: FATF Risks Political Backlash over Poor AML Scores for US, China, Australia – Accused of Ignoring Professional Enablers', *money-laundering.com*, 8 July 2024, www.amlintelligence.com/2024/07/latest-fatf-risks-political-backlash-as-it-accuses-us-china-australia-of-fuelling-illicit-finance-by-ignoring-professional-enablers/.

Muslim-majority country, joined in 2024, along with negotiations on its potential accession to the OECD.[270]

Still, the FATF's institutional setup is fraught with challenges and contradictions. The most visible one relates to the two-tier system the FATF is based upon. The FATF proper includes forty members, among them two international agencies: the European Commission and the Gulf Cooperation Council. The FATF adopts the Recommendations and approves MERs at regular plenary sessions, which gives it significant power over more than 200 jurisdictions that have committed to complying with the FATF Recommendations. Those other jurisdictions are members of FATF-style regional bodies (FSRBs), which the FATF describes as being part of the FATF Global Network alongside the FATF proper.[271]

While FSRBs are represented at the FATF meetings, this means that FSRB members can only participate in the development of FATF Recommendations indirectly, via the relevant FSRB's intermediation. This two-tier hierarchy also has implications for the conduct of MERs. The evaluations of FSRB members are conducted by the FSRBs themselves (or, in the case of joint FATF/FSRB members, such as Australia,[272] by both the respective FSRB and the FATF) but need to be approved by the FATF proper at a plenary meeting. Therefore, despite the FATF's insistence on there being 'no organisational hierarchy between FATF and the FSRBs',[273] the perception of there being rule-givers (FATF) and rule-takers (FSRBs) has more than a grain of truth to it.

In some respects, though, the FSRBs' independence is real and not merely symbolic. For instance, following Russia's suspension from the FATF, it has continued to exercise a leading role in the Eurasian Group on Combating Money Laundering and Terrorist Financing (EAG), the Eurasian FSRB chaired by a Russian diplomat and headquartered in Moscow. Russia has also applied for an observer status with the Eastern and Southern Africa Anti-Money Laundering Group (ESAAMLG), one of the African FSRBs.[274] This demonstrates how the regional nature of the FSRBs not only provides opportunities for democratic participation but also breeds the risk of capture by states with regional influence.

Therefore, it would be simplistic to suggest that further empowerment of the FSRBs alone is the best solution to the FATF's current democratic deficit. Likewise, the expansion of the FATF proper remains a difficult prospect. In the early 2000s, the

[270] FATF, 'Outcomes: FATF Plenary', 25–27 October 2023.

[271] FATF, 'The FATF Global Network', undated, available at www.fatf-gafi.org/en/countries/global-network.html.

[272] Australia is a member of both the FATF proper and the Asia/Pacific Group on Money Laundering (APG).

[273] FATF, *High-Level Principles and Objectives for FATF and FATF-Style Regional Bodies*, updated February 2019, 9.

[274] Koos Couvée, 'EXCLUSIVE: Despite Suspension, Russia Still Wields Power inside FATF', *money-laundering.com*, 5 April 2024.

Bush administration was a major champion of including Russia and China within the FATF to ensure the organisation's global reach.[275] The benefits of a broader coalition are obvious, but they come with the risks of undermining the unity of purpose and quality of governance that a more close-knit coalition would enjoy. For now, the FATF remains torn between its origins as a taskforce on drug money set up by the G7 and its aspirations as the global standard-setter across multiple areas of financial crime (money laundering, terrorist financing and proliferation financing).

This leads us to the second facet of the FATF's expansion, namely the spread of its recommendations from money laundering to terrorist financing and, subsequently, proliferation financing. The latter two areas came within the ambit of the FATF's rules at two pivotal points: for terrorist financing, it was the attacks of 9/11, which also led to the adoption of the Patriot Act in the US; for proliferation financing, it was the revelations about the proliferation network set up by A. Q. Khan, a Pakistani nuclear scientist who helped his home country develop the nuclear bomb before selling nuclear technology to multiple other governments around the world.[276] The transposition of AML approaches to those distinct areas of law and policy has its detractors, and Chapter 4 considers in greater detail the synergies – and differences – between AML and CTF regulation.

The third aspect of the FATF's expansion is the growing number of predicate offences that its AML requirements address. The current edition of the FATF Recommendations requires that the offence of money laundering should extend to the proceeds of 'all serious offences, with a view to including the widest range of predicate offences'. Some flexibility is allowed as to what 'serious crime' means: for instance, it can simply encompass all crimes altogether; be defined by reference to a specific list of offences; or be defined based on the applicable maximum penalty.[277] The latter approach is consistent with the requirements of the UN Convention against Transnational Organized Crime (UNTOC), adopted in 2000 and also known as the Palermo Convention, which defines 'serious crime' as offences that attract a maximum term of imprisonment of four years or above under the relevant state's domestic law.[278]

There are multiple reasons for this extension of predicate offences. For one thing, the limitation of AML measures to the proceeds of a particular crime suggests that either the seriousness of the offence or the scale of associated money laundering stands out, as was originally the case with drug trafficking. With multiple forms of crime each being harmful in their own way and linked to significant criminal ecosystems, those sorts of determinations become difficult to maintain. Furthermore,

[275] Zarate, *Treasury's War*, 159.

[276] Emil Dall, Andrea Berger and Tom Keatinge, 'Out of Sight, Out of Mind? A Review of Efforts to Counter Proliferation Finance', *RUSI Whitehall Report*, June 2016, 3.

[277] FATF, *International Standards on Combatting Money Laundering and the Financing of Terrorism & Proliferation*, updated November 2023, 38 (Interpretive Note to Recommendation 3).

[278] Article 2(b).

on a practical level, regulated businesses are frequently unable to determine what offence suspect funds may relate to beyond identifying their generally suspicious quality. As a result, the FATF's retreat from a drug-bound AML regime to a more all-encompassing one is both a reflection of the evolving policy thinking on the subject and a concession to the realities of private-sector compliance.

Finally, yet another side to the FATF's expansion is the growing coverage of the sectors that must be subject to regulation under the FATF Recommendations. The first edition of the Recommendations applied to banks and non-bank financial institutions, such as insurance companies and money remitters. In 2003, the Recommendations extended their reach to designated non-financial businesses and professions (DNFBPs), which include casinos, real estate agents, dealers in precious metals and precious stones, lawyers, accountants, and trust and company service providers.[279] The next significant change to this list occurred in 2019, when virtual asset service providers (VASPs) were added to address the risks related to virtual assets, also known as virtual currencies, digital assets or crypto-assets.[280]

All those different dimensions of the FATF's evolution are indicative of the ever-greater role that the organisation itself and its standards are meant to play in governing everyday commercial interactions. As discussed in Chapter 3, these changes accentuate the question of the objectives that AML measures pursue, and therefore of the contribution that regulated businesses are expected to make to the achievement of those objectives. Before proceeding to that discussion, it is also useful to consider the implementation of the FATF Recommendations in one of the world's largest geopolitical blocs, namely the EU.

2.4.6 *EU AML Directives and Regulations: Europe against Cash*

The EU is not the only organisation shaping AML policies on the European continent. As already mentioned, the Council of Europe's recommendation issued in 1980 was arguably the forerunner of contemporary European AML efforts. Another key document stemming from the Council of Europe is the Convention on Laundering, Search, Seizure and Confiscation of the Proceeds from Crime, which was adopted in 1990 and provided for the criminalisation of money laundering on an all-crimes basis unless a state party made a declaration specifically excluding a particular offence from the ambit of the Convention.[281]

Those initiative notwithstanding, the EU has been the leading force in the promulgation of AML measures in Europe. Its primary vehicle for doing so has

279 FATF, *The Forty Recommendations*, 2003, Recommendation 12.

280 FATF, *International Standards on Combatting Money Laundering and the Financing of Terrorism & Proliferation*, Recommendation 15. See also FATF, *Targeted Update on Implementation of the FATF Standards on VAs and VASPs*, July 2024.

281 Article 1(e) and Article 6(4).

traditionally been a series of directives known as MLDs, although this has now changed.[282] Directives are legally binding instruments that need to be implemented by member states into their legislation, unlike Regulations, which are directly applicable across the EU without any further implementation.[283] Like the FATF Recommendations, the MLDs also exhibit a tendency towards the steady accretion in the number of regulated sectors but with slight adjustments compared to the FATF's approach. For instance, 5MLD extended AML/CTF regulation to freeport operators when trading art,[284] in response to the EU's longstanding concerns about tax evasion.[285]

In May 2024, the EU adopted a package of reforms to its AML framework, which includes a repackaging of the obligations faced by regulated sectors into a 'Single Rulebook' Regulation instead of a Directive.[286] Meanwhile, a newly adopted 6MLD will govern the obligations of EU member states to establish a proper AML regime, including by ensuring adequate supervision of private-sector compliance and maintaining beneficial ownership registers.[287] Both the Single Rulebook Regulation and 6MLD entered into force in July 2024, although some of their provisions apply from later dates.[288]

The Single Rulebook Regulation envisages the extension of AML/CTF obligations to professional football clubs, professional football agents and investment migration operators.[289] These changes address issues that, while not unique to EU

[282] Council Directive 91/308/EEC of 10 June 1991 on prevention of the use of the financial system for the purpose of money laundering [1991] OJ L 166 (1MLD); Directive 2001/97/EC amending Council Directive 91/308/EEC on prevention of the use of the financial system for the purpose of money laundering [2001] OJ L 344 (2MLD); Directive 2005/60/EC on the prevention of the use of the financial system for the purpose of money laundering and terrorist financing [2005] OJ L 309 (3MLD); Directive (EU) 2015/849 on the prevention of the use of the financial system for the purposes of money laundering or terrorist financing [2015] OJ L 141 (4MLD); and Directive (EU) 2018/843 amending Directive (EU) 2015/849 on the prevention of the use of the financial system for the purposes of money laundering or terrorist financing, and amending Directives 2009/138/EC and 2013/36/EU [2018] OJ L 156 (5MLD).

[283] Panos Koutrakos, *Trade, Foreign Policy and Defence in EU Constitutional Law* (Hart Publishing, 2001) 58–63.

[284] Article 1(1)(j).

[285] European Parliament, *Report on Financial Crimes, Tax Evasion and Tax Avoidance*, 2018/2121(INI), March 2019.

[286] Regulation of the European Parliament and of the Council on the Prevention of the Use of the Financial System for the Purposes of Money Laundering or Terrorist Financing [2024] OJ L, 2024/1624. See also European Council and Council of the European Union, 'Anti-Money Laundering: Council Adopts Package of Rules', 30 May 2024; European Council and Council of the European Union, 'Anti-Money Laundering: Council and Parliament Strike Deal on Stricter Rules', 18 January 2024.

[287] Directive on the mechanisms to be put in place by Member States for the prevention of the use of the financial system for the purposes of money laundering or terrorist financing, amending Directive (EU) 2019/1937, and amending and repealing Directive (EU) 2015/849 [2024] OJ L, 2024/1640.

[288] Norton Rose Fullbright, 'The New EU AML/CFT Regime Has Arrived – Are You Ready?', July 2024, www.nortonrosefulbright.com/en-au/knowledge/publications/644c5392/the-new-eu-amlcft-regime-has-arrived-are-you-ready.

[289] Article 3(3)(n)–(o).

member states, have garnered particular attention in the EU and become subjects of the EU's supranational money laundering and terrorist financing risk assessment.[290] The casting of AML/CTF obligations across these categories of businesses further speaks to the fluid, ever-changing composition of regulated sectors.

Another major development in the EU's reform package is the €10,000 limit on cash payments, which will replace existing US-style CTRs.[291] This measure, too, draws on a series of studies on the use of cash in criminal transactions.[292] Occasionally, governments worldwide have attempted to clamp down on cash use to curb its criminal abuse. The European Central Bank ended the issuance of €500 banknotes in 2016 because of 'concerns that this banknote could facilitate illicit activities'.[293] By that time, multiple EU countries had introduced upper limits on cash payments, among them Belgium, Bulgaria, Croatia, Czechia, France, Greece, Italy, Poland, Portugal, Romania, Slovakia and Spain.[294] The European Commission first proposed an EU-wide cash limit in 2017, and several other countries worldwide had introduced cash purchase limits from 2013 onwards, including Jamaica, Mexico, Uruguay and India.[295] By and large, however, the EU stands out in imposing a blanket ban on large cash purchases rather than requiring their reporting – and, therefore, offering an alternative to the less far-reaching CTR model.[296]

A challenge peculiar to the EU is the division of responsibilities for AML policies between the EU and its member states. The imposition of AML rules across the Union by means of a directly binding Regulation is a recognition of the limitations inherent in a patchwork regime that relies on member states' domestic implementation – as discussed in Chapter 4, this is also the case in relation to financial sanctions. However, centralised rulemaking at the EU level does not entirely alleviate the challenges of decentralised enforcement by member states. Therefore, the 2024 reform package provides for the establishment of an EU-wide Anti-Money Laundering and Countering the Financing of Terrorism Authority (AMLA), with the power to directly supervise high-risk financial institutions and VASPs as well as providing guidance for domestic supervisory authorities.[297] In February 2024, an agreement was reached for Frankfurt to be the AMLA's seat.[298]

290 European Commission, Brussels, *Report from the Commission to the European Parliament and the Council on the Assessment of the Risk of Money Laundering and Terrorist Financing Affecting the Internal Market and Relating to Cross-Border Activities*, COM(2022) 554, October 2022, 12, 24.

291 Article 80 of the Single Rulebook Regulation.

292 See Kenneth S. Rogoff, *The Curse of Cash* (Princeton University Press, 2017) 59–79.

293 European Central Bank, 'ECB Ends Production and Issuance of €500 Banknote', 4 May 2016.

294 Peter Sands, Haylea Campbell, Tom Keatinge and Ben Weisman, 'Limiting the Use of Cash for Big Purchases: Assessing the Case for Uniform Cash Thresholds', *RUSI Occasional Paper*, September 2017, 13.

295 Ibid, 19–21.

296 For a call for similar measures in Australia, see Christian Chamorro-Courtland, 'Ensuring Equitable Payment Options: A Legal Perspective on Banning "No Cash" Policies in Australia' (2024) *Federal LR*.

297 European Council and Council of the European Union, 'Frankfurt to Host the EU's New Anti-Money Laundering Authority (AMLA)', 22 February 2024.

298 Ibid.

The EU's centralisation drive is a sensible response to the reality of EU member states approaching money laundering with varying degrees of vigour, urgency and capacity. Its flipside is the taking of this crucial area of criminal justice from the hands of states, who ultimately are responsible for the vast majority of law enforcement across the EU, and therefore potentially impeding the effective integration of AML measures into each relevant country's own criminal justice policy. This structural disconnect between the EU-driven AML agenda and state-level criminal justice priorities adds another layer of complexity to the consideration of objectives that the AML regime should pursue, which is the topic of Chapter 3.

2.5 CONCLUSION

This concludes the broad overview of the history of AML rules that this chapter has provided. An understanding of this history is essential to appreciating that the contemporary AML regime is neither a product of logical and systematic planning nor an irrational outburst of 'moral panic'. The corpus of AML rules we now have has emerged in response to well-founded and persistent concerns about the accumulation of wealth by organised crime groups and the legitimate economy's complicity in it – in moral and, sometimes, legal terms. This, in essence, is the substance of the FATF's and domestic governments' concern with the 'integrity of the financial system', a vague concept that is often cited as the raison d'être of AML rules.

The earliest manifestation of these concerns dates back to the Anglo-American offence of handling stolen goods, itself originally a species of the broader concept of complicity in crime. With time and experience, the need for a discrete crime of money laundering, distinct from the offence of handling stolen goods or the law of complicity, became apparent. So did the necessity of regulating certain categories of businesses, which would otherwise be tempted to facilitate the 'laundering' of the proceeds of crime.

The emergence of some form of an AML system is therefore as close to inevitable as a legal development can be. It is not merely a consequence of the FATF's first meeting held in Paris in 1989. Some of the elements of the current regime had already been percolating across multiple countries for decades. What is not inevitable is the precise configuration of the existing regulatory scheme.

For example, CDD obligations are conceivable without the concomitant obligation to report suspicious activities. In turn, reporting obligations can either be suspicion-based, as required by the FATF, or predicated on some other criteria found in the international experience, be they a predefined monetary threshold (US$10,000 in the US), the objectively unusual features of the transaction (the Netherlands) or its cross-border nature (Australia). These approaches are summarised in Table 2.1, with a distinction made between those that are required by the FATF and those that are not.

TABLE 2.1 *Key elements of the current AML framework*

Element	Emergence	Current status
FATF-required		
Criminalisation of money laundering	Criminalised in relation to drug trafficking in the US and UK in 1986 but could be prosecuted as a form of complicity before then.	Now required to be criminalised on an 'all crimes' basis under the FATF Recommendations and UNTOC.
Confiscation of proceeds of crime	Facilitated through the adoption of bespoke legislation in the US and UK in 1986, despite being possible before then to some extent.	Conviction-based confiscation required by the FATF, while states are encouraged to consider non-conviction-based confiscation.
Customer due diligence (CDD)	Introduced in a limited fashion by the Swiss Due Diligence Agreement in 1977.	Subject to detailed FATF-imposed requirements and forms the basis for identifying and reporting suspicious activities.
Suspicious activity report (SAR)	Traceable to the US Trading with the Enemy Act 1917 in the form of unusual transaction reports, and first postulated in its current form in the inaugural edition of the FATF Recommendations in 1989.	Continues to be the only form of mandatory reporting required by the FATF Recommendations in contrast to other, non-FATF-mandated forms of reporting.
Controls on cross-border cash movement	Introduced in the US under the Bank Secrecy Act 1970.	Part of the FATF Recommendations since their inception.
Non-FATF-required		
Unusual transaction report (UTR)	Originates in the US Trading with the Enemy Act 1917 but was never adopted as a measure against financial crime in the US or other common law countries, with the exception of the Canadian province of British Columbia.	Currently used in several countries, most notably in the Netherlands, whose authorities receive and analyse a substantial number of UTRs.
Cash transaction report (CTR)	One of the earliest components of the US response against money laundering under the Bank Secrecy Act 1970 alongside controls on cross-border cash movement.	Used in a variety of countries besides the US, including Australia, where it was introduced in 1988.[299]
International fund transfer instruction (IFTI)	Introduced in Australia in 1992 as a result of both money laundering and tax evasion concerns.	Continues to be used in Australia and some other countries, e.g. Indonesia,[300] but not otherwise widely adopted internationally.

(*continued*)

[299] Financial Transaction Reports Act 1988 (Cth).

[300] See FATF, *Anti-Money Laundering and Counter-Terrorist Financing Measures – Indonesia: Fourth Round Mutual Evaluation Report*, April 2023.

TABLE 2.1 *(continued)*

Element	Emergence	Current status
Geographic targeting order (GTO)	Enabled in the US since 1988 to limit the application of AML requirements to high-risk areas.	Despite some discussions of GTOs as a means of tailoring AML obligations to high-risk situations,[301] not yet adopted in any other country.
Cash payment limits	Introduced in the 2010s in a dozen countries including a number of EU member states, Jamaica, Mexico, Uruguay and India.	Will be put in place in the EU for transactions over €10,000 once the Single Rulebook Regulation comes into effect.

On the other hand, while not inevitable, the basic features of our current AML framework are not random, either. They reflect an evolution of international and domestic standards in response to emerging challenges and ideas. One can often come across financial crime professionals saying that, if one were to design the AML regulatory regime from scratch today, one would not come up with the framework we now have. There is a kernel of truth to this, but it is also worth remembering that we, as society, have tried other approaches in the past: from a complete absence of financial crime rules, through a due diligence-oriented regime, all the way to various forms of reporting obligations. This experience should be recalled and drawn upon as we consider the tensions underpinning AML regulation, which are considered in Chapter 3.

[301] Helena Wood, David Artingstall, Haylea Campbell and Anton Moiseienko, 'Known Unknowns: Plugging the UK's Intelligence Gaps on Money Laundering Involving Professional Services Providers', *RUSI Occasional Paper*, 2018, 54–55.

3

Servant of Many Masters

The Objectives of Anti-money Laundering

3.1 INTRODUCTION

The growth of AML rules in the late twentieth and early twenty-first centuries has been spectacular. From the complete absence of AML laws before the 1970s to the emergence of a truly global legal and regulatory framework, the extent of the change is stark. There are costs involved. Governments have to supervise compliance and enforce the rules, whereas regulated businesses need to ensure that they fulfil the obligations imposed on them.[1] The data company LexisNexis estimates the cost of private-sector AML compliance measures at US$206 billion globally: an amount almost equal to the GDP of Hungary and more than twice that of Luxembourg.[2] This figure also gives a sense of the non-financial commitment involved, or the time and effort associated with giving effect to AML rules.

This raises the question of what the point of it all is. Often, the answers are less than encouraging. It is common to encounter policymakers, practitioners and academics with a profoundly sceptical view of the effectiveness of the AML regime they have dedicated much of their careers to – and, occasionally, the soundness of the objectives it pursues and the premises it rests upon. One can often hear that the AML regime floods governments with largely worthless reporting while excluding legitimate customers from financial services and displacing criminal activity into overtly non-compliant sectors. This summary is bleak, but also wholly mainstream.

[1] These costs are not always quantified. For instance, Australia's Treasury Department confirmed in May 2024 that it was not aware of it ever having conducted a cost–benefit analysis of AML measures: Australian Government, The Treasury, 'Freedom of Information Request 3584: Decision Letter', 17 May 2024 (on file with the author). The freedom of information request pertained to 'any assessments by the Treasury of the costs and benefits of implementing the Anti-Money Laundering and Counter-Terrorism Financing Act 2006 (Cth) and Anti-Money Laundering and Counter-Terrorism Financing Rules Instrument 2007 (No. 1) (Cth)'. By contrast, the UK's impact assessment of the Money Laundering Regulations 2019 estimated their cost to regulated businesses at only £0.5 million per year: UK Government, 'Money Laundering and Transfer of Funds (Information) (Amendment) (EU Exit) Regulations 2019: De Minimis Impact Assessment', 13 September 2019.

[2] Forrester Consulting, 'True Cost of Financial Crime Compliance Study, 2023', *LexisNexis Risk Solutions*, 2023, 9.

This chapter revisits the challenges with which the regime is fraught and recasts them in a new light. The argument here is that, at their core, those challenges are the product of two levels of unresolved tension: between exclusion and surveillance as the primary objectives of AML regulation; and between those objectives and other competing values and principles, specifically the presumption of innocence and privacy. So long as governments and legislatures refuse to confront the difficult choices relating how those values should be balanced, the AML regime will remain a patchwork of one-off solutions that do not pursue a single design. For instance, while outlawing anonymous bank accounts evinces a certain conception of how privacy should be balanced against financial crime prevention, that conception of privacy has only partially manifested itself in the context of corporate or trust structures or virtual assets.

In the absence of coherent governmental responses to those dilemmas, regulated businesses are required to fill the blanks. Thus, for example, it is up to banks to decide whether an overly cautious approach to the 'onboarding' of new customers with a view to exclude a potentially criminal clientele outweighs the collateral effects of rendering certain categories of (probably innocent but high-risk) customers unbankable. Governments' non-response to those conundrums tends to be the invocation of the 'risk-based approach', which is a version of saying 'do what you think is best for you'. This results in some regulated businesses erring on the side of caution while others intentionally cater to high-risk segments of the market, as did the German digital bank Wirecard until its implosion as a result of a massive fraud by its management.[3] Moreover, while each element of the contemporary AML framework makes sense on its own terms, they combine to give rise to a set of incentives that are at once blunt and contradictory, as explicated in this chapter.

The analysis that follows is essential for proper understanding of the challenges that bedevil countermeasures against money laundering. There is nothing wrong with treating money laundering as a serious problem; nor with prosecuting it as a crime; nor with setting up a regulatory regime that supports the prosecution of money laundering and confiscation of the proceeds of crime, even if that regime entails significant costs. What is problematic is the uncoordinated, undirected nature of today's regime that requires regulated businesses to confront unresolved policy dilemmas on a daily basis, with misplaced reliance on the 'risk-based approach' as the solution. Furthermore, while this chapter is concerned with money laundering as the original crime upon which the entire anti-financial crime system has been based, it also foreshadows later analysis of responses to terrorist financing and sanctions evasion.

This chapter begins by addressing law enforcement responses to money laundering, namely the prosecution of money launderers and the confiscation of proceeds of crime. It proceeds to discuss regulatory responses, with a focus on the tensions

[3] See Dan McCrum, *Money Men* (Penguin Books, 2023).

they entail, namely exclusion versus surveillance, exclusion versus the presumption of innocence, and surveillance versus privacy. It then explores the challenges presented by the misalignment between law enforcement priorities and private-sector compliance efforts, including defensive reporting, derisking, the displacement effect and tick-box compliance. The chapter then outlines potential solutions, including a modified reporting regime, public–private partnerships and privacy-enhancing technologies, and the implementation of a risk-based approach. The last substantive topic in this chapter is the special case of the legal profession, which presents particularly difficult choices in connection with both exclusion and surveillance. Finally, the conclusion brings together this analysis to elucidate the limitations of the existing FATF-mandated framework.

3.2 LAW ENFORCEMENT RESPONSES TO MONEY LAUNDERING

In exploring the objectives of the AML framework, it is useful to adopt Michael Levi and Peter Reuter's distinction between 'enforcement' measures (criminalisation of money laundering and confiscation or proceeds of crime) and 'preventative' measures (regulatory requirements such as customer due diligence and suspicious activity reporting).[4] As discussed in Chapter 2, prosecutions of whom we would now describe as money launderers are the historical wellspring of AML law. In common law systems, they date back to the prosecutions of vendors knowingly supplying goods for criminal purposes in the prohibition era in the US, as well as complicity-based prosecutions of those handling organised crime money in the 1970s. Likewise, the imperative of confiscating the proceeds of crime has been a key driver behind the evolution of AML rules, as evidenced by the swift reaction to the House of Lords' judgment in *Cuthbertson* in the UK.

The desirability of both prosecution of money launderers and confiscation of the proceeds of crime is largely uncontested. One might have therefore expected the entire corpus of AML rules to be solely focused on supporting those two responses, but the reality is more complicated. Considerations of excluding suspected criminals from the legitimate economy, and therefore ensuring that legitimate businesses are not complicit in their activities, appear to have strong purchase irrespective of whether they ultimately serve the goals of prosecution or confiscation. Furthermore, the relationship between money laundering prosecutions and prosecutions for predicate offences throws up challenges of its own given that any acquisitive crime by definition leads to money laundering. Sections 3.2.1 and 3.2.2 that follow consider those issues.

4 Michael Levi and Peter Reuter, 'Money Laundering' in Michael Tonry (ed), *Crime and Justice: A Review of Research* (Volume 34, Chicago University Press, 2006) 333.

3.2.1 *Prosecution of Money Launderers*

If one accepts that laundering the proceeds of crime is socially harmful, then the criminalisation of such behaviour, whether through the means of complicity law or via a dedicated criminal offence, is largely free of controversy. Every once in a while, the notion of money laundering being a victimless crime – and therefore not truly harmful – is floated.[5] But, like the idea of the Earth being flat, it is almost invariably raised only to be refuted, with only the rarest of exceptions.[6] In the legal academia, the loudest sceptical voice is that of Peter Alldridge, who writes as follows:

> The obstacle faced by those who want to present money laundering as one of the great problems of the world is that they cannot limit their claim merely to saying that laundering is a form of complicity in crime, because that will not make it bad enough to justify the erection of the AML edifice. The gravity of any form of complicity in crime is, to some extent at least, a function of the gravity of the predicate offence that generates the profit.[7]

The argument being made here is making an implicit distinction between the harm of money laundering as a justification for two separate policies: the criminalisation of money laundering (of which Alldridge is broadly supportive, even if only in the form of complicity in the predicate offence) and the creation of the AML regulatory regime (which Allridge argues, in common with many other scholars and practitioners, is bad value for money – and so requires dramatic rhetoric to justify its existence). This distinction is a fair one to make, and it is therefore useful to consider law enforcement and regulatory responses to money laundering separately.

As relates to the criminalisation of money laundering, its historical roots in the law of complicity speak to the mischief that the offence is calculated to address. The responsibility of the money launderer lies in the creation of economic conditions for the commission of crimes, specifically through enabling criminals to retain and enjoy the wealth they generate illegally. For instance, recent ethnographic studies of drug traffickers and cybercriminals, each based on hundreds of interviews, attest to the central role that the professional money launderer plays in the respective criminal ecosystem.[8]

5 For instance, criminal law theorist Douglas Husak suggests that money laundering is a perfect example of a *malum prohibitum* offence, that is, conduct that is not morally wrongful as such but is designated as a crime by the law. However, Husak's analysis is so heavily caveated and focused on self-laundering (see below) that he does not, in fact, appear to argue that money laundering is victimless or not harmful: Douglas Husak, *Overcriminalization: The Limits of the Criminal Law* (Oxford University Press, 2008) 105.

6 One such exception is a legal philosophy paper that posits money laundering as an example of a victimless crime (while conceding that many might disagree): Stephen P. Garvey, 'Was Ellen Wronged?' (2013) 7(2) *Crim L & Phil* 185.

7 Peter Alldridge, *What Went Wrong with Money Laundering Law?* (Palgrave Macmillan, 2016) 35.

8 Rajeev V. Gundur, *Trying to Make It: The Enterprises, Gangs, and People of the American Drug Trade* (Cornell University Press, 2022) 231–234; Jonathan Lusthaus, *Industry of Anonymity: Inside the Business of Cybercrime* (Harvard University Press, 2018) 86–91.

Still, there is a genuine concern about the propriety of bringing money laundering prosecutions against those who commit the underlying offence (known as 'self-laundering' prosecutions), as opposed to helping others launder the proceeds of their crimes ('third-party' laundering). Self-laundering is a logical consequence of the criminalisation of money laundering: if Alice successfully robs a bank, Alice will also commit money laundering any time she handles the proceeds. On many definitions of money laundering, even the hiding of criminally obtained cash under the mattress can constitute an offence since it involves 'concealing' the proceeds of crime. This can result in a multiplicity of prosecutions and, potentially, excessive punishment for any form of acquisitive crime. For these reasons, some domestic legislatures or courts have ruled out the prosecution of self-laundering in most cases.[9]

In some circumstances, however, good reasons may exist to bring a self-laundering prosecution. Primary among them are situations where the predicate crime is committed in one jurisdiction, but the proceeds are laundered elsewhere. Treating money laundering as a distinct offence extends the range of states that can prosecute the offence. This can be particularly positive in cases of large-scale corruption, which often involve the subversion of domestic criminal justice systems by 'kleptocrats', meaning that accountability at home may be wholly unattainable. In that way, treating money laundering as a separate offence fulfils a valuable 'jurisdictional function'.[10] There are manifold instances of this being crucial for the prosecution of large-scale corruption, such as the conviction of a Nigerian state governor James Ibori in the UK,[11] the conviction of Ukraine's ex-Prime Minister Pavlo Lazarenko in the US[12] or the conviction of the Equatoguinean vice president Theodorin Obiang in France mentioned in Chapter 2.[13] As a result, objections against prosecutions

9 For instance, in Australia self-laundering prosecutions were rejected by the courts in *Thorn v R* [2009] NSWCCA 294 and *Nahlous v R* [2010] NSWCCA 58. While, technically, these judgments are confined to the law of New South Wales, there is no reason to believe that a different approach would be taken in other states or at the Commonwealth level: FATF and APG, *Anti-Money Laundering and Counter-Terrorist Financing Measures: Australia, Fourth Round Mutual Evaluation Report*, April 2015, 57, para 3.43. For global context, see Roberto Durrieu, *Rethinking Money Laundering & Financing of Terrorism in International Law: Towards a New Global Legal Order* (Martinus Nijhoff Publishers, 2013) 29.

10 Bruce Zagaris, *International White Collar Crime: Cases and Materials* (Cambridge University Press, 2010) 138; Guy Stessens, *Money Laundering: A New International Law Enforcement Model* (Cambridge University Press, 2000) 216–217; Heba Shams, 'The Fight against Extraterritorial Corruption and the Use of Money Laundering Control' (2001) 7 *Law & Bus Rev Americas* 85, 129–132. Immunities might occasionally present an impediment to prosecution: see Yuliya Zabyelina, *Between Immunity and Impunity* (Cambridge University Press, 2023) Ch 3.

11 *R v Ibori* [2013] EWCA Crim 815, [2014] 1 Cr App Rep (S) 73.

12 *US v Lazarenko*, Case No 00-cr-0284-01 CRB (ND Cal 4 February 2010) Amended Judgment.

13 Shirley Pouget and Ken Hurwitz, 'French Court Convicts Equatorial Guinean Vice President Teodorin Obiang for Laundering Grand Corruption Proceeds', *Global Anticorruption Blog*, 30 October 2017, https://globalanticorruptionblog.com/2017/10/30/french-court-convicts-equatorial-guinean-vice-president-teodorin-obiang-for-laundering-grand-corruption-proceeds/.

of self-laundering are strongest in a purely domestic context that does not involve cross-border money laundering.

The 'parasitic' nature of money laundering, in the sense that it always involves laundering the proceeds of some other crime, has further implications. One of those is the potentially paradoxical mismatch in the levels of punishment for some acquisitive crimes and money laundering. To take a UK example, the sale or distribution of illicit streaming devices, which enable unlawful access to copyrighted material, carries a maximum penalty on indictment of two years' imprisonment or a fine in England and Wales.[14] By contrast, becoming concerned in an arrangement that one knows or suspects facilitates the retention of criminal property is punishable by up to fourteen years' imprisonment.[15]

This differential opens up questions about the harm of money laundering: surely it is a function of the harm of the predicate offence involved, such that the laundering of the proceeds of, say, selling illicit streaming devices is not the same as that of laundering the proceeds of child sexual exploitation.[16] But, having originally evolved in the context of drug trafficking and then extended on an all-crimes basis, the substantive criminal law of money laundering does not make any such link between the seriousness of the predicate offence and the seriousness of the resulting money laundering. Instead, such considerations are relegated to the sentencing stage. While this is a pragmatic solution to ensuring that the treatment of money laundering is not wholly divorced from the severity of the predicate offence (to the extent that the predicate offence can be ascertained!), there has been no research to date on whether sentencing in money laundering cases in fact reflects the nature of the predicate offence involved.

Subject to applicable rules on self-laundering prosecutions, this also provides prosecutorial agencies with the opportunity to 'upgrade' almost any charges stemming from acquisitive crimes to those of money laundering. This is of a feather with the similar practice of charging criminals with tax offences on the basis of their failure to report criminal income, discussed previously in Chapter 2. Such 'pretextual' prosecutions are both ubiquitous and controversial because they violate what criminal law theorists describe as the 'fair labelling' principle, that is, the idea that criminal charges should accurately convey the precise nature of the wrongful conduct.[17] A much less often discussed but similar tactic is what one might term 'pretextual investigations',

[14] Section 296ZB of the Copyright, Designs and Patents Act 1998 (UK).

[15] Sections 328 and 334 of the Proceeds of Crime Act 2002 (UK).

[16] This is not to suggest that the former is trivial: in some cases, IP piracy may be connected to major organised crime enterprises. See Ardi Janjeva, Alexandria Reid and Anton Moiseienko, 'Taking the Profit Out of Intellectual Property Crime: Piracy and Organised Crime', *RUSI Whitehall Report* 4–20, March 2021.

[17] Peter Alldridge, *Criminal Justice and Taxation* (Oxford University Press, 2017) 158. See also Daniel C. Richman and William J. Stuntz, 'Al Capone's Revenge: An Essay on the Political Economy of Pretextual Prosecution' (2005) 105(2) *Columbia LR* 583.

where the investigation of a certain crime is re-branded into a money laundering investigation specifically to obtain access to a broader range of investigative techniques, such as the covert monitoring of a suspect in his or her home or vehicle.[18]

The FATF's engagement with these issues, which could be thought of as going to the heart of prosecutorial (or, indeed, investigatory) discretion, has been light touch. Its principal foray into those matters is an ongoing study of the authoritarian abuses of FATF standards, which involve governments subverting AML rules to shut down civil society organisations or prosecute their political opponents on spurious financial crime charges.[19] In fact, one could fault the FATF for unwittingly contributing to the problem by focusing on whether a given country vigorously prosecutes money laundering in its MERs. This approach incentivises the 'rebranding' of investigations into money laundering ones even where an investigation into the predicate offence would be perfectly sufficient. This is indicative of the risk that, with the benefit of the global momentum that the FATF Recommendations generate, AML measures might occasionally become an end in themselves rather than one of the means of tackling criminal conduct.[20]

Occasional difficulties surrounding 'self-laundering' and pretextual money laundering prosecutions both stem from the dilemma of whether predicate offence charges or money laundering charges should be proffered. Another example is the years-long schism among US appellate courts on whether a payment for drugs was punishable as a financial transaction intended to promote unlawful activity.[21] This challenge is not always present. In some cases, the prosecution would have evidence that the proceeds of *some* predicate offence have been laundered but would not be able to prove beyond a reasonable doubt what the offence was or the circumstances of its commission. Multiple states have adopted rules that facilitate money laundering

[18] For instance, under Subsection 32(3)(b) of the Regulation of Investigatory Powers Act (UK), such monitoring, termed 'intrusive surveillance', can be ordered 'for the purpose of preventing or detecting serious crime'. Under Subsections 81(2) and 81(3), serious crime is taken to mean crime that satisfies one of the following tests:

(a) that the offence or one of the offences that is or would be constituted by the conduct is an offence for which a person who has attained the age of twenty-one and has no previous convictions could reasonably be expected to be sentenced to imprisonment for a term of three years or more;
(b) that the conduct involves the use of violence, results in substantial financial gain or is conduct by a large number of persons in pursuit of a common purpose.

The consideration of money laundering charges, which carry a penalty of up to fourteen years' imprisonment, makes it much easier to bring any form of acquisitive crime, whether or not otherwise matching the characteristics of serious crime, within the ambit of paragraph (a).

[19] FATF, 'High-Level Synopsis of the Stocktake of the Unintended Consequences of the FATF Standards' 27 October 2021, 4–6.

[20] Interview with an Australian AML/CTF expert (B), 1 July 2024.

[21] See Jimmy Gurulé, 'The Money Laundering Control Act of 1986: Creating a New Federal Offense or Merely Affording Federal Prosecutors an Alternative Means of Punishing Specified Unlawful Activity?' (1995) 32(3) *Am Crim LR* 823.

prosecutions in such cases, for instance, by removing the requirement that the predicate offence be indicated, let alone proven, with any degree of certainty.[22] Some commentators have described these changes as obliterating the concept of a predicate offence from AML law.[23] This is an overstatement in the sense that a predicate offence remains conceptually necessary: one can only have proceeds of crime if there is a crime that generates the proceeds. However, it is true that the requirement to *prove* that crime has been significantly diluted in some cases. In the absence of direct proof of the predicate offence, this means that such money laundering prosecutions need to be brought on the basis of circumstantial evidence leading to an 'irresistible inference' that the property is, in fact, proceeds of crime.[24]

Beyond the predicate crime versus money laundering prosecutorial dilemma, the criminalisation of money laundering also requires governments to ponder the balance between prosecutorial and regulatory responses. The legal feasibility of a criminal prosecution does not necessarily mean that it is in the public interest. Corporate criminal liability has long presented a particular challenge in that respect: in the words of the eighteenth-century Lord Chancellor Edward Thurlow, corporations have 'no body to kick, no soul to damn'.[25] They are legal fictions that bring people together for a common purpose, primarily to make money.[26] There is a risk that the criminal liability of a company will primarily affect an innocent constituency, such as shareholders, rather than the guilty parties, such as (former) managers – to say nothing of the broader economic risks presented by institutions that are 'too big to fail'.

The resulting tensions are well known. Governments are often accused of handling major corporations with kids' gloves.[27] In the money laundering context, the British Chancellor of the Exchequer, George Osborne, is reported to have requested the US government to drop the criminal prosecution of HSBC for its Mexican branch's knowing laundering of funds for drug cartels.[28] Some of such situations are

22 For instance, for a range of money laundering offences under Division 400 of the Criminal Code (Cth) in Australia, it is sufficient to establish that the property constitutes proceeds of 'general crime', that is, any crime, including non-indictable offences. These provisions were specifically introduced in 2020 to cover cases where the category of predicate crime could not be conclusively established: Australian Government, *Explanatory Memorandum, Crimes Legislation Amendment (Economic Disruption) Bill 2020 (Cth)*, 2020, paras 5–8. I would like to acknowledge Holly Ashburner, who wrote an excellent undergraduate thesis about this legislation from which I have learned a lot.

23 R. E. Bell, 'Abolishing the Concept of "Predicate "Offence"' (2002) 6 *J Money Laundering Control* 137.

24 *Explanatory Memorandum, Crimes Legislation Amendment (Economic Disruption) Bill 2020 (Cth)*, para 8.

25 'Edward, Lord Thurlow 1731–1806, English Jurist' in Susan Ratcliffe (ed), Oxford Essential Quotations (4th edn, Oxford University Press, 2016), www.oxfordreference.com/display/10.1093/acref/9780191826719.001.0001/q-oro-ed4-00010943.

26 The purposes of corporations, and whether they should be solely (or even primarily) focused on the pursuit of wealth for their shareholders, is a source of some contention. See William Magnuson, *For Profit: A History of Corporations* (Basic Books, 2022).

27 Jesse Eisinger, *The Chickenshit Club* (Simon & Schuster, 2017).

28 Chris Blackhurst, *Too Big to Jail* (Macmillan, 2022) 220–221.

nothing else but instances of governmental timidity, such as the UK government's discontinuation of a foreign bribery investigation into BAE Systems in 2006,[29] but there may also be entirely legitimate reasons to resort to non-criminal regulatory alternatives, such as public censure in the UK,[30] appointment of corporate monitors in the US[31] or enforceable undertakings in Australia.[32]

A by-now classic way of thinking about these choices is using John Braithwaite's 'responsive regulation' theory.[33] This theory, which can be more accurately described as a set of regulatory precepts rather than a theory per se, posits that well-meaning but non-compliant businesses ought to be educated and encouraged, whereas wilfully non-compliant ones should bear the full force of the law. This idea is often presented in the form of a 'compliance pyramid', or alternatively a spectrum, where different enforcement options correspond to varying levels of recalcitrance.[34]

The common-sense appeal of the responsive regulation theory is evident. Few would deny that a heavy-handed response should not always be the government's first choice, or that well-meaning businesses ought to be supported to do the right thing. This simple notion of treating different categories of actors differently goes back to Jerome Hall's critique of the criminal offence of handling of stolen goods, which normally does not differentiate between the activities of professional fences and one-off handlers of stolen goods.[35] As we shall see, this approach also poses some challenges when considering the regulatory dilemmas that AML regulation presents.

3.2.2 *Confiscation of Proceeds of Crime*

Before moving on to regulatory dilemmas, though, it is worth considering the second pillar of the enforcement response to money laundering, namely the confiscation of proceeds of crime, also often known as asset recovery. As discussed previously, along with the perceived centrality of professional money launderers to the criminal economy, the need to divest criminals of the proceeds of their activities has been a driving force in the evolution of the global AML framework.

This need is as close to an axiom in criminal justice policy as one can encounter.[36] No serious dissent from it has ever been detected, although some scholars have

29 *R (Corner House Research) v Director of the Serious Fraud* Office [2008] UKHL 60; [2009] 1 AC 756.

30 See Section 205 of the Financial Services and Markets Act 2000 (UK).

31 Brandon L. Garrett, *Too Big to Jail: How Prosecutors Compromise with Corporations* (Harvard University Press, 2017) Ch 7.

32 Michael Legg, Olivia Dixon and Stephen Speirs, *Corporate Misconduct & White-Collar Crime in Australia: Regulation, Investigation & Enforcement* (Thomson Reuters, 2022) 307–334.

33 See the list of relevant publications at John Braithwaite, 'Regulatory Theory', https://johnbraithwaite.com/regulatory-theory/.

34 See, e.g., John Braithwaite, 'Minimally Sufficient Deterrence' (2018) 47(1) *Crime & Justice* 69, 74.

35 See Chapter 2.

36 Colin King and Jennifer Hendry, *Civil Recovery of Criminal Property* (Oxford University Press, 2023) 102; Jordan English, Sam Hickey and Simon Bronitt, *Federal Proceeds of Crime Law* (Thomson Reuters, 2023) 11–12.

rightly suggested that the practical consequences of parting criminals with their money have remained largely unexplored.[37] There are plenty of anecdotes of hardened criminals being blasé about the prospect of a length prison term but reduced to tears by the confiscation of their property. There has, however, never been a systematic study of the effect that confiscation has on the criminals' resolve to engage in further crime: for instance, it is theoretically possible that having part of their income taken away would only incentivise them to work harder. A rare empirical study of this topic was carried out by the Crime and Corruption Commission in Queensland, Australia, which explored the correlation between confiscation and the rates of future reoffending – which proved to be lower than otherwise predicted, suggesting that confiscation did have a positive impact.[38]

Like prosecution of money laundering, states' ability to confiscate the proceeds of crime is meant to benefit directly from the operation of their regulatory AML frameworks. Confiscation of criminal property requires it to be identified to begin with, and this is where effective financial surveillance may prove indispensable. As multiple governmental reviews across the common law world demonstrate, lacking financial investigation skills and resources are often the main cause of underwhelming confiscation rates.[39]

Those disappointments are then frequently sought to be overcome through legal reforms, with a view to making confiscation easier to achieve. Perhaps the most significant of such reforms is the adoption throughout the world of non-conviction-based confiscation laws, known as non-conviction-based asset forfeiture in the US and civil recovery in the UK.[40] As the term suggests, such laws enable confiscation of alleged proceeds of crime in a notionally civil proceeding without the need for

37 Johan Boucht, *The Limits of Asset Confiscation* (Hart Publishing, 2017) 95–116; Michael Levi, 'Criminal Asset-Stripping: Confiscating the Proceeds of Crime in England and Wales' in Adam Edwards and Peter Gill (eds), *Transnational Organised Crime: Perspectives on Global Security* (Routledge, 2003) 218–222.

38 Queensland Crime and Corruption Commission, *The Impact of Proceeds of Crime Action on Offending Trajectories*, May 2022, www.ccc.qld.gov.au/publications/impact-proceeds-crimeaction-offending-trajectories.

39 See, e.g., Australian reviews carried out in Western Australia and Tasmania, respectively: Wayne Martin AC QC, *Review of the Criminal Property Confiscation Act 2000 (WA)*, May 2019; Damian Bugg AM QC, *Independent Review of Part 9 Crime (Confiscation of Profits) Act 1993*, June 2017. Similar findings and recommendations were made by the Cullen Commission in British Columbia: The Hon. Austin F. Cullen, *Commission of Inquiry into Money Laundering in British Columbia: Final Report*, June 2022, 1609–1613, building on the work of previous Canadian inquiries: Peter M. German, QC, *Dirty Money: An Independent Review of Money Laundering in Lower Mainland Casinos Conducted for the Attorney General of British Columbia*, 31 March 2018; Peter M. German, QC, *Dirty Money, Part 2: Turning the Tide – An Independent Review of Money Laundering in B.C. Real Estate, Luxury Vehicle Sales & Horse Racing*, 31 March 2019; Dan Perrin, *Real Estate Regulatory Structure Review*, 2018; and Maureen Maloney, Tsur Somerville and Brigitte Unger, *Combatting Money Laundering in BC Real Estate*, 31 March 2019.

40 See, generally, King and Hendry, *Civil Recovery of Criminal Property*; Stefan D. Cassella, *Asset Forfeiture Law in the United States* (3rd edn, Juris Publishing, 2021).

compliance with criminal trial safeguards. In common law countries, this means – crucially – that the civil standard of proof applies, and not the criminal one. When the UK's Proceeds of Crime Act 2002 was debated in the House of Lords, Lord Llord of Berwick famously – and, in hindsight, erroneously – predicted that civil recovery provisions would be struck down by the European Court of Human Rights (ECtHR):

> [I]f we design an agricultural implement for digging and it has a handle and four or five prongs, we have designed a fork. We can call it a spade, if we like, but it remains, in fact and in law, a fork. Likewise, if we design a piece of legislation with the object of depriving a man of some or all of his possessions, after he has been found guilty of unlawful conduct under Part 5 [money laundering], we can describe that as a recovery order, but the European Court will call our bluff and will call it what it is – a confiscation order by another name.[41]

The ECtHR never called the bluff, and nor did any other international human rights court or domestic court.[42] One can legitimately continue to question the supposedly civil nature of non-conviction-based confiscation based on first principles,[43] and in particular the almost undeniably punitive impact on those affected by such confiscation, but the reality remains that multiple countries have adopted such legislation with no demur from the judiciary.[44] What has proved considerably more contentious is mechanisms that combine non-conviction-based confiscation with a reversal in the burden of proof, such that the respondent bears the burden to prove the property is of legitimate origin lest it should be liable to confiscation.[45]

In 2023, the FATF launched a workstream on confiscation jointly with Interpol to ensure that the Recommendations and the MER process better deliver on the imperative of depriving criminals of ill-gotten property.[46] Some commentators have criticised the FATF's exercise as too focused on legal arguments about the most appropriate modes of confiscation, such as conviction-based or non-conviction-based, with less attention devoted to the operational measures that can support the

41 HL Deb 13 May 2002 Vol 635 Col 67.

42 In fact, the first case considering the point was decided by the European Commission of Human Rights long before the entry into force of UK legislation that Lord Lloyd was commenting upon: *M v Italy*, European Court Human Rights, App No 12386/86, Decision on Admissibility of 15 April 1991 (*Yearbook of the ECHR, Martinus Nijhoff*, 1991) 86. The same approach was then followed in multiple later cases, for example, *Gogitidze et al v Georgia*, European Court Human Rights, App No 36862/05, Judgment of 12 May 2015. For more analysis, see Boucht, *The Limits of Asset Confiscation*.

43 See, e.g., Liz Campbell, 'The Recovery of "Criminal" Assets in New Zealand, Ireland and England: Fighting Organised and Serious Crime in the Civil Realm' (2010) 41(1) *Victoria University of Wellington LR* 15.

44 See, e.g., Colin King, 'Civil Forfeiture and Article 6 of the ECHR: Due Process Implications for England & Wales and Ireland' (2014) 34(3) *Legal Studies* 371; Theodore Greenberg et al, *Stolen Asset Recovery: A Good Practices Guide for Non-Conviction Based Asset Forfeiture*, Stolen Asset Recovery Initiative, 2011.

45 Anton Moiseienko, 'The Limitations of Unexplained Wealth Orders' [2022] (3) *Criminal LR* 230.

46 FATF, 'FATF and INTERPOL Intensify Global Asset Recovery', 13 September 2022, www.fatf-gafi.org/en/publications/Methodsandtrends/FATF-INTERPOL-intensify-global-asset-recovery.html.

identification of criminally obtained property.[47] It is too early to draw any definitive conclusions as to whether the FATF's work on confiscation ultimately lives up to this critique, but at the very least it serves as a welcome reminder of the confiscation of criminal property being one of the key objectives behind the entirety of AML law. How the rest of the AML framework supports the attainment of that objective, along with that of prosecuting money launderers, is something that we can now consider.

3.3 KEY REGULATORY DILEMMAS

The most intuitive way of thinking about the entire corpus of AML rules is either as directly enabling the prosecution of money launderers and confiscation of proceeds of crime, through the adoption of rules that make this legally possible, or as supporting the attainment of those objectives through the provision of information by regulated businesses. Viewed in this manner, the AML framework presents as a coherent whole united around a single core of key objectives, even if the achievement of those objectives is at times not as effective or efficient as it could be.

In reality, this simple and attractive conception of the AML framework must be qualified. The main reason for this is that AML regulatory requirements, including CDD and suspicious activity reporting, do not appear to be limited solely to the provision of information required for law enforcement purposes. Instead, they also pursue the exclusion of proceeds of crime from the legitimate economy as a self-standing objective of the entire AML regime. Furthermore, prosecutions of potential 'professional enablers', such as banks or lawyers, can also be plausibly interpreted as an attempt to insulate the legitimate economy from criminal infiltration. With the exclusion of proceeds of crime thus emerging as a central tenet of AML rules, questions arise about how it fits with the other objectives, values and principles that underpin the system – and what trade-offs it presents.

3.3.1 *Exclusion versus Surveillance*

As discussed previously, standard-setting organisations including the FATF, EU and Basel Committee all speak of financial integrity as a key value that AML measures seek to protect.[48] The Oxford English Dictionary defines 'integrity' as a moral concept to mean 'soundness of moral principle; the character of uncorrupted virtue, especially in relation to fair dealing; uprightness, honesty, sincerity'.[49] Those are all valuable qualities, and it is only natural to wish that they define our financial system.

[47] Helena Wood, 'The Courage of Its (Non) Convictions: The FATF Review of Asset Recovery', *RUSI Commentary*, 19 January 2023, https://rusi.org/explore-our-research/publications/commentary/courage-its-non-convictions-fatf-review-asset-recovery.

[48] See Chapter 2.

[49] 'Integrity' in *Oxford English Dictionary*, www.oed.com/dictionary/integrity_n?tl=true.

Making money by helping criminals amass and retain their wealth is antithetical to those features of integrity. Whether one has in mind the Bank of New York's laundering of the proceeds of Russian corruption in the 1990s,[50] the Riggs Bank's work for African dictators in the early 2000s,[51] or HSBC's laundering of drug cartel money in the 2010s,[52] no one would seriously contend that collusion with criminals in pursuit of self-enrichment is compatible with any meaningful conception of integrity. Therefore, the FATF's and other standard-setting bodies' invocation of financial integrity as a core value is not a cliché devoid of substance but a genuine explanation of the origins of the AML framework.

The design of criminal laws against money laundering reflects that value. With only some oversimplification, they can be described as criminalising assisting someone in retaining proceeds of crime with the knowledge of their criminal origins. Consider, for example, Article 6 of the UNTOC, which is worth quoting at length:

> 1. Each State Party shall adopt, in accordance with fundamental principles of its domestic law, such legislative and other measures as may be necessary to establish as criminal offences, when committed intentionally:
>   (a)
>   (i) The conversion or transfer of property, knowing that such property is the proceeds of crime, for the purpose of concealing or disguising the illicit origin of the property or of helping any person who is involved in the commission of the predicate offence to evade the legal consequences of his or her action;
>   (ii) The concealment or disguise of the true nature, source, location, disposition, movement or ownership of or rights with respect to property, knowing that such property is the proceeds of crime;
>   (b) Subject to the basic concepts of its legal system:
>   (i) The acquisition, possession or use of property, knowing, at the time of receipt, that such property is the proceeds of crime;
>   (ii) Participation in, association with or conspiracy to commit, attempts to commit and aiding, abetting, facilitating and counselling the commission of any of the offences established in accordance with this article.
>
>   (…)
>   (f) Knowledge, intent or purpose required as an element of an offence set forth in paragraph 1 of this article may be inferred from objective factual circumstances.

50 US Attorney's Office, Southern District of New York, 'The Bank of New York Resolves Parallel Criminal Investigations through Non-Prosecution Agreement with the United States', 8 November 2005, www.justice.gov/archive/usao/nye/pr/2005/2005nov08.html.

51 US Senate, Permanent Subcommittee on Investigations, *Money Laundering and Foreign Corruption: Enforcement and Effectiveness of the PATRIOT Act – Case Study Involving Riggs Bank*, 2002.

52 See Blackhurst, *Too Big to Jail*.

A domestic criminal law provision drafted in line with the UNTOC is apt to capture the activities of professional third-party money launderers, such as the IRS undercover agent Robert Mazur's alter ago Robert Musella, the make-believe money launderer for the Sinaloa drug cartel.[53] It also serves as a deterrent to banks, money remitters, law firms and any other businesses who may come into contact with proceeds of crime and be requested to facilitate their investment. This might appear to be an unalloyed positive, but we need to recognise the potential for a clash with another facet of AML laws, namely the deputisation of regulated businesses to collect and transmit to the government information about the financial activities of suspected criminals.

The dilemma was brought home to me at a financial crime conference I attended at the Royal United Services Institute (RUSI) in London in around 2017. During the Q&A session after one of the panels, an audience member – most of them, financial crime compliance professionals – mentioned the UK government's then-estimate that around 5,000 organised crime groups were active in the UK. The audience member asked why UK law enforcement or intelligence agencies could not share information about suspected members of those groups with banks on a confidential basis so as to generate better, more targeted intelligence on their activities than the hundreds of thousands of SARs filed by regulated businesses in an undirected fashion. The speaker, a senior bank compliance officer with extensive prior law enforcement experience, said this would not produce the desired result: any bank's instinct would be to 'derisk', that is, drop all customers with organised crime links. Substantially the same observation has been repeated by scores of compliance professionals I have spoken to since, including interviewees for this book.[54]

This is because the two key pillars of AML rules, the criminalisation of knowing involvement in money laundering and the reporting of suspicious activities, are contradictory in practice even though they are fully compatible in theory. The FATF's Recommendation 20, which deals with SARs, provides as follows:

> If a financial institution suspects or has reasonable grounds to suspect that funds are the proceeds of a criminal activity, or are related to terrorist financing, it should be required, by law, to report promptly its suspicions to the financial intelligence unit (FIU).

Other FATF Recommendations extend this requirement to DNFBPs and VASPs.[55] The threshold for suspicion is invariably lower than knowledge. Therefore, the FATF's scheme requires that regulated businesses report activities that reach the

53 Robert Mazur, *The Infiltrator: Undercover in the World of Drug Barons and Dirty Banks* (Corgi Books, 2015).

54 Interview with a Canadian law enforcement expert, 27 November 2023; interview with two international AML/CTF experts, 18 January 2024; interview with an Australian AML/CTF expert (B), 1 July 2024.

55 FATF, *International Standards on Combatting Money Laundering and the Financing of Terrorism & Proliferation*, updated November 2023, Recommendation 15 (VASPs) and Recommendation 22 (DNFBPs).

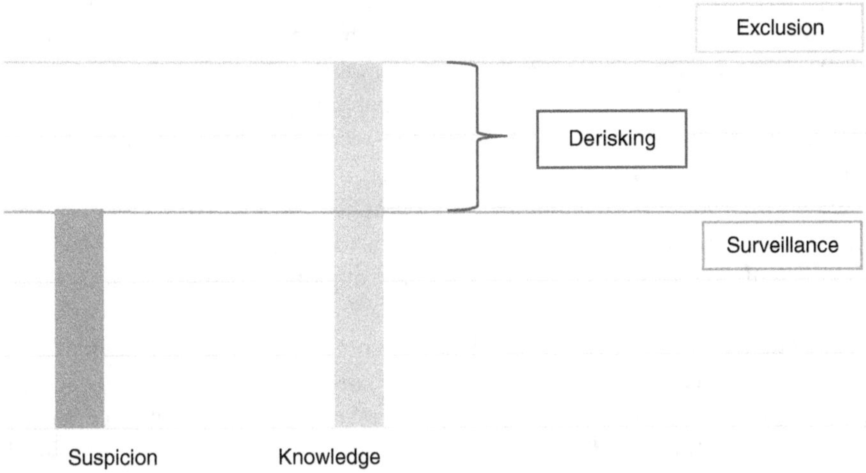

FIGURE 3.1 Mental states thresholds (FATF requirements)

threshold of suspicion while foregoing activities that they know involve the proceeds of crime. In reality, once the level of suspicion is reached, the regulated business is overwhelmingly likely to drop the customer ('derisk'), as depicted in Figure 3.1.

As a result of this offboarding of high-risk customers, their financial surveillance by any given bank or other regulated business is likely to be short-lived. But those customers' potentially malicious activities will continue: once dropped by one bank, they will simply move on to another one. If that second bank does not have the same financial crime detection capabilities, a useful source of financial intelligence may be lost forever. In any event, the second bank is likely to require some time, typically months, to adequately assess whether its new customer's activities are suspicious. This creates a time gap that a criminal can exploit.[56]

Some appreciation of banks' financial crime controls is useful in order to understand why the gap emerges. The FATF Recommendations do not prescribe *how* regulated businesses are to identify suspicious activities. The approach universally required by domestic regulators is known as 'transaction monitoring', a term that is never mentioned in the FATF Recommendations but is essential to AML compliance in practice.[57] It involves ongoing automatic monitoring of a user's transactions to identify 'red flags', that is, indicators of high-risk transactions that need to be reviewed by a human analyst to ascertain whether they give rise to a reportable suspicion.[58]

56 Interview with two international AML/CTF experts, 18 January 2024.

57 See Matthew R. Redhead, 'The Future of Transaction Monitoring: Better Ways to Detect and Disrupt Financial Crime', *SWIFT Institute*, May 2021.

58 Federal Financial Institutions Examination Council, *BSA/AML Manual; Appendix F: Money Laundering and Terrorist Financing 'Red Flags'*, https://bsaaml.ffiec.gov/manual/Appendices/07.

Some red flags are universal: for example, it is unusual for a legitimate business to regularly both send money to and receive money from another company (one would normally pay suppliers and receive payment from customers, but those would not be one and the same).[59] Others are a function of the customer's individual circumstances: for example, a student is unlikely to be receiving substantial payments from anyone other than his or her family. Still other red flags reflect identified money laundering 'typologies': for example, if a particular jurisdiction is known to be a major money laundering hub, all fund transfers to that country could be flagged – especially if they also fit the typology in some other way, such as the amounts or timings involved.[60]

Depending on the would-be launderer's brazenness and sophistication, discrepancies between expected activities and actual transaction profile may only become evident with time. Therefore, in terms of generating financial intelligence, there is a real opportunity cost to displacing potential criminals from a bank that has already done its homework on that customer to one that has not. The inability to share information about such customers among banks has been a persistent gripe in the sector, but there are good reasons to eschew such information-sharing on the grounds of the presumption of innocence and privacy, as discussed in Sections 3.3.2 and 3.3.3. For now, regulated businesses have to make do with the framework they have. For instance, one senior bank compliance officer interviewed for this book mentioned how, in the aftermath of any regulatory action against another bank, he would warn his staff to exercise special diligence in anticipation of an influx of offboarded customers from that other bank.[61]

The problem is serious and ubiquitous, and it is crucial to understand that its main cause is the structural incentives that AML rules produce. No legitimate bank – to stay for the moment with banks as the avatar of all regulated sectors – would wish to become the target of a money laundering prosecution. This fear tends to spread across the entire chain of the individuals involved, too: from the compliance officer, who would dread a money laundering scandal breaking out on his or her watch; to the bank management, to whom the risk would likely outweigh the advantage of keeping any particular customer on the books; to regulatory agencies' field examiners, who are in charge of supervising a given bank.

As a senior compliance expert interviewed for this book observed, individually rational actions by multiple actors could therefore combine to give rise to irrational results.[62] Further still, those actions are not only rational if taken in isolation but also serve the genuinely useful purpose of excluding the proceeds of crime from

59 One of the best introductions to 'red flags' is the 'Risky Business' episode of The Dark Money Files podcast hosted by Ray Blake and Graham Barrow: https://podcasts.apple.com/us/podcast/risky-business/id1448635132?i=1000457866936.

60 The Wolfsberg Group, *Country Risk Frequently Asked Questions (FAQs)*, 2024.

61 Interview with two international AML/CTF experts, 18 January 2024.

62 Ibid.

the financial system. The drawback of this is the lack of incentives to account for trade-offs that single-minded pursuit of that objective entails. Therefore, a cultural rift may emerge in AML regulatory agencies between policy experts, who might be more open to thinking about the systemic effects of compliance practices on fighting crime, and field examiners, who would inevitably be the ones facing uncomfortable questions if a scandal erupted on their watch.[63]

These structural incentives are a product of legal rules, but they do not appear to depend much on the nuances of the drafting. It is exceedingly unlikely that adjusting the relevant legal thresholds, such as raising the standard of knowledge required of a bank to face prosecution for money laundering, would make any meaningful difference. Comparative international experience across the US, UK and Australia offers illuminating examples.

One of those is the UK's system of using a special category of SARs, now officially described as 'defence against money laundering' SARs or 'defence against terrorist financing' SARs – and previously known by the more convenient moniker of 'consent' SARs, which I shall use here.[64] For context, consider one of the three money laundering offences under the Proceeds of Crime Act 2002:

> (1) A person commits an offence if he enters into or becomes concerned in an arrangement which he knows or suspects facilitates (by whatever means) the acquisition, retention, use or control of criminal property by or on behalf of another person.[65]

This offence provides for a *mens rea* element (suspicion) that is considerably lower than what the UNTOC or the FATF Recommendations require (knowledge). On its own terms, this provision would have required UK businesses to take an even more of a 'belt and braces' approach to money laundering than their overseas counterparts. However, the following subsection provides as follows:

> (2) But a person does not commit such an offence if –
> (a) he makes an authorised disclosure under Section 338 and (if the disclosure is made before he does the act mentioned in Subsection (1)) he has the appropriate consent;
> (b) he intended to make such a disclosure but had a reasonable excuse for not doing so;
> (c) the act he does is done in carrying out a function he has relating to the enforcement of any provision of this Act or of any other enactment relating to criminal conduct or benefit from criminal conduct.

63 Ibid.

64 NCA, 'SARs Regime Good Practice – Frequently Asked Questions: Defence Against Money Laundering (DAML)', May 2019, www.nationalcrimeagency.gov.uk/who-we-are/publications/167-defence-against-money-laundering-daml-faq-may-2018/file.

65 Section 328(1).

An 'authorised disclosure under Section 338' is precisely what a consent SAR is. In essence, it is a notification made to the National Crime Agency (NCA) via the UK Financial Intelligence Unit (UKFIU) to (a) set out the grounds for suspecting that the customer's proposed activity involves money laundering and (b) request the NCA's consent to proceed with this activity notwithstanding. If the consent is granted, the filer of the SAR can proceed with the transaction without incurring criminal or civil liability for money laundering or terrorist financing in connection with that transaction.

The money laundering offences in the UK have been framed in this fashion since their introduction in 1993.[66] This form of SARs is a UK innovation evidently meant to alert the NCA to criminal activity without requiring the filer of the SAR to refuse the transaction, let alone offboard the customer concerned. With the filer of the SAR benefiting from a defence to money laundering charges, one might expect such SARs to fulfil the uniquely valuable function of breaking the link between the submission of a SAR and the offboarding of the customer. In other words, in theory it could be the perfect vessel for the provision of information to law enforcement agencies, as summarised in Figure 3.2.

The problem with consent SARs is the significant resourcing and timing pressures they entail, for filers and the UKFIU alike. SARs in general are a costly and time-consuming exercise. For instance, the staff costs involved in producing a complex SAR on a cross-jurisdictional transaction or series of transactions could come up to US$50,000–60,000 and take several days to prepare.[67] While not all consent SARs will be that costly, overall they are likely to be on the more demanding end of the spectrum because of the need to provide information of the quality sufficient to enable the UKFIU to decide on the SAR in close to real time.

Just how close to real time this determination has to be, has been a stumbling block for a while. Once a consent SAR is filed, the 'moratorium' period starts to run during which the transaction must not be attempted.[68] The UKFIU must notify the filer within the moratorium period. If no decision is communicated to the filer during that period, the consent is deemed to have been granted. The UKFIU has often struggled to respond to consent SARs within the moratorium period, in part because a meaningful response frequently requires consultation with the relevant local police force. Until the enactment of the Criminal Finances Act 2017, the moratorium period constituted thirty-one days.[69] It can now be extended on application to the court

[66] Sections 29 and 30 of the Criminal Justice Act 1993 (UK), amending the Criminal Justice Act 1988 (UK).

[67] Interview with two international AML/CTF experts, 18 January 2024; Jim Richards' *LinkedIn* post, 1 May 2024, available at www.linkedin.com/posts/richards1_sars-take-2-hours-on-average-ctrs-take-activity-7201931794890280961-pBys/ (see also replies from various compliance officers in comments, including from Anna Palmer, Charlene Cieslik, Jay P. Gentile and Maria Escoto).

[68] Section 335(3) of the Proceeds of Crime Act 2002 (UK).

[69] Transparency International UK, *Empowering the UK to Recover Corrupt Assets: Unexplained Wealth Orders and Other New Approaches to Illicit Wealth and Asset Recovery*, 2015 (updated March 2016) 16.

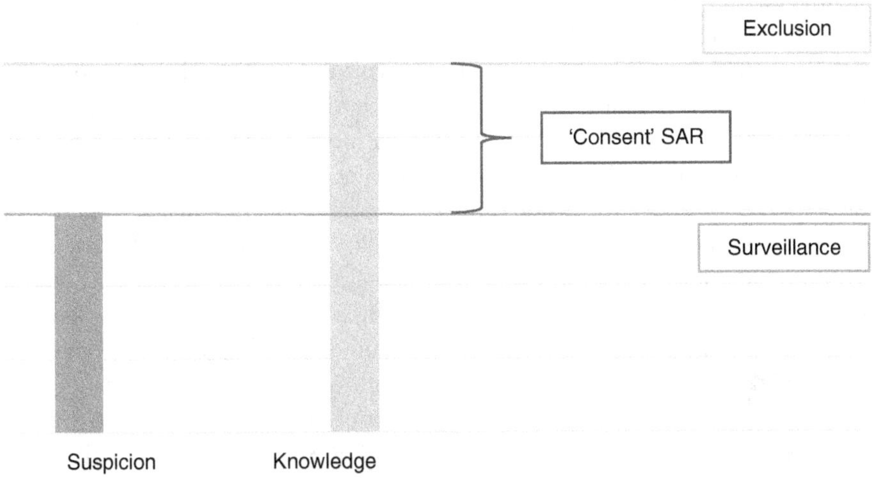

FIGURE 3.2 Mental states thresholds (UK model)

for a total of up to 186 days.[70] During that period, the filer of the SAR is placed in the rather awkward position of holding up the transaction without disclosing to the customer that a SAR has been submitted lest the criminal offence of 'tipping off' be committed. The contrived nature of any explanation that a bank can provide without disclosing the existence of a SAR will lead an astute customer to deduce that a SAR has been filed – a phenomenon described by some as 'reverse tipping-off'.[71]

In short, the consent SAR regime has not proved to be panacea against the challenges borne of the tension between the objectives of exclusion and surveillance – or other problems with the SAR regime, which are discussed in more detail below. Those challenges are as pressing in the UK as they are elsewhere. In recognition of the systemic weaknesses of the SAR regime, the UK government referred its operation for the Law Commission's consideration in 2017.[72] The Law Commission produced its report in 2019, with a series of modest recommendations, some of them related to oversight of the UK's AML regime or priorities for further research.[73] The Law Commission's approach prompted a gentle rebuke from those commentators who had hoped for a root-and-branch reform of the regime, but ultimately it reflects the deep-seated nature of the issues involved, which are not amenable to a technical legal fix.[74]

70 Section 336A of the Proceeds of Crime Act 2002 (UK).

71 Interview with two international AML/CTF experts, 18 January 2024.

72 Law Commission, 'Anti-Money Laundering', https://lawcom.gov.uk/project/anti-money-laundering/.

73 Law Commission, *Anti-Money Laundering: The SARs Regime Report*, Law Com No 384, March 2019.

74 Helena Wood, 'Kicking the Can Down the Road: The Law Commission's Report on UK Anti-Money Laundering Law', *RUSI Commentary*, 9 July 2019, https://rusi.org/explore-our-research/publications/commentary/kicking-can-down-road-law-commissions-report-uk-anti-money-laundering-law.

Another illustration of this latter point is the Australian experience. At the federal level, the Commonwealth Criminal Code contains dozens of money laundering offences structured across different tiers – with different maximum penalties – depending on the amount involved, the nature of the crime (indictable offences versus all other offences) and the defendant's mental state.[75] A number of those offences criminalise dealing with proceeds of crime while being negligent as to their provenance.[76] Negligence is one of the lowest standards of culpable *mens rea* in Anglo-American criminal law and falls short of knowledge or even recklessness as to the criminal origins of the property.[77] In the absence of a consent SAR-style mechanism, one would expect Australian banks and other businesses to be even more risk-averse in their dealings than their US or UK counterparts. But there is absolutely no evidence that these nuances of the criminal law provisions on money laundering play any significant role at all in shaping behaviour in the regulated sectors. So long as money laundering is criminalised and SAR/STR/SMR reporting is required, the incentives discussed above manifest themselves in a powerful way.[78]

One must also acknowledge the significant role of non-regulatory reputational considerations in determining organisations' stance towards the risk of involvement in money laundering. In recent years, a great deal of attention has been focused on the propriety or otherwise of business dealings with criminal or even controversial clients, such as the convicted financier Jeffrey Epstein or likewise convicted media mogul Harvey Weinstein.[79] Major banks, law firms and accountancy firms have become the subjects of book-long exposés of their entanglements with criminal or simply controversial clients.[80]

The proliferation of various 'name and shame' lists, many of them published by pressure groups and activists, speaks to these developments. They span a wide gamut of alleged transgressions, such as manufacturing weapons or dealing with the arms industry[81]; supporting fossil fuel trade[82]; failing to provide modern slavery

75 Division 400 of the Criminal Code (Cth).

76 See, e.g., Section 400.2B(8) of the Criminal Code (Cth).

77 See Findlay Stark, *Culpable Carelessness: Recklessness and Negligence in the Criminal Law* (Cambridge University Press, 2016).

78 Interview with an Australian AML/CTF expert (A), 14 June 2024; interview with an Australian AML/CTF expert (B), 1 July 2024.

79 See, e.g., Kalyeena Makortoff, 'Deutsche Bank Agrees to Pay $75m to Settle Jeffrey Epstein Lawsuit', *The Guardian*, 18 May 2023; Nupur Anand, Lananh Nguyen and Jonathan Stempel, 'JPMorgan Pays $75 million to Settle Lawsuit over Jeffrey Epstein Ties', *Reuters*, 27 September 2023.

80 See, e.g., Richard Brooks, *Bean Counters* (Atlantic Books, 2019) 211–232 (discussing KPMG's alleged involvement in the FIFA corruption scandal); David Enrich, *Dark Towers* (HarperCollins, 2020) (detailing Deutsche Bank's history of dealing with controversial clients, including US President Donald Trump); David Enrich, *Servants of the Damned* (Marine Books, 2022) (same for the law firm Jones Day).

81 'Don't Bank on the Bomb', www.dontbankonthebomb.com/; Ethical Consumer, 'Banks and Financial Institutions Profiting from Weapons', www.ethicalconsumer.org/money-finance/banks-weapons.

82 'Fossil Banks', www.fossilbanks.org/fossil-banks; Law Students for Climate Accountability, 'Climate Change Scorecard', www.ls4ca.org/scorecard.

disclosures[83]; lacking in gender diversity,[84] and so on. They also target a wide array of industries, from obvious ones – such as finance – to pharmaceuticals, fashion and others.

Even governments resort to such lists. For instance, for some time the Ukrainian government was maintaining a list of 'sponsors of the war', that is, Western companies that continue to operate in Russia following its full-scale invasion of Ukraine.[85] The list had no consequences under Ukrainian law and was explicitly conceived as a means of exerting public pressure on the companies who find themselves on it. In 2024, Ukraine took the list offline, reportedly after pressure from foreign governments who were upset with the inclusion of companies from their countries.[86]

Taken together, these developments – including the rise of AML legislation, sustained and ubiquitous press reporting of dubious business dealings and the proliferation of 'name and shame' campaigns – give strong reasons to argue that there has occurred a shift in public sentiment such that there truly is no such thing as amoral business anymore. It is easy to see a connection here to the emergence of exclusion, as distinct from surveillance, as a key objective of AML efforts. As the US federal judge John Noonan wrote in his treatise *Bribes*, '[l]aws do not testify to social fact; they do testify to social consciousness'.[87] AML laws do not mean that the complicity of major corporations in money laundering is a thing of the past, but they do underscore that public indifference to such complicity is largely gone.

One noteworthy illustration of this point is the publication by the International Consortium of Investigative Journalists (ICIJ) in 2020 of a series of leaks dubbed the FinCEN Files, which disclosed confidential information about SAR filings held by FinCEN, the US FIU and AML/CTF regulator.[88] The FinCEN Files followed on the heels of other high-profile journalist investigations carried out by the ICIJ, including Panama Papers, Paradise Papers and Pandora Papers.[89] The principal revelation of the FinCEN Files was that several US banks continued to do business with Russian oligarchs after filing SARs in connection with their activities.[90] Broadly speaking, the reaction within professional AML circles was the proverbial collective

[83] Nga Pham, Bei Cui and Ummul Ruthbah, 'Modern Slavery Disclosure Quality Ratings: ASX100 Companies Update 2022', *Monash Centre for Financial Studies, Monash Business School*, 2022.

[84] Chief Executive Women, 'CEW Senior Executive Census 2023: Incremental Change Failing to Solve the Crisis', 2023.

[85] Tom Balmforth, Pavel Polityuk and Liz Lee, 'Exclusive: China Tells Ukraine to Remove Its Firms from "Sponsors of War" List', *Reuters*, 2 February 2024.

[86] Tom Balmforth and John O'Donnell, 'Ukraine Drops Russia Business Blacklist after Backlash', *Reuters*, 23 March 2024.

[87] John Noonan, *Bribes* (University of California Press, 1987) 97.

[88] ICIJ, 'FinCEN Files', www.icij.org/investigations/fincen-files/.

[89] ICIJ, 'The Panama Papers: Exposing the Rogue Offshore Finance Industry', www.icij.org/investigations/panama-papers/; ICIJ, 'Paradise Papers: Secrets of the Global Elite', www.icij.org/investigations/paradise-papers/; ICIJ, 'Pandora Papers', www.icij.org/investigations/pandora-papers/.

[90] 'Global Banks Defy U.S. Crackdowns by Serving Oligarchs, Criminals and Terrorists', *ICIJ*, 20 September 2020.

shrug: not only had the banks followed the letter of the law, but they had also done the right thing by avoiding unnecessary derisking. What this reaction does not fully acknowledge is that, in most cases, the banks would have offboarded the customer immediately following the filing of a SAR. It is therefore legitimate to ask why the reaction was different when wealthy customers were concerned, although the question contains the complete answer.

This is yet another example of banks acting upon the incentives they face. A natural instinct to derisk can be outweighed by the financial rewards of keeping a well-paying client, but this is only likely to be true for a narrow sliver of the bank's customer base. Therefore, the broader problem of banks labouring under the operation of several conflicting objectives remains. This is also evident from a landmark statement by the Wolfsberg Group, a grouping of thirteen global banks convened in the 2000 to develop non-binding industry standards in response to the FATF Recommendations.[91] In 2019, the Wolfsberg Group published a statement setting out its views on what effective AML/CTF compliance looks like, which involves three 'key elements':

1. Comply with AML/CTF laws and regulations;
2. Provide highly useful information to relevant government agencies in defined priority areas; and
3. Establish a reasonable and risk-based set of controls to mitigate the risks of a financial institution being used to facilitate illicit activity.[92]

These three 'Wolfsberg factors' are a useful encapsulation of what banks should aspire to, but they do not help resolve the tensions between the second and third elements. In essence, doing so requires governments to make policy choices about when exclusion should be prioritised over surveillance, or the other way around. Those are the choices that governments have been loath to make so far, and engaging with them seriously is further complicated by the other values and principles that push against either exclusion or surveillance, as discussed below.

3.3.2 *Exclusion versus Presumption of Innocence*

In light of their AML obligations, regulated businesses need to consider the risk of their customers being engaged in money laundering. One may argue that, practically speaking, this means treating customers other than presumptively innocent. To appreciate the argument, it is useful to briefly lay out the competing visions of what the presumption of innocence could mean.

[91] See Mark Pieth, 'The Wolfsberg Process' in Wouter Muller et al (eds), *Anti-Money Laundering: International Law and Practice* (John Wiley & Sons, 2007) 95.

[92] The Wolfsberg Group, 'Demonstrating Effectiveness', June 2021.

The presumption of innocence can be understood in at least four ways. These are, from the least to the most controversial:

- In a narrow criminal law sense, as a legal rule that the prosecution bears the burden of proof in relation to all elements of the alleged offence in a criminal trial.[93] The standard of proof being beyond reasonable doubt is often seen as a corollary of that rule.[94]
- In a broader criminal procedure sense, as a principle that government authorities must treat a person before charges have been laid, or after that person has been found not guilty, as innocent.[95]
- In a still broader criminal justice policy context, as a precept that the framing of laws should not undermine the guarantees afforded by the presumption of innocence narrowly understood. The best example is non-conviction-based confiscation, where the protections afforded by the presumption of innocence are removed by taking the confiscation of proceeds of crime out of the setting of a criminal trial. The courts' unanimous approval of this form of confiscation rests on a narrow conception of the presumption of innocence, whereas abiding academic criticism of it espouses a broader conception of the presumption.[96] Another example is the offence of illicit enrichment, that is, an unexplained increase in the wealth of a public official, which can be viewed as a means of circumventing the need to prove that the official has engaged in bribery or another form of corruption.[97]
- In a general civic sense, as a notion that all of us – or, at the very least, the state itself – should treat our fellow citizens as presumptively innocent of crime.[98] This, the argument goes, is a manifestation of civic trust and solidarity that all of us owe to each other. This conception of the presumption of innocence evinces not a legal rule, nor even a criminal justice policy principle, but a philosophical postulate about how we should deal with each other.

That latter, broadest view of the presumption of innocence has been criticised by some as an amorphous substitute for civil rights that is too vague in terms of its impact to be useful.[99] Theorists all the way back to Jeremy Bentham have observed that

93 In English and Australian criminal law, the rule is conventionally traced to *Woolmington v DPP* [1935] AC 462.

94 Paul Roberts, *Roberts & Zuckerman's Criminal Evidence* (3rd edn, Oxford University Press, 2022) Ch 6.

95 Antony Duff, 'Who Must Presume Whom to Be Innocent of What?' (2013) 42(3) *Netherlands J Leg Phil* 170.

96 See footnotes 41–45.

97 See the discussion in Andrew Dornbierer, *Illicit Enrichment: A Guide to Laws Targeting Unexplained Wealth* (Basel Institute on Government, 2021) 122–141; Lindy Muzila et al, *On the Take: Criminalizing Illicit Enrichment to Fight Corruption* (Stolen Asset Recovery Initiative, 2012) 30–31.

98 Dale A. Nance, 'Civility and the Burden of Proof' (1994) 17(3) *Harvard J Law & Pub Policy* 647.

99 Thomas Weigend, 'There Is Only One Presumption of Innocence' (2013) 42(3) *Netherlands J Leg Phil* 193.

certain circumstances leave the state no choice but to treat an individual as other than innocent.[100] The exercise of arrest powers is one such example. True, the individual may then be acquitted, but the implication of criminality that the arrest instils in the minds of the general public may never be entirely dispelled. No one would suggest that arresting suspects is therefore illegitimate, but on the other hand it is generally accepted that the legal status of those in pre-trial detection is substantially different to the status of those sentenced to a term of imprisonment – the latter person is being subjected to a criminal punishment, whereas the former one is merely awaiting trial.

For those who favour the broad, civic notion of the presumption of innocence, the principal implication of this stance is that legal protections should constrain the state's ability to treat people as other than innocent. Here is how Liz Campbell, a professor of criminal law at Monash University, describes the raft of situations where legal protections should attach to governments' encroachments on the presumption of innocence broadly conceived:

> Where state agents describe a person as suspect, as problematic, as risky, or as criminal, an official view is being conveyed that separates her from the 'law-abiding' majority. (…) Though public preconceptions about individuals who come into contact with the justice system may be unavoidable, as Husak has said 'it is one thing to have such feelings, and quite another to express them through an institution'.[101]

The protections involved need not be as extensive as those afforded in a criminal trial, but nor should they be wholly absent. This view of the presumption of innocence, with its focus on the expressive aspect of conveying an imputation that someone might be other than innocent, is closely related to the protection of individual reputation. Therefore, the Swiss jurist Stefan Trechsel writes of a reputation-based vision of the presumption of innocence in his analysis of the ECtHR's case law on insinuations of guilt by state authorities.[102] (The case law of the ECtHR and Court of Justice of the European Union (CJEU) occupies an odd intermediate position where post-acquittal imputations of guilt are deemed to be in contravention of the ECHR, but the same imputations of guilt in circumstances where no criminal prosecution was ever brought do not trigger the presumption of innocence.)[103]

100 See the discussion in Pamela Ferguson, 'The Presumption of Innocence and Its Role in the Criminal Process' (2016) 27(2) *Crim L Forum* 131, 141–143.

101 Liz Campbell, 'Criminal Labels, the European Convention on Human Rights and the Presumption of Innocence' (2013) 76(4) *MLR* 681, 688 (citations omitted).

102 Stefan Trechsel, *Human Rights in Criminal Proceedings* (Oxford University Press, 2006) 189–190.

103 Compare *Butkevičius v Lithuania*, European Court of Human Rights, App No 48297/99, Judgment of 26 March 2002, paras 53–54 with *Zollmann v UK*, European Court Human Rights, App No 62902/00, Decision on Admissibility of 27 November 2003 and *Franchet and Byk v Commission*, European Court of Justice, Judgment of 8 July 2008 in Case T-48/05. For analysis, see Anton Moiseienko, *Corruption and Targeted Sanctions: The Law and Policy of Anti-Corruption Entry Bans* (Brill, 2019) 198–203.

This kind of analysis applies squarely to some state-issued allegations of criminality, such as targeted financial sanctions discussed in Chapter 4. The issues arising in the AML context are subtly different. Here, too, someone is treated as other than innocent if they are denied access to services that people otherwise obtain as a matter of course – for example, opening a bank account or preparing conveyancing documents for a real estate transaction. But, without more, this confidential denial of services or offboarding lacks the expressive aspect that a public allegation of criminality would have. Nor are those measures imposed directly by state authorities. Instead, they are adopted by private businesses *because of* the AML rules set by the state, as well as the associated reputational incentives.

Despite those important differences, the conundrum remains. Is it appropriate for regulated businesses to second-guess their customers' potential engagement in criminal activity? This question can be expressed in terms of concerns about financial exclusion, which this second-guessing can lead to, but it can also be considered through the lens of the presumption of innocence understood as a broad civic virtue. As with any such conflict between competing objectives or values – here, the exclusion of proceeds of crime from the legitimate economy and the presumption of innocence – the contradiction cannot be resolved through some form of scientific measurement to determine which one is weightier. Which one to prioritise is ultimately a policy choice for governments and legislatures to make.

In pondering this choice, one may well feel that we have drifted too far towards a world where businesses are incentivised to drop customers on the basis of no more than a whiff of potential involvement in crime. Sometimes, this is true for entire categories of legitimate business, for example, virtual asset exchanges, money remitters or, in countries where they are legal, cannabis producers. However, it is also useful to remember that we have experience of the alternative. An environment where businesses truly embrace the presumption of innocence, broadly understood, harbours its own risks.

In British journalist Oliver Bullough's *Butler to the World*, the book's central metaphor is encapsulated in its title.[104] It speaks of the UK as a butler to the world due to its role in transnational money laundering schemes – by contrast to the US, often described as the world's policeman. Bullough's narrative deftly paints the picture of an erstwhile imperial power reduced to the Jeeves-like role facilitating the machinations of the *nouveau riche*. But if one put the unflattering connotations of the metaphor to one side, this non-judgmental attitude to other people's wealth, combined with extending the benefit of the doubt even when no benefit of the doubt is due, is precisely what the presumption of innocence, broadly understood, requires. Embracing it involves a return to the business environment that is amoral, in the literal sense of being unconcerned with morality, that we have collectively retreated from – with all the dilemmas that entails.

[104] Oliver Bullough, *Butler to the World* (Profile Books, 2022).

3.3.3 *Surveillance versus Privacy*

Financial surveillance of transactions potentially involving money laundering is another key objective behind AML measures. The development of AML regulations from the 1970s onwards has made significant inroads into financial privacy. The most visible manifestations of this initial encroachment on financial privacy were the introduction of reporting requirements for banks and the abolition of anonymous bank accounts.[105] The magnitude of the departure this marked from the traditional deference to privacy was clear to the contemporaries, as is evident from this passage in the US Supreme Court Justice William Rehnquist's judgment dismissing the challenge to the constitutionality of the Bank Secrecy Act, delivered in 1974:

> While an Act conferring such broad authority over transactions such as these might well surprise or even shock those who lived in an earlier era. The latter did not live to see the time when bank accounts would join chocolate, cheese, and watches as a symbol of the Swiss economy. Nor did they live to see the heavy utilization of our domestic banking system by the minions of organized crime as well as by millions of legitimate businessmen.[106]

Jason Sharman, a scholar of economic crime based at the University of Cambridge, has captured this change by arguing that 'the dominance of the principle of transparency, justified on the grounds of a "nothing to hide, nothing to fear" logic, and the equation of privacy with roguery, mean that the decline of financial privacy looks set to continue'.[107] Sharman is probably correct in identifying the direction of travel. Crucially, though, the ongoing expansion of the AML framework fell short of a comprehensive renegotiation of the boundaries between criminal justice needs and financial privacy protections. Those boundaries remain highly contested to this day. To appreciate the challenge, it is useful to distinguish between seven forms of AML-related information-sharing, each with their own distinct purposes:

- **Provision of information by regulated businesses in response to a valid law enforcement request.** This is the most straightforward and uncontentious form of information-sharing. The FATF-derived AML framework shapes this form of information-sharing in a few ways. First, since their first edition, the FATF Recommendations have provided that bank secrecy cannot form a reason to reject a law enforcement request.[108] Second, CDD and record-keeping

[105] See Chapter 2.

[106] *California Bankers Ass'n v Shultz*, 416 US 21 (1974).

[107] J. C. Sharman, 'Privacy as Roguery: Personal Financial Information in an Age of Transparency' (2009) 87(4) *Pub Administration* 717.

[108] This proposition is most recently found in FATF, *International Standards on Combatting Money Laundering and the Financing of Terrorism & Proliferation*, Recommendation 9.

obligations determine what information must be collected from the customer with a view to potentially being shared with law enforcement agencies upon a lawful request.[109] Third, the FATF-mandated 'wire transfer rule', also known as the 'travel rule' in the context of VASPs, requires that, in the context of cross-border financial or virtual asset transactions, certain information about the payor be collected and passed on the payee's financial institution or VASP.[110] This is to ensure that the latter financial institution or VASP has information about both sides of the transactions and can share it with law enforcement agencies if required.

- **Private-to-public reporting**. This is perhaps the most recognisable category of AML obligations, which involves regulated businesses providing the government with information about suspicious, unusual or otherwise reportable activities. Depending on the applicable regulatory framework, it can take the form of SAR, CTR, UTR or IFTI reporting, or reporting pursuant to GTOs – of which only SAR reporting is required by the FATF.[111]
- **Private-to-public information-sharing (other than reporting).** Formal reporting does not exhaust the modalities of private-to-public information-sharing. Other modes of such information-sharing can be either wholly informal or take place via public–private partnerships, discussed in greater detail below. Informal information-sharing can involve no more than a bank compliance officer placing a phone call to the FIU directing their attention to a particularly noteworthy SAR – but, due to applicable data protection restrictions, can typically involve no more than that. By contrast, public–private partnerships provide participants with the legal basis for exchanging information about observed typologies as well as operational details of investigations. As discussed below, they serve to enable information-sharing that is more fluid and responsive to law enforcement needs than various reporting regimes can ensure. No such arrangements are required by the FATF.
- **Private-to-private information-sharing.** Several states, including the UK and the US, enable regulated businesses to share information about suspicious activities with each other subject to certain conditions.[112] This information-sharing is meant to enable them to consolidate the information they hold about a particular person with a view to making a report to law enforcement agencies, that is, filing a SAR. This mode of information-sharing is not required by the FATF. Some jurisdictions also have non-AML-oriented but AML-relevant information-sharing arrangements in place, for example,

[109] Ibid, Recommendations 10 and 11.

[110] Ibid, Recommendations 15 and 16. The Interpretive Note to Recommendation 15 clarifies that Recommendation 16 is among those FATF requirements that should be applied to VASPs.

[111] See Chapter 2.

[112] Section 314(b) of the Patriot Act (US); Section 339ZB of Proceeds of Crime Act 2002 (UK).

to share information about customers found to have engaged in fraudulent activity among banks.[113]

- **Public-to-private information-sharing.** One of the persistent complaints among AML experts has been that information-sharing tends to be wholly unidirectional, that is, law enforcement agencies receive the information reported to them but provide little to no indication of its usefulness or otherwise.[114] Despite multiple discussions of the issue, no tangible progress appears to have been made. Instead, two other forms of public-to-private information-sharing have emerged, both of which are discussed below. One is the sharing of general information about law enforcement AML priorities done in some jurisdictions. The other is the identification of law enforcement priorities and needs via public–private partnerships. None of these modes of information-sharing is required by the FATF.
- **International information-sharing.** The international sharing of information about potential money laundering can happen either in the context of mutual legal assistance (MLA) or, more swiftly and with a specific focus on money laundering or terrorist financing, via the Egmont Group, an international platform for FIUs' cooperation. The information-sharing system used by the Egmont Group enables participating FIUs to first identify another FIU that might hold relevant information and then liaise with it on a bilateral basis.[115] The FATF Recommendations contain a general requirement that jurisdictions afford each other the widest range of international cooperation in the prevention, detection, investigation and prosecution of money laundering, including via cooperation among FIUs.[116]
- **Disclosure of beneficial ownership information.** The identification of potential crimes, or the location of the proceeds of those crimes, often entails the need to ascertain who owns or controls a particular company or property.[117]

[113] An example from the UK is the National Fraud Database run by Cifas: www.cifas.org.uk/fraud-prevention-community/member-benefits/data/nfd. For a brief discussion, see Anton Moiseienko and Kayla Izenman, 'What's in a Name? Corruption and Fraud in the UK', *RUSI Occasional Paper*, June 2019, 49–50.

[114] Interview with a Canadian law enforcement expert, 27 November 2023; interview with a Swiss banking expert, 17 January 2024; interview with a UK AML/CTF expert, 30 January 2024; interview with Dr Katie Benson, 1 July 2024. For an early articulation of the problem, see John J. Byrne, 'The Bank Secrecy Act: Do Reporting Requirements Really Assist the Government' (1993) 44(3) *Ala L Rev* 801, 832.

[115] See Egmont Group of Financial Intelligence Units, *Operational Guidance for FIU Activities and the Exchange of Information*, 2013 (updated February 2017).

[116] FATF, *International Standards on Combatting Money Laundering and the Financing of Terrorism & Proliferation*, Recommendation 40.

[117] See Alberto Aziani, Joras Ferwerda and Michele Riccardi, 'Who Are Our Owners? Exploring the Ownership Links of Businesses to Identify Illicit Financial Flows' (2022) *European J Criminology* 1542; A. F. Steinko, 'Financial Channels of Money Laundering in Spain' (2012) 52(5) *Brit J Criminology* 908; Emile van der Does De Willebois et al, *The Puppet Masters: How the Corrupt Use Legal Structures to Hide Stolen Assets and What to Do about It*, Stolen Asset Recovery Initiative, 2011.

The difficulties of doing so as a result of criminals concealing property or control via complex corporate arrangements have given rise to multiple initiatives aimed at advancing beneficial ownership transparency.[118] Those initiatives tend to involve the collection of beneficial ownership information in a centralised state-run register and its disclosure to either a certain category of users, such as law enforcement agencies, tax authorities and regulated businesses, or the public at large. The FATF requires states to collect beneficial ownership information but leaves it up to them to decide whether a centralised register is necessary or who exactly has access to it.[119] These issues have proved to be intensely controversial over the past decade.[120]

These forms of AML information-sharing are summarised in Table 3.1.

In connection with each of these forms of information-sharing, privacy and data protection concerns arise. These two concepts are broadly similar, but in the law enforcement context, privacy is ordinarily taken to refer to whether an individual's data can be collected at all, whereas data protection rules govern how information is used once collected.[121] The thresholds for collection and use of information can vary, and views differ on which of these two should be more exacting (should it be more difficult to collect data but easier to query it once collected, or the other way around?).[122] For the purposes of this discussion, 'privacy' is treated as an all-encompassing concept that also embraces data protection concerns.

The manner in which privacy is treated in the AML context is at once rigid and marked by uncertainty. It is rigid in the sense that, generally speaking, the sharing of customers' financial information by regulated businesses is subject to tight constraints. This creates multiple difficulties. For example, a bank who has conducted analysis on a high-risk customer's activities generally cannot share its results with other banks, subject to certain exceptions discussed later, such as acting in the confines of a public–private partnership. More strikingly, a bank's branch or subsidiary in one country may not be able to share AML-relevant information with

[118] These include programmes run by non-governmental organisations, such as Open Ownership, and international agencies, such as the Stolen Asset Recovery Initiative, a joint programme set up by the World Bank and UN Office on Drugs and Crime.

[119] FATF, *International Standards on Combatting Money Laundering and the Financing of Terrorism & Proliferation*, Recommendations 24 and 25.

[120] For an overview of key issues, see Tom Keatinge and Anton Moiseienko, 'For Whose Benefit? Reframing Beneficial Ownership Disclosure around Users' Needs', *RUSI Occasional Paper*, November 2020.

[121] Serge Gutwirth and Paul de Hert, 'Privacy, Data Protection and Law Enforcement: Opacity of the Individual and Transparency of Power' in Eric Claes, Antony Duff and Serge Gutwirth (eds), *Privacy and the Criminal Law* (Intersentia, 2006).

[122] See Michael Chertoff, *Exploding Data* (Grove Press, 2018) 127–132 (arguing for 'considerable latitude' in governmental collection of data but stringent controls on its access, on the basis that it is difficult to predict in advance what data might become necessary for law enforcement or national security purposes).

TABLE 3.1 *Forms of AML information-sharing*

Form of information-sharing	Objective	Legal status
Responses to valid law enforcement requests	Provision of information about potential money laundering.	The FATF Recommendations require that bank secrecy must not prevent such information-sharing; set out requirements as to the CDD information to be collected and recorded; and require certain information to be sent alongside financial or virtual asset transfers.
Private-to-public reporting	Provision of information about potential money laundering.	The FATF Recommendations require SAR reporting, but not any of the other reporting models, to be implemented.
Other private-to-public information-sharing	Provision of information about potential money laundering.	Not required by the FATF but introduced domestically in some jurisdictions via dedicated legislative provisions.
Private-to-private information-sharing	Collation of information from different regulated businesses for further reporting.	Not required by the FATF but introduced domestically in some jurisdictions via public–private partnerships.
Public-to-private information-sharing	Communication of law enforcement priorities; communication of operational information to regulated businesses; and provision of feedback on their reporting.	Not required by the FATF but introduced domestically in some jurisdictions via public–private partnerships.
International information-sharing	Communication of information internationally to support law enforcement investigations.	Required by the FATF as part of a broader provision on international cooperation.
Disclosure of beneficial ownership information	Support of regulated businesses' efforts to conduct CDD and identify suspicious activities.	Required by the FATF in broad terms, without defining whether a centralised register must be used or who, beyond law enforcement agencies and tax authorities, must have access to it.

the same bank's branch or subsidiary elsewhere due to data protection rules.[123] The impediments these rules create are well known. As recently as in March 2024, Paul Jevtovic, the former head of AUSTRAC and current head of financial crime

[123] The FATF has recognised that group-wide AML information-sharing is highly desirable but sometimes is challenging in practice: FATF, *Guidance on Private Sector Information Sharing*, November 2017, 7–14.

compliance at the National Australian Bank, identified reconsideration of the boundaries between privacy and AML measures as a priority.[124]

Some governments' heavy-handed treatment of information-sharing by regulated businesses might suggest prioritisation of financial privacy over AML information-sharing. Yet, as the discussion above highlights, in reality both the forms of AML information-sharing and its extent have been rapidly increasing. This contradiction underscores the lack of depth and consistency in how the AML framework accounts for privacy concerns. This depth and consistency is lacking on multiple levels.

The first of these is in relation to the *choice of the AML reporting model*. It is worth returning again to the FATF's preference for SARs as the only mandatory mode of private-to-public information-sharing. One might have expected it to be the result of a thorough consideration of the law enforcement benefits of SARs weighed against their drawbacks, including their impact on individual privacy. If that calculus were more advantageous for SARs than other modes of reporting, that would convincingly explain the FATF's preference for SARs. However, there is no evidence of any such comparative analysis of various forms of reporting ever having taken place, whether undertaken by the FATF or by any other organisation. The analysis that is perhaps closest to that description is a RUSI paper published by Olivier Kraft, which focuses on the contribution of advanced analytics to the detection and prevention of financial crime but does not explicitly compare and contrast various alternative approaches to reporting with the FATF model.[125] In short, the current design of the FATF Recommendations insofar as the reporting of potential money laundering is concerned is due to 'an accident of birth', or the fact that the SAR model was proffered at the FATF's inaugural meeting, as described by Mark Pieth.[126]

The second, and arguably more important, area where privacy concerns have not been treated satisfactorily relates to *consistency across settings*. As already mentioned, the FATF Recommendations require that bank secrecy must prevent no obstacle to compliance with them, including SAR filing.[127] This could be viewed, not unfairly, as a policy commitment to prioritising financial crime prevention and detection over privacy. However, this is only partly true. In fact, battles over AML measures and privacy continue to rage in different settings in a fashion that makes one wonder whether we have any coherent concept of the value of privacy vis-à-vis financial crime at all – meaning the criminal justice policy writ large, not only the

[124] Sumeyya Ilanbey, 'Balance the Right to Privacy with Stamping out Organised Crime: NAB', *The Age*, 10 March 2024, www.theage.com.au/business/banking-and-finance/balance-the-right-to-privacy-with-stamping-out-organised-crime-nab-20240308-p5fauy.html.

[125] Olivier Kraft, 'Sharpening the Money-Laundering Risk Picture: How Data Analytics Can Support Financial Intelligence, Supervision and Enforcement', *RUSI Occasional Paper*, November 2018.

[126] See Chapter 2.

[127] FATF, *International Standards on Combatting Money Laundering and the Financing of Terrorism & Proliferation*, Recommendation 9.

FATF's approach. There are two particular areas that throw this lack of consistency into focus, those being 'corporate entities and legal arrangements' in the FATF's terminology (i.e. companies, partnerships and trusts) and virtual assets.[128]

For many decades, companies, partnerships and trusts have been used to obscure ownership.[129] This is possible because each of these forms of commercial organisation can entail a separation between the formal (legal) ownership of an asset and its ownership in economic terms. For instance, if I hold a house via a company whose shares I own 100 per cent, I can rightfully describe the house as my property for virtually any practical purpose. In short, I am the beneficial owner of the house. However, technically speaking, the legal owner of the house is the company, not me.[130] Likewise, the legal owner of a property held on trust is the trustee, not the beneficiary – nor the settlor.

Each of these forms of commercial organisation have evolved for contexts having nothing to do with hiding the ownership of wealth or the identity of a person engaging in a particular transaction. The two key features that have transformed the limited liability company into a preeminent vehicle for commercial transactions are separate legal personality and limited liability. These concepts entered legal usage in England and the US in the nineteenth century to finance large-scale, high-risk commercial enterprises, especially the construction of railroads.[131] The investing public could from then on participate in the funding of those endeavours without fear of personal exposure to significant losses if the firm went bust – they would only risk the extent of their investment. From the early days of the truly modern corporation, as opposed to its historical forerunners such as the East India Company, *limited liability* was central to its operation.

By contrast, *limited visibility* into corporate ownership (or corporate opaqueness) emerged organically and was never the focus of any sustained examination in terms of its benefits and disadvantages. It is a product of the distinct legal personality that a company enjoys extending into multiple domains beyond the mere ability to enter into commercial relations independently of its shareholders. Such extensions are perennially controversial. One high-profile example is the US Supreme Court's

[128] Covered in FATF, *International Standards on Combatting Money Laundering and the Financing of Terrorism & Proliferation*, Recommendations 24, 25 and 15, respectively.

[129] See footnote 117.

[130] The classic English case establishing this separation is *Salomon v A Salomon & Co Ltd* [1896] UKHL 1; [1897] AC 22.

[131] Philip Lipton, 'Limited Liability in the English and Australian Companies Acts' (2018) 41(3) *Melb Uni LR* 1278, 1293. Limited liability was introduced in England, Wales and Ireland by the Limited Liability Act 1855 (18 & 19 Vict. c. 133), whereas the notion of separate corporate personality is more ancient pedigree: see Tom Bathurst, 'The Historical Development of Corporations Law' (2013) 37(3) *Aust BR* 217. Some scholars argue that limited liability predated those nineteenth-century developments, but the precise historical chronology is not essential for our purposes: Ron Harris, 'A New Understanding of the History of Limited Liability: An Invitation for Theoretical Reframing' (2020) 16(5) *J Institutional Economics* 643.

ruling that companies enjoy free speech, and that free speech entails the right to make campaign contributions to the campaign of one's favoured candidate.[132] More broadly, Mariana Pargendler of the University of São Paulo argues that the law is ridden with the 'fallacy of complete corporate separateness', that is, the view that because companies are treated as distinct persons in some contexts (e.g. their ability to act as commercial counterparties), they therefore need to be treated as distinct persons in *all* contexts (e.g. it is sufficient *for all purposes* to say that a particular piece of property is owned by a company, as opposed to the individuals behind that company).[133]

If one accepts this reasoning, limited visibility is nothing but a poorly thought through consequence of applying the logic of separate personality and limited liability outside its proper remit. The same can be said of trusts, originally developed as a means of arranging family affairs in the Roman and then medieval times,[134] and of partnerships, which came about as a means for various categories of professionals to organise their business dealings – from solicitors in England to farmers in Scotland.[135] The point is not that limited visibility is an invariably undesirable consequence of distinct legal personhood of corporations or the fiduciary nature of trusts, but that it has emerged without any serious, sustained consideration of its merits and flaws. This, for example, is how we ended up in a world with a flourishing supply of 'off-the-shelf' companies incorporated specifically to be sold to someone who wishes to have a company that looks as though it was set up some time ago.[136]

Suppose a government agency proposed the establishment of a Limited Visibility Company, a corporate form whose sole purpose would be to conceal from the public the beneficial owners of the property that such a company legally owns. One might expect such a proposal to generate a great deal of disquiet and debate. Yet, when this benefit of limited visibility is packaged together with the other accoutrements of the corporate form, such as limited liability, and emerges organically over decades and centuries rather than being implemented by design, the level of scrutiny is markedly lower. (Ironically, during the writing of this book, Scotland legislated to introduce the private purpose trust, which would separate legal and beneficial ownership without being subject to any registration requirements – described by Dan Neidle, former UK head of tax at the law firm

[132] *Citizens United v Federal Election Commission*, 558 US 310 (2010).

[133] Mariana Pargendler, 'The Fallacy of Complete Corporate Separateness' (2024) 14 *Harvard Business LR Online* 1.

[134] Stephen Kos, 'A Short History of the Trust', June 2019, www.courtsofnz.govt.nz/assets/speechpapers/trt_1.pdf.

[135] Department for Business, Energy & Industrial Strategy (UK), *Limited Partnerships: Reform of Limited Partnership Law*, April 2018, 16 (see the textbox on 'agricultural uses of Scottish limited partnerships').

[136] Masarah Paquet-Clouston, Nicholas Lord, Jade Philibert and Celine Giese, 'Incorporating the Illicit: Assessing the Market Supply of Shelf Companies' (2024) *Eur J Crim Pol Res*, https://link.springer.com/article/10.1007/s10610-024-09594-w.

Clifford Chance, as 'an amazing new legal vehicle for money launderers, tax evaders and sanctions-busters').[137]

This state of affairs is indicative of how we lack any coherent conception of financial privacy and its limitations. This becomes ever more apparent with the growing focus on beneficial ownership transparency, which has been prompted in part by recurrent journalist investigations about the use of corporate structures and trusts to conceal property ownership.[138] The benefits of beneficial ownership transparency include speeding up law enforcement work and facilitating regulated sectors' CDD efforts.[139] The downsides are often framed in terms of examples of celebrities, kidnappings and global corporations.[140] If you were a celebrity and bought a house, you would not want people to know that it is you who is the purchaser; corporate ownership would provide a welcome screen from the prying eyes of the public.[141] Relatedly, it is often said that wealthy individuals in less secure countries where kidnappings are rife, such as certain Latin American jurisdictions, are rightly anxious to be discrete about their wealth lest it should attract violence against them.[142] Finally, in a somewhat less visceral example, if you are a major corporation, people will charge you more for buying their land or other property – hence the legitimate incentive to keep your ownership under wraps.[143]

There genuinely are various perspectives to be brought to this debate, and therefore differing opinions as to where the balance between preventing financial crime

[137] Section 46 of the Trusts and Succession (Scotland) Act 2024. For commentary, see Dan Neidle, Twitter (X) post, 24 June 2024, https://x.com/DanNeidle/status/1805170391855313048. The Scottish Law Commission's reform paper recommending the creation of such a trust contains no observations on AML or tax evasion implications save for its criticism of the beneficial ownership transparency requirements in 4MLD and 5MLD: Scottish Law Commission, *Report on Trust Law*, Scot Law Com No 239, August 2014, 20–23.

[138] A classic 'mystery shopping' experiment demonstrating the limited effectiveness of the existing regulation of trust and corporate service providers is laid out in Michael G. Findley, Daniel L. Nielson and J. C. Sharman, *Global Shell Games: Experiments in Transnational Relations, Crime, and Terrorism* (Cambridge University Press, 2014). The banking sector-oriented follow-up study is in Michael G. Findley, Daniel L. Nielson and J. C. Sharman, 'Banking Bad? A Global Field Experiment on Risk, Reward, and Regulation' (2024) *Am J Pol Sci* https://doi.org/10.1111/ajps.12861.

[139] Keatinge and Moiseienko, 'For Whose Benefit'.

[140] Ibid, 28.

[141] Open Ownership, The B Team and The Engine Room, *Data Protection and Privacy in Beneficial Ownership Disclosure*, May 2019, 42.

[142] Ibid; Andres Knobel, 'Privacy Washing & Beneficial Ownership Transparency', *Tax Justice Network*, March 2024, 18.

[143] US Senate Committee on Banking, Housing, and Urban Affairs, *Hearing on Combating Money Laundering and Other Forms of Illicit Finance: Opportunities to Reform and Strengthen Bank Secrecy Act Enforcement*, 115th Congress, 9 January 2018, Testimony of Greg Baer:

> Everybody uses the example of, you know, when the Disney Corporation was buying up half of Orlando, they did not want to have to pay exorbitant rates for the last piece of land. And there may be valid privacy reasons where you do not want people to know who owns your company. But we cannot think of any valid reason you would not want law enforcement to know who owns your company.

and safeguarding privacy should lie. If one considers the global AML landscape, what is striking is not that a 'wrong' answer has been reached, but that key issues remain unsettled. The one area of consensus among policymakers worldwide appears to be that law enforcement agencies and tax authorities ought to have access to information about assets and transactions, regardless of the financial medium used. Difficult questions remain as to the information that should be available to other stakeholders in the financial surveillance system, such as regulated businesses, or the public at large.

An example is the judgment delivered by the CJEU in November 2022, which struck down the provision of 5MLD requiring EU member states to institute centralised beneficial ownership registers accessible to 'any member of the general public'.[144] The previous iteration of this provision in 4MLD spoke instead of 'any person or organisation that can demonstrate a legitimate interest'.[145] The CJEU found that 5MLD's provisions involved an interference with the right to privacy under EU law and that opening up property ownership information to the public at large went beyond what was 'strictly necessary'.[146]

This reasoning implies that corporate ownership opacity is a corollary of the right to privacy, such that any deviations from it constitute an interference with the right. This is not the only possible view. For instance, one could argue that corporate ownership transparency should be the price shareholders pay for the benefits of limited liability – limited liability and limited visibility, in one package, are too much of a good thing.[147] Of course, the CJEU's position is perfectly plausible too, and it aligns more closely with the status quo, which is marked by opacity of corporate ownership. What is striking, though, is that the crucial policy choice in favour of opacity was never explicitly made or even articulated. It developed organically as a consequence of unreservedly treating companies as distinct legal persons in all contexts alike – Pargendler's fallacy.

Corporate entities and legal arrangements are one example of abiding uncertainties about the boundaries of financial privacy; virtual assets are another. The advent of virtual assets has provided the public with a new medium for conducting transactions and storing wealth in addition to those available in the traditional financial system, such as banks and money remitters.[148] Problematically, one of the first major use cases of Bitcoin, the original cryptocurrency, turned out to be as a payments means for the online drug marketplace Silk Road.[149] Well-documented money

144 *WM and Sovim SA v Luxembourg Business Registers*, Grand Chamber, Joined Cases C-37/20 and C-601/20, Judgment of 22 November 2022; Article 30(5)(c) of 5MLD.

145 Article 30(5)(c) of 4MLD.

146 *WM and Sovim SA*, paras 68–73.

147 This point is often made by Ray Blake and Graham Barrow in the Dark Money Files podcast.

148 An engaging illustration of how cryptocurrency came to be used to launder the proceeds of, among other things, 'offline' crime such as drug trafficking is available in Geoff White, *Rinsed* (Penguin, 2024) Ch 2.

149 See Nick Bilton, *American Kingpin* (Portfolio, 2017).

laundering risks in virtual assets have led to the swift extension by the FATF of AML/CTF regulation to VASPs, although domestic implementation remains patchy as of this writing.[150] The instantiation of such regulation may create the impression that there is a general agreement, at least among regulators, on the appropriate limits of financial privacy in the virtual asset context. That is not the case.

The best example of the lingering uncertainties is the legal status of virtual asset mixers. While Bitcoin was developed in part to secure its users' financial privacy from the prying eyes of banks, it is based on a publicly available record of all transactions, known as the blockchain. The same is true of many other cryptocurrencies, including the most widely used ones, such as Ethereum. Through a variety of investigative techniques, law enforcement agencies and dedicated blockchain analytics companies, such as Chainalysis and Elliptic, can connect a given user's cryptocurrency address to their real-life identity and thereby obtain a record of the entirety of his or her transactions in the relevant cryptocurrency.[151] Virtual asset mixers are designed to counteract this by injecting artificial intermediaries into the transaction trail to impede the identification of the payor and the payee.[152]

There are two schools of thought as to what mixers are. On one view, they are a means of vindicating the original vision behind cryptocurrency and safeguarding financial privacy. As the proponents of mixers point out, you or I would hardly be happy with any open-source intelligence analyst being able to reconstruct the entire history of your or my bank transactions – nor should a different standard apply in the cryptocurrency ecosystem.[153] The other viewpoint is that they are an inherently criminal service that exists for the sole purpose of frustrating legitimate law enforcement activities. Somewhere between the two extremes is the nuanced and sober position articulated by Chainalysis:

> Virtually everyone would acknowledge that privacy is valuable, and that in a vacuum, there's no reason services like mixers shouldn't be able to provide it. But the data suggest that 25% of mixed funds come from illicit addresses, and that cybercriminals associated with hostile governments are among those taking the most advantage.[154]

150 For a general overview of AML issues in the cryptocurrency context, see David Carlisle, *The Crypto Launderers* (Wiley, 2023). For a review of progress in the implementation of the FATF's Recommendation 15, see FATF, *Targeted Update on Implementation of the FATF Standards on Virtual Assets and Virtual Asset Service Providers*, June 2023.

151 For an account of the emergence of blockchain analytics, see Andy Greenberg, *Tracers in the Dark* (Knopf Doubleday Publishing Group, 2022).

152 Anton Moiseienko and Olivier Kraft, 'From Money Mules to Chain Hopping: Targeting the Finances of Cybercrime', *RUSI Occasional Paper*, November 2018, 42–43.

153 Andrea O'Sullivan, 'What Are Mixers and "Privacy Coins"?', *Coin Center*, 7 July 2020, www.coincenter.org/education/advanced-topics/what-are-mixers-and-privacy-coins/.

154 'Crypto Mixer Usage Reaches All-time Highs in 2022, With Nation State Actors and Cybercriminals Contributing Significant Volume', *Chainalysis*, 14 July 2022, www.chainalysis.com/blog/crypto-mixer-criminal-volume-2022/.

Whichever side of the debate one gravitates towards, it speaks to the unsettled boundaries of financial privacy. So far, the FATF and domestic governments' response has been rather nuanced. In 2019, FinCEN indicated that the US government viewed mixers as 'money transmitters' on the basis that they were involved in transferring virtual assets, meaning that they were subject to AML obligations on a par with any money remitters.[155] That, of course, entails CDD and SAR filing obligations that are entirely incompatible with the raison d'être of mixers, although in theory one could imagine an AML-compliant mixer that shares information with law enforcement agencies but shields it from the world at large.

US law enforcement agencies have carried out multiple actions against mixers and their operators, the most well-known one being that against Tornado Cash, a mixer used particularly heavily by the North Korea-affiliated Lazarus Group, whose track record includes stealing US$81 million from the Bank of Bangladesh.[156] Other countries have likewise conducted numerous mixer takedowns, including Germany and the Netherlands, based on allegations that the mixers involved catered to a criminal clientele.[157] Still, those developments fall short of an unambiguous policy choice that virtual asset transactions should be traceable and that their traceability should therefore be preserved in the face of technological and commercial developments.

The most radical and internally coherent move in that direction to date is the EU's prohibition on EU-regulated VASPs engaging in mixing or otherwise facilitating the anonymisation of cryptocurrency transactions. Specifically, Article 79(1) of the Single Rulebook Regulation provides as follows:

> Credit institutions, financial institutions and crypto-asset service providers shall be prohibited from keeping anonymous bank and payment accounts, anonymous passbooks, anonymous safe-deposit boxes or anonymous crypto-asset accounts as

[155] FinCEN, *Application of FinCEN's Regulations to Certain Business Models Involving Convertible Virtual Currencies*, FIN-2019-G001, May 2019, 18–20. This followed on from an earlier indication by the FinCEN director that mixers were money transmitters in August 2018: Kenneth A. Blanco, 'Prepared Remarks of FinCEN Director Kenneth A Blanco', speech given at the 2018 Chicago-Kent Block (Legal) Tech Conference, 9 August 2018. A separate bill proposed in the US Congress in May 2024 (the Blockchain Integrity Act) would prohibit financial institutions to interact with virtual asset mixers: https://casten.house.gov/imo/media/doc/blockchain_integrity_act.pdf.

[156] For sanctions, see US Department of the Treasury, 'US Treasury Sanctions Notorious Virtual Currency Mixer Tornado Cash', 8 August 2022, https://home.treasury.gov/news/press-releases/jy0916. For criminal prosecutions, see US Attorney's Office, Southern District of New York, 'Tornado Cash Founders Charged with Money Laundering and Sanctions Violations', 23 August 2023, www.justice.gov/usao-sdny/pr/tornado-cash-founders-charged-money-laundering-and-sanctions-violations; *US v Storm and Semenov*, Southern District New York 23 Cr. 430, www.justice.gov/usao-sdny/file/1311391/dl?inline.

[157] 'One of the Darkweb's Largest Cryptocurrency Laundromats Washed Out', *Europol*, 16 March 2023, www.europol.europa.eu/media-press/newsroom/news/one-of-darkwebs-largest-cryptocurrency-laundromats-washed-out; 'Multi-Million Euro Cryptocurrency Laundering Service Bestmixer.io Taken Down', *Europol*, 23 May 2019, www.europol.europa.eu/media-press/newsroom/news/multi-million-euro-cryptocurrency-laundering-service-bestmixerio-taken-down.

well as any account otherwise allowing for the anonymisation of the customer account holder or the anonymisation or increased obfuscation of transactions, including through anonymity-enhancing coins.

The EU's placing of credit institutions, financial institutions and crypto-asset service providers on the same footing insofar as financial anonymity is concerned is welcome. It reflects a consistent vision of an economy where complete financial anonymity, including vis-à-vis the government, is no longer allowed.[158] By contrast, the US has not yet taken the bold step of enacting such a vision into law. In October 2023, FinCEN proposed the designation of all virtual asset mixing transactions as transactions of 'primary money laundering concern', which would trigger additional record-keeping requirements and likely dissuade most legitimate VASPs from engaging with mixers.[159] Despite FinCEN's publication of the notice of proposed rulemaking, no final rule has been published as of February 2025.

Even if countries worldwide gravitated towards the EU's position on mixers, there would still remain pockets of the cryptocurrency ecosystem defying the precept that financial privacy should not shield one's transactions from legitimate government or law enforcement oversight. This is especially apparent in connection with the ongoing debates about the implications of decentralised finance (DeFi), a category of virtual asset projects, most of them commercial, operated in a decentralised manner such that law enforcement or regulatory action against any particular individual – or even a group of individuals – will have little to no effect on the DeFi project's ability to continue to operate.[160] This has shifted the discussion to whether it would be desirable, or even appropriate, to regulate the development of DeFi protocols.[161] As a potential restriction on the development of software, such proposals implicate civil liberties, including free speech in some jurisdictions.[162] The wish to avoid these complications has prompted a search for workarounds, such as suggestions that governments should proactively help design lawful cryptocurrency privacy techniques so as to minimise the risk of use of illicit mixers.[163]

[158] Whether this development amounts to a complete ban on mixers within the EU depends on what it takes for a mixer to be subject to EU regulation. For analysis of the challenges of determining whose jurisdiction applies in a cross-border cryptocurrency setting, see Louis de Koker, Talha Ocal and Pompeu Casanovas, 'Where's Wally? FATF, Virtual Asset Service Providers, and the Regulatory Jurisdictional Challenge', in Doron Goldbarsht and Louis de Koker (eds), *Financial Technology and the Law: Combating Financial Crime* (Springer, 2022).

[159] FinCEN, *Proposal of Special Measure Regarding Convertible Virtual Currency Mixing, as a Class of Transactions of Primary Money Laundering Concern*, 88 FR 72701, October 2023.

[160] See, e.g., Dirk A. Zetzsche, Douglas W. Arner and Ross P. Buckley, 'Decentralized Finance' (2020) 6(2) *Journal of Financial Regulation* 172.

[161] For instance, the proposed Crypto-Asset National Security Enhancement Act 2023 in the US.

[162] Jerry Brito, 'The CANSEE Act Is a Messy, Arbitrary, and Unconstitutional Approach to DeFi', *Coin Center*, 20 July 2023, www.coincenter.org/the-cansee-act-is-a-messy-arbitrary/.

[163] Alex O'Neill, 'Upholding North Korea Sanctions in the Age of Decentralised Finance', *Royal United Services Institute*, March 2024, 27–28.

These, too, are all difficult questions. Still, it is important not to lose sight of the broader context. Imagine that a technological solution emerged in the banking sector that would allow anonymous transactions. They can be little doubt that such a technology would not be allowed to flourish. The agonising over DeFi is symptomatic of the continued uncertainty over the limits of financial privacy, with debates about it relitigated anew across various domains. This surveillance versus privacy dilemma adds to the range of trade-offs that the AML regime entails, whose implications are outlined in greater depth in Section 3.4.

3.4 THE CHALLENGES OF UNDIRECTED DEPUTISATION

As we have seen, the AML regime involves three sets of key dilemmas that have not been satisfactorily resolved. With the exception of the surveillance versus privacy dilemma, which tends to benefit from exhaustive regulation (even if inconsistent in policy terms), their resolution is therefore passed down to the level of regulated businesses. It is up to regulated businesses to decide whether the exclusion of proceeds of crime from the economy outweighs other considerations; whether the law enforcement benefits of having information about the financial activities of an organised crime group justify keeping that group on the books as a client; and it whether overzealous reporting of marginally suspicious activities is worthwhile.

It would be foolhardy to expect resulting choices by regulated businesses to be often well aligned with law enforcement needs. Furthermore, those needs might not be static. They may differ depending on the criminal threat involved and a country's law enforcement priorities. For instance, wholesale exclusion of domestic drug traffickers from the financial system is likely to be rather pointless. The traffickers will still make their money and rely on the unregulated sectors of the economy, such as international trade, to move and spend them – or simply hoard cash. All the while, a valuable source of financial intelligence will be lost. Contrast this to the proceeds of large-scale corruption by foreign officials: excluding them from a country's financial system may be the best it can do, even if this means that the money will instead flow into some other jurisdiction.[164]

The FATF-mandated AML framework is not sensitive to any of that as the incentives it creates are truly blunt. It is often said that AML obligations entail the deputisation of the private sector to carry out government's criminal justice policy.[165]

[164] For the argument that a global policy norm has emerged against states harbouring the proceeds of overseas corruption, see J. C. Sharman, *The Despot's Guide to Wealth Management: On the International Campaign Against Grand Corruption* (Cornell University Press, 2017).

[165] See, e.g., 'Frequently Asked Questions on the Use of AI as a Tool to Accelerate Effectiveness in Fighting Financial Crime in the Private Sector for Financial Institutions', *Global Coalition to Fight Financial Crime*, March 2024, 4, www.gcffc.org/wp-content/uploads/2024/03/GCFFC-AI-Paper-FULL-PAPER_v3.pdf.

This is true, although the criticism that is sometimes implicit in this observation[166] is not entirely justified because there are good reasons for such deputisation.[167] What is problematic is its virtually entirely *undirected* nature. The obligations of regulated businesses can be summarised as not engaging in transactions that they know involve money laundering, and reporting transactions that they suspect involve money laundering. This engenders the incentives to derisk and over-report, rather than to use exclusion and surveillance in a strategic fashion to support law enforcement priorities, which in any event are unknown to regulated businesses most of the time. We can now consider the main implications of these incentives.

3.4.1 *Tick-Box Compliance*

The broadest implication is the overall concern, which is often raised, that regulated businesses engage in 'tick-box compliance' instead of a genuine attempt to fight money laundering.[168] Tick-box compliance is a term laden with assumptions. It presupposes that punctilious fulfilment of applicable obligations is insufficient. A more purposive quality to compliance is implicitly required by the pejorative invocation of 'tick-box' compliance. Such purposive compliance might be contrasted with tick-box compliance or outright non-compliance, as indicated in Figure 3.3.

This demanding approach might be considered an anomaly. For instance, we hardly hear about tick-box compliance with capital adequacy requirements in banking, although one could come across instances of non-compliance being concealed through off-balance-sheet transactions. There are, however, good reasons to treat tick-box compliance as a genuine concern in the financial crime context – although, as discussed below, solutions to this lie with additional clarity provided by governments, not with soul-searching among regulated businesses.

For one thing, some of the key obligations that attach to regulated businesses involve a significant degree of discretion or judgement. Suspicious activity reporting is a case in point. What is suspicious is inherently subjective. The absence of any detailed explanation of what suspicion should mean for reporting purposes is notorious. In the UK, the Court of Appeal defined 'suspicion' for the purposes of money laundering offences in *Da Silva*:

[166] See, e.g., R. T. Naylor, 'Follow-the-Money Methods in Crime Control Policy' in Margaret E. Beare (ed), *Critical Reflections on Transnational Organized Crime, Money Laundering, and Corruption* (University of Toronto Press, 2003) 280.

[167] Nor is it unusual for private-sector organisations to be involved with criminal justice matters. See Ric Simmons, *Private Criminal Justice* (Cambridge University Press, 2023).

[168] See, e.g., HM Treasury, *Review of the UK's AML/CFT Regulatory and Supervisory Regime*, June 2022, 1, 14, 25–26; Sarah Prichard, 'Calibrating Controls to Build Confident Markets', FCA, 6 September 2023, www.fca.org.uk/news/speeches/calibrating-controls-build-confident-markets; Jemma Slingo, '"Tick Box" AML Regime Isn't Working, Society Tells Treasury', *The Law Society Gazette*, 20 October 2021, www.lawgazette.co.uk/news/tick-box-aml-regime-isnt-working-society-tells-treasury/5110210.article.

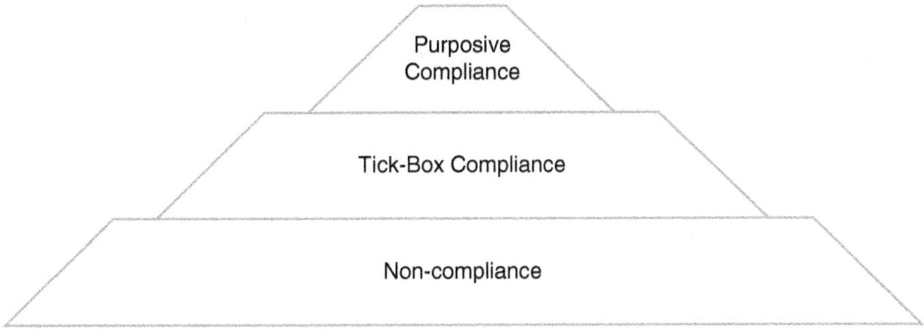

FIGURE 3.3 Taxonomy of compliance

> [T]he defendant must think that there is a possibility, which is more than fanciful, that the relevant facts exist. A vague feeling of unease would not suffice.[169]

The sufficiency of this explanation has been occasionally contested,[170] but the UK Law Commission declined to provide any further gloss on it in its report into the UK AML regime.[171] Nor does the FATF define any specific threshold for suspicion. This means that it is up to bank or another regulated business to determine what a suspicion means and whether that threshold has been reached. It is natural, and arguably desirable, that in doing so the business should take account of the broader purposes of AML regulation and seek to be useful in their attainment.

But there is also another aspect to purposive compliance. That pertains to the tensions between the values and principles involved: the exclusion of proceeds of crime from the legitimate economy versus the surveillance of their movement; the exclusion of proceeds of crime versus the presumption of innocence, broadly understood as a civic virtue; and financial surveillance versus financial privacy. Any sustained enforcement of AML measures involves a trade-off. The question therefore arises of how far they ought to be pursued before they do more harm than good. One example is whether citizens of a high-risk jurisdiction should be excluded from financial services to minimise the risk of proceeds of crime entering the legitimate financial system. Many would be instinctually uncomfortable with the idea and argue that the negative consequences of financial exclusion outweigh the benefit of fighting financial crime in such a no-holds-barred manner.

Problematically, governments often prove loath to make those policy choices, and therefore the burden of doing so falls upon the regulated businesses, who are obliged to implement policies based on unarticulated policy preferences. Tick-box compliance is best understood as a state of affairs where those difficult dilemmas are not engaged with in a meaningful way but are resolved based on cost and convenience.

[169] *R v Da Silva* [2006] EWCA Crim 1654; [2006] 4 All ER 900, para 16.

[170] Sarah Kebbell, *Anti-Money Laundering Compliance and the Legal Profession* (Routledge, 2022) Ch 6.

[171] Law Commission, *Anti-Money Laundering*, 99–101.

In fairness, this mode of solving problems is what one must expect of any for-profit enterprise. The problem that tick-box compliance is symptomatic of is not that businesses are doing a bad job of addressing those fundamental policy dilemmas, but that they are relied upon to address them to such a significant extent in the absence of any tangible incentives to produce desired outcomes. There is no genuine incentive, financial or otherwise, for regulated businesses to ponder whether exclusion or surveillance is best suited to support law enforcement efforts in relation to a particular criminal threat, or whether the exclusion of vast swathes of unbanked customers from the financial system is justified by keeping the proceeds of crime out of it.

To be sure, businesses might still take all those issues seriously because they, too, consist of good citizens trying to support law enforcement work. One experienced law enforcement officer has suggested that a genuinely collaborative attitude from Australian banks has been essential to the high quality of their SMR reporting from the 1990s onwards.[172] These days, in multiple jurisdictions such a collaborative attitude may be a product of former law enforcement officers taking up senior AML compliance roles.[173] These cultural factors should not be overlooked, but it does not take a cynic to suggest that relying on culture alone is fraught with risk in the absence of aligned commercial or regulatory incentives.

In short, the term 'tick-box compliance' can be best thought of as a description of the natural state of the AML regime. It is characterised by regulated businesses doing what they must do, but no more than that, while giving no particular consideration to broader law enforcement objectives or societal values. Such a state of affairs is bound to give rise to socially suboptimal outcomes that are determined by regulated businesses' risk/reward calculus rather than an attempt to contribute to a whole-of-society effort against money laundering.

Sometimes, internal culture within a particular business leads it towards more thoughtful, purposive compliance, which then forces such a business to confront the difficult and unresolved questions about the trade-offs that the AML regime entails. One could view fostering that sort of compliance culture as the answer to the perils of tick-box compliance. That, to a significant extent, is the mission of public–private partnerships, such as those discussed below, or professional associations such as the Association of Certified Anti-Money Laundering Specialists (ACAMS).[174] Greater recognition by governments of good-faith compliance efforts, through a

[172] Interview with an Australian AML/CTF expert (A), 14 June 2024.

[173] Interview with two UK law enforcement experts, 28 June 2024. This is consistent with the findings of empirical research in France reported in Gilles Favarel-Garrigues, Thierry Godefroy and Pierre Lascoumes, 'Sentinels in the Banking Industry: Private Actors and the Fight against Money Laundering in France' (2008) 48(1) *Brit J Criminology* 1, 10–11.

[174] Interview with an Australian AML/CTF expert (B), 1 July 2024.

form of 'regulatory praise', also has its proponents.[175] Ultimately, however, one must question whether culture-building alone can redress the imbalances introduced by the skewed incentives that are the product of a system of binding AML rules.

3.4.2 *Defensive Reporting*

A concept related to tick-box compliance is that of defensive reporting, or the filing of SARs solely to mitigate the risk of having failed in one's reporting duties rather than genuinely to help detect money laundering.[176] The issues around defensive reporting not only highlight some of the problematic incentives that AML rules create, but also involve serious consideration of the value of SARs, which – as mentioned previously – are the only form of reporting required by the FATF.

The FATF's reliance on SARs is noteworthy in two respects. First, their filing constitutes a presumptively important source of financial intelligence for law enforcement activities, although its genuine utility occasionally comes into question, as discussed below. Second, the FATF's and domestic governments' endorsement of suspicious activity reporting signals an implicit policy choice about privacy. That choice is that reaching the threshold of suspicion justifies the provision by a regulated business of information about the respective customer's activities to the government. Depending on other applicable regulation, this may not be the only one such threshold, for example, cash reporting might be in place, but it certainly is one. This is so even though the concept of suspicion is a subjective one that is notoriously difficult to pin down with any precision.

Defensive reporting calls into question both the utility of SARs and the privacy bargain to which they give expression. Excessive filing of SARs that have little to no law enforcement value is arguably not useful, but it also results in the government having access to a greater array of financial information than it ought to have. It can have further implications in placing a strain on FIUs' ability to process the reporting they receive. This has been the case in the UK, where long-overdue reform of the UKFIU's Elmer Database has been a key item on the Home Office's SAR Reform Programme for well over a decade.[177] These problems are intuitively easy to grasp and, as discussed in Chapter 2, had been correctly anticipated even before the introduction of mandatory SAR reporting.[178]

175 Sneha Dawda, Ardi Janjeva and Anton Moiseienko, 'The UK's Response to Cyber Fraud: A Strategic Vision', *RUSI Occasional Paper*, February 2021, 52.

176 See, e.g., FATF, *Guidance on AML/CFT-Related Data and Statistics*, October 2015, 12–13; Clare Sullivan and Evan Smith, 'Trade-Based Money Laundering: Risks and Regulatory Responses', *Australian Institute of Criminology*, 2011, 22.

177 The UK's current Economic Crime Plan envisages the delivery of a new SARs database in Q3 2024: HM Government, *Economic Crime Plan 2: 2023–2026*, 2023, 35.

178 Michael Levi, 'Pecunia Non Olet: Cleansing the Money-Launderers from the Temple' (1991) 16(3) *Crime, Law and Social Change* 217, 298.

Still, the issue of SARs' utility, which is a crucial part of any discussion of defensive reporting, often proves more nuanced than it appears at first sight.[179] A natural understanding of the purpose of SARs is that they should lead to law enforcement investigations. Sometimes, this is precisely what happens[180]; but often, it does not. According to Europol, only 10 per cent of SARs submitted across the EU result in an investigation.[181] The Home Affairs Committee of the House of Commons channelled similar concerns:

> The private sector shared the concerns. Laurence Sacker, Partner, Corporate Finance and Money Laundering Reporting Officer at UHY Hacker Young LLP said that his perception was that the system was so overloaded, that many SARs were never actually investigated. He believed that many firms were submitting SARs simply so that the reporting officers were 'in the clear' in terms of having met their statutory requirement and that investigators 'probably only look in detail at the consent SARs that go to them, which is about 15,000 in a year. The others are just recorded somewhere and may get passed on eventually.'[182]

However, there may also be value in 'sleeping SARs' that neither trigger an investigation nor are otherwise immediately useful. Sometimes, a SAR can become useful later on once an investigation into its subject is launched for other reasons. Sleeping SARs can also form the basis for an FIU's analysis of trends in suspicious activity reporting that may be worthwhile in and of itself, for instance, by identifying geographic areas of concern linked with higher rates of SAR submissions. Finally, even if a SAR does trigger an immediate investigation, this may or may not be a function of the quality of the information contained therein. Instead, a rather feeble SAR may provide an impetus for an investigation once matched with other forms of financial reporting (such as, depending on the jurisdiction, CTRs or IFTIs).[183]

This means that the simple equivalency between a timely and well-formed SAR and the launch of an investigation into suspicious activity is one that, while widespread, is lacking in nuance. One way to think of the role of SARs in a more holistic fashion is to consider them as having a dual purpose. One is the 'alert' function that is typically associated with SARs, namely the identification of activities that

[179] For a good overview of the issues involved, see Jayesh D'Souza, *Terrorist Financing, Money Laundering, and Tax Evasion: Examining the Performance of Financial Intelligence Units* (CRC Press, 2012) 143–168.

[180] For example, a SAR submitted by a Czech bank led to the arrest of the administrator of a major cybercriminal marketplace: Moiseienko and Kraft, 'From Money Mules to Chain-Hopping', 54. SARs filed by Swedish banks led to counter-proliferation financing investigations on multiple occasions: Jonathan Brewer, 'Study of Typologies of Financing of WMD Proliferation', *Project Alpha, King's College London*, October 2017, 91, 101.

[181] Europol, *From Suspicion to Action: Converting Financial Intelligence into Greater Operational Impact*, 2017, 5.

[182] Home Affairs Committee, House of Commons (UK), *Proceeds of Crime*, HC 25, June 2016, para 22.

[183] John Madinger, *Money Laundering: A Guide for Criminal Investigators* (3rd edn, CRC Press, 2012) 61.

the FIU might wish to look into – even if the information about those activities is already available to the FIU, for example, through other forms of reporting. The other is the 'information-provision' function, namely the provision of the FIU with the information about a particular person's activities that law enforcement agencies would otherwise have no access to. Once a SAR is filed, the 'alert' aspect of the filling might not lead to much if the FIU is unconcerned about the situation or overstretched, but the 'information-provision' facet to the SAR submission could become useful later on.

This duality of purpose is explicitly acknowledged in the Netherlands, where regulated businesses submit UTRs rather than SARs. UTRs must be filed when either 'objective' indicators, such as the €10,000 transaction threshold, or 'subjective' indicators, that is, a suspicion of financial crime, are present.[184] The Dutch FIU explicitly states that 'the subjective reports provide a lead in themselves, whereas the objective reports generally provide additional information'.[185] That SARs, too, can fulfil the same two functions, is essential to appreciating the ways in which they can be valuable.

Misunderstandings of the role of 'sleeping SARs' have led to situations that border on the darkly comical.[186] In 2021, a court in the German town of Osnabrück ordered the search of the premises of the German FIU on suspicion of perverting the course of justice because the FIU had not been forwarding each and every SAR to law enforcement agencies.[187] This led to a change in German law enacted in November 2023, which now expressly requires the FIU to triage and prioritise SARs using a risk-based approach.[188] There is no expectation, nor should there be one, that every SAR, or even a significant proportion of them, *trigger* an investigation. It is important, however, that they be *useful* in investigations.[189]

None of this is to deny that there is widespread perception that large swathes of SAR filings in multiple jurisdictions are not particularly helpful because of defensive reporting. The point is that it is exceedingly difficult to devise a metric that will meaningfully corroborate or disprove this perception. This is aptly captured by Matthew Redhead:

[184] FIU-the Netherlands, 'Banks', www.fiu-nederland.nl/en/reporting_group/banks/.

[185] FIU-the Netherlands, *Annual Review 2021*, February 2023, 8. See the discussion in Miles Kellerman, 'FinCEN and the Data Dilemma', *False Positive*, 16 June 2024, https://mileskellerman.substack.com/p/fincen-and-the-data-dilemma.

[186] Tim Szent-Ivanyi and Andreas Niesmann, 'Wie würden Sie eine Milliarde waschen, Herr Thelesklaf?' *RedaktionsNetzwerkDeutschland*, 9 March 2024, www.rnd.de/politik/chef-der-deutschen-anti-geldwaesche-behoerde-wie-wuerden-sie-eine-milliarde-waschen-herr-thelesklaf-5YGLZRAPDZA5BINLIGMPNL3ABQ.html.

[187] 'Gericht erklärt Durchsuchung im Finanzministerium für rechtswidrig' *RedaktionsNetzwerkDeutschland*, 11 November 2022, www.rnd.de/politik/gericht-durchsuchung-im-finanzministerium-war-rechtswidrig-DMW3JDM5GVDWRNLAOQVC5TBMEE.html.

[188] Szent-Ivanyi and Niesmann, 'Wie würden Sie eine Milliarde waschen, Herr Thelesklaf?'.

[189] For a useful discussion, see Nicholas Gilmour and Tristram Hicks, *Dirty Money* (Bristol University Press, 2023) 182.

> In addition, although SARs are often valuable for trend analysis and as an investigative database, they are of variable quality as immediate investigative leads. In a RUSI workshop in 2017, one national FIU represented reported that 97% of SAR information they received had no immediate value to their investigations. Moreover, linked surveys conducted with 135 financial crime professionals in Hong Kong, Singapore and Argentina found that across the surveys, 85–95% of participants disagreed or strongly disagreed with the view that SARs lead to the effective discovery and disruption of crime. In interviews conducted for this paper, former senior officials suggested that no more than 1–2% of conventional SARs were likely to be of immediate investigative value for LEAs.[190]

The statistics Redhead cites are noteworthy. We also know for sure that the rates of SAR filings have been growing consistently across common law jurisdictions, if not all countries that have committed to complying with the FATF Recommendations. It is exceedingly likely that at least part of the increase is due to defensive reporting, which has long been acknowledged.[191] Like tick-box compliance, this is the sort of behaviour that is rational for an organisation that wishes to minimise the risk of adverse regulatory action.

These well-known problems with SARs are aptly encapsulated in the Wolfsberg Group's Statement on Effective Monitoring for Suspicious Activity published in Jule 2024. The Wolfsberg Group observes how perverse incentives that regulated businesses operate under translate to similarly skewed priorities within institutions, where mechanistic expansion of the range of 'red flags' utilised and the alert-to-SAR ratio become treated as indicators of effectiveness.[192] All of that leads to over-reporting or, at least, useless reporting.

For all those drawbacks, the future of SARs appears secure for now as the FATF has exhibited no inclination to reconsider suspicious activity reporting. However, there are two places where significant change can come from. One of these is the extension by countries of their reporting regimes to provide for a more varied array of information-gathering models alongside SARs, such as CTRs, UTRs, IFTIs and GTOs. This could help overcome the limitations of SARs as suspicion-based reports and enrich them with other data. Multiple countries are already doing precisely that, including all of the jurisdictions that have obtained a 'high

[190] Matthew Redhead, 'Deep Impact? Refocusing the Anti-Money Laundering Model on Evidence and Outcomes', *RUSI Occasional Paper*, October 2019, 16.

[191] John J. Byrne, 'Improving Financial Oversight: A Private Sector View of Anti-Money Laundering Efforts', Testimony on behalf of the American Bankers Association before the US House of Representatives, Committee on Financial Services, Subcommittee on Oversight and Investigations, 18 May 2024, www.govinfo.gov/content/pkg/CHRG-108hhrg95012/html/CHRG-108hhrg95012.htm, discussed in Levi and Reuter, 'Money Laundering', 301, 335. By contrast, some authors are more optimistic about the incidence of defensive reporting while not denying that it occurs: Stavros Gadinis and Colby Mangels, 'Collaborative Gatekeepers' (2016) 73(2) *Washington & Lee LR* 797, 877–878.

[192] 'The Wolfsberg Group Statement on Effective Monitoring for Suspicious Activity', July 2024, 3.

effectiveness' rating from the FATF under Immediate Outcome 6 (use of financial intelligence).[193]

The other key development could be the maturation of central bank digital currencies (CBDCs) into a widely used medium of storing and moving wealth. There are multiple CBDC models being explored or trialled around the world.[194] Among them are retail CBDCs, which are a central bank-issued digital currency that can be held directly by retail customers, and not only by commercial banks. What role commercial banks might play in the issuance of retail CBDCs or transactions involving them is a subject of discussion. For instance, in some 'hybrid' models customers will hold retail CBDCs via commercial banks but their deposits will be backed up with those banks' CBDC holdings with the central bank, effectively eliminating the counterparty risk inherent in holding one's funds in a commercial bank.[195] By contrast, in 'direct' CBDC models, customers will hold retail CBDCs directly with the central bank without any intermediation by commercial banks.[196]

In either case, one could conceive of an arrangement whereby all customer transactions in CBDCs will be directly known to the central bank without the need for any form of reporting, including SARs. In a hybrid model, this could be a feature of how the system is set up. In a direct model, this is likely to be inevitable because existing reporting entities – in this case, commercial banks – will be out of the picture.[197] Either way, the transition towards CBDCs could mark the most far-reaching renegotiation of the bounds of financial privacy in recent history, with total access to one's financial activities being granted to the government. One could think of this in terms of the continuum between financial privacy and financial surveillance with the toggle pushed towards the latter, as illustrated in Figure 3.4.

The implications of this potential shift towards a qualitatively different financial surveillance environment have not yet been properly considered, including by the FATF. There is a strong argument to be made that, on the whole, entrusting governments with the complete details of one's financial life would not be desirable.

[193] As of July 2024, these include Israel (using CTRs and UTRs), the Netherlands (using CTRs and UTRs), Russia (using various forms of reporting based on objective thresholds) and Spain (using CTRs and certain other forms of objective reporting, e.g. on transactions over €30,000 involving high-risk jurisdictions). The FATF's consolidated ratings and links to relevant MERs can be found at www.fatf-gafi.org/en/publications/Mutualevaluations/Assessment-ratings.html.

[194] 'Central Bank Digital Currencies for Cross-Border Payments: A Review of Current Experiments and Ideas', *World Bank*, November 2021.

[195] Rainer Böhme and Raphael Auer, 'CBDC Architectures, the Financial System, and the Central Bank of the Future', *CEPR*, 2 October 2020, https://cepr.org/voxeu/columns/cbdc-architectures-financial-system-and-central-bank-future; Raphael Auer and Rainer Boehme, 'The Technology of Retail Central Bank Digital Currency', *BIS Quarterly Review*, 1 March 2020, www.bis.org/publ/qtrpdf/r_qt2003j.htm.

[196] Ibid.

[197] Besides privacy issues, this is likely to have profound macroeconomic implications, such as in relation to commercial banks' role in creating money supply. See Böhme and Auer, 'CBDC Architectures, the Financial System, and the Central Bank of the Future'.

FIGURE 3.4 The privacy/surveillance continuum

Even leaving aside broader privacy risks, critical though they are, the complete abrogation of SAR reporting would deprive the government of the benefit of regulated businesses alerting the FIU to what they consider, based on their own experience and expertise, to constitute suspicious activity. The significance of that foregone benefit depends on the governments' ability to set up systems that counteract the natural trends towards defensive reporting. Before considering potential solutions to dealing with defensive reporting, though, it is useful to outline several further consequences of poor and inflexible incentive structures that the FATF-mandated AML framework creates.

3.4.3 *Derisking and Financial Exclusion*

So far, this book has primarily considered the exclusionary effects of the criminalisation of money laundering. That is, compliant regulated businesses are likely to derisk far before they reach the threshold of knowing involvement in money laundering. While the criminalisation of money laundering is likely to be a significant driver of derisking, empirical research commissioned by the UK's Financial Conduct Authority (FCA) suggests that the costs of internal compliance processes within banks, such as ongoing monitoring of customers identified as high risk, are themselves a notable contributor to derisking.[198] In other words, so long as certain customers cost more than others to maintain on the books, there is an incentive to derisk and get rid of the higher-cost segment of the customer base.

This could be thought of as an unintended consequence of AML rules, but whether it truly is unintended is open to question. In her historically informed analysis of the US framework, Courtney Linn noted how, in the late 2000s, a 'deterrence rationale', focused on excluding proceeds of crime from the financial system rather than surveilling their activities, began to emerge.[199] That deterrence rationale was

[198] David Artingstall, Nick Dove, John Howell and Michael Levi, 'Drivers & Impacts of Derisking', *John Howell & Co*, February 2016, www.fca.org.uk/publication/research/drivers-impacts-of-derisking.pdf.

[199] Courtney J. Linn, 'Redefining the Bank Secrecy Act: Currency Reporting and the Crime of Structuring' (2010) 50(2) *Santa Clara LR* 407, 432–433.

manifested not only in the threat of criminal prosecution of businesses knowingly involved in money laundering but also in the notion that preventative controls, such as CDD, made it more difficult for criminals to be onboarded in the first place. Even if this does not prevent them from accessing the legitimate economy, this may raise the cost of money laundering and therefore eat into the profitability of crime. (Whether that also reduces the incidence of crime has never been, and perhaps cannot be, empirically tested).

The problem is that legitimate customers can also be caught up in the operation of AML rules and experience the same adverse effects. These effects manifest themselves in two ways. First, certain segments of the population may not be in possession of documents required to undergo CDD checks, such as passports or proof of address. This is often the issue with 'unbanked' populations from rural regions or disadvantaged strata of the society.[200] The FATF's and some domestic governments' solution to this has been to allow the application of simplified due diligence measures, which do not involve the provision of documents that would otherwise be required, in certain situations deemed to present low risks of financial crime.[201] The limitation of this approach is that it does not address the second facet of derisking. From a regulated business's standpoint, any compliance measures, including the resources spent on justifying why simplified due diligence is sufficient, may not be worth the revenue generated by the respective part of its customer base. So, commercial incentives continue to point towards derisking.[202]

These incentives are powerful, and so are their effects. For instance, the difficulties experienced by Iranian citizens in opening bank accounts in the UK have been well documented,[203] as are those faced by charities.[204] Those difficulties are likely to be the product of a set of overlapping regulatory regimes, including AML, CTF and sanctions laws,[205] but in either case the issue boils down to the same commercial imperative to derisk rather than evaluate each customer's position. Resulting financial exclusion, including the inability to access a basic bank account, has profound adverse implications for certain segments of the population in a modern economy.

[200] Isabella Chase, Jonathan van der Valk and Tom Keatinge, 'Assessing the Financial Action Task Force's Impact on Digital Financial Inclusion', *RUSI Occasional Paper*, June 2021, 8, 40.

[201] FATF, *Guidance for a Risk-Based Approach: The Banking Sector*, 2014, 9–11.

[202] Chase, van der Valk and Keatinge, 'Assessing the Financial Action Task Force's Impact on Digital Financial Inclusion', 14.

[203] Saeed Kamali Dehghan, 'UK Bank Accounts of Iranian Customers Still Being Closed, Says Law Firm', *The Guardian*, 22 April 2017.

[204] Anna Gross and Akila Quinio, 'England's Charities Watchdog Hits Out at High Street Lenders over Debanking', *Financial Times*, 7 March 2024.

[205] The latter two regimes are discussed in Chapter 4. For an outline of various issues contributing to derisking, see Council of Financial Regulators, AUSTRAC, ACCC and the Attorney-General's Department, *Potential Policy Responses to De-banking in Australia*, 8 August 2022.

Neither the true extent of the problem nor its nature was anticipated when the regime was being stood up. As discussed in Chapter 2, in the Congressional hearings preceding the adoption of the Money Laundering Control Act 1986 in the US, a representative of the ABA brought up the concern that 'any person with a reputation for being connected to organized crime may be effectively isolated from completing ordinary, day-to-day, financial transactions because the other party will fear incurring "receipt of criminal proceeds" liability'.[206] That is a fair concern, but today's financial exclusion problem extends far beyond it. The incentive to derisk lies not only in incurring criminal liability for money laundering but also in the costs attendant on CDD and ongoing monitoring in relation to high-risk customers. Furthermore, what makes a person high risk has moved beyond personally having a reputation for organised crime connections. In a cross-border setting, being a citizen or resident of a high-risk jurisdiction is often sufficient, which leads to much more widespread financial exclusion than one might have anticipated in the 1980s. The same goes for certain high-risk professions or industries, such as sex workers or legalised cannabis production.[207] These activities may be legal in a certain jurisdiction but still be associated with elevated risks of other crimes, such as human trafficking or illegal drug dealing.

For the first decade since the adoption of the FATF Recommendations, the problem of financial exclusion remained unacknowledged. That began to change in the early 2000s. Research conducted at the University of Bristol in 1999 found that 7 per cent of UK population lacked access to a basic bank account and identified AML requirements as a contributing factor, for example, for people who could not prove their address.[208] This conclusion was echoed by the Financial Services Authority, the FCA's predecessor, in 2000.[209] Academic studies of the tensions between AML requirements and the objectives of financial inclusion began appearing in the mid 2000s.[210] From then on, the issue has consistently been on the experts' agenda, but the extent to which it has shaped policymaking is debatable. In particular, it took the FATF until 2021 to launch a workstream on the intended consequences of the

[206] Jeffrey Glekel and Lawrence B. Pedowitz, 'Statement on Behalf of the American Bar Association Concerning Money Laundering Legislation', Subcommittee on Financial Institutions Supervision, Regulation and Insurance, 14 May 1986, 1129.

[207] See, e.g., CFATF, *Potential Implications of Decriminalisation, Legalisation or a Hybrid Decriminalisation Approach of Cannabis on AML/CFT*, December 2023. CFATF is the Caribbean FSRB. See also Emilia Terzon, 'Sex Worker Takes on Financial Sector "Debanking", with Outcome Hailed as Transformative for Adult Industry', *ABC News*, 30 May 2024.

[208] Elaine Kempson and Claire Whyley, *Kept Out or Opted Out? Understanding and Combating Financial Exclusion* (Policy Press, 1999) 34, 47.

[209] Financial Services Authority, *In or Out? Financial Exclusion: A Literature and Research Review*, July 2000, 52.

[210] For an early analysis of the problem, see Louis de Koker, 'Money Laundering Control and Suppression of Financing of Terrorism: Some Thoughts on the Impact of Customer Due Diligence Measures on Financial Exclusion' (2006) 13(1) *J Financial Crime* 26.

FATF Recommendations, financial exclusion among them, and the full text of the ensuing FATF report remains confidential.[211]

Ironically, the cases that propelled derisking and financial exclusion towards greater public awareness are not the experiences of migrant communities or underbanked rural populations, but the difficulties faced by high-ranking public officials. Under the FATF Recommendations, individuals currently or formerly entrusted with prominent public functions, known as politically exposed persons (PEPs), should undergo enhanced due diligence.[212] Such enhanced due diligence involves, among other things, ascertaining the PEP's overall source of wealth and his or her source of funds for the particular transaction involved.[213] The decision to onboard a PEP must be escalated to the institution's senior management.[214] All of that entails a degree of compliance effort that, in the eyes of certain banks and other regulated businesses, raises the same question of whether the effort is worth the financial reward involved.

These rules originally only applied to foreign PEPs. They were clearly meant to address the archetypal case of overseas potentates arriving in major Western capitals to spend the proceeds of their graft.[215] The current iteration of the FATF Recommendations requires regulated businesses to identify domestic PEPs and ascertain whether they involve 'a higher risk business relationship', in which case enhanced due diligence should likewise apply.[216] In line with the FATF Recommendations, multiple jurisdictions, including all EU member states, now apply PEP controls to domestic officials.[217] This addresses the very real corruption risks that all PEPs can present but also gives rise to an entirely new constituency of well-heeled and successful people who suddenly find themselves subject to derisking. For instance, in 2014, the Liberal Democrat peer Lord Clement-Jones, formerly the managing partner at the London office of the law firm DLA Piper, spoke as follows on the floor of the UK's House of Lords:

> Even before the [EU's 4MLD] has come in, many Members of this House and their relatives are being treated as PEPs. I myself and my son were unable to access an ATM and my brother was unable to exercise a joint power of attorney.[218]

[211] FATF, 'High-Level Synopsis of the Stocktake of the Unintended Consequences of the FATF Standards', 27 October 2021.

[212] FATF, *International Standards on Combatting Money Laundering and the Financing of Terrorism & Proliferation*, Recommendation 12.

[213] Ibid.

[214] Ibid.

[215] See consistent references to corruption risks in FATF, *FATF Guidance: Politically Exposed Persons (Recommendations 12 and 22)*, June 2013.

[216] FATF, *International Standards on Combatting Money Laundering and the Financing of Terrorism & Proliferation*, Recommendation 12.

[217] In the latest iteration, Article 2(1)(34) of the 'Single Rulebook' AML Regulation. Analogous rules have been in place since 4MLD.

[218] HL Deb 14 October 2014 Vol 756 Col 114.

Seven years later, Baroness Hayter from the Labour Party echoed the same frustrations:

> My Lords, it seems that genuine money launderers can bring in foreign money and buy up property with no disclosure of ownership, but we PEPs get this ridiculous six-page questionnaire, which I have just received, wanting to know about my past employers, my family wealth – I have not got any – my lottery wins, my jewellery, and not just my car but 'cars'; I have only got one. Many of your Lordships have approached me to say that they and their families have been similarly inconvenienced.[219]

Lord Vaizey from the Conservative Party was likewise afflicted:

> My Lords, with impeccable timing, my building society wrote to me yesterday to say that it was reviewing its approach to PEPs, following my throwing my toys out of my pram when it emailed me and my 83-year-old mother to ask, among other things, about my casino winnings. It is quite clear that the banks and building societies are ignoring the FCA's advice, which is to approach each person as an individual and assess the risk individually.[220]

Similar issues have been registered in the context of senior diplomats or, indeed, embassies. For instance, it has been reported that, following the revelations of criminal activities of the North Korean embassy facilitated by Riggs Bank, multiple major US banks discontinued their customer relations with the embassies of overseas nations, which prompted the latter to seek banking facilities in smaller, regional banks.[221] The issue of the 'derisking of the rich' reached a crescendo in the UK after Nigel Farage, then-former member of the European Parliament widely associated with the successful Brexit campaign, was dropped as a customer by Coutts, a British bank forming part of the NatWest group.[222] A subsequent review conducted by the law firm Travers Smith found that Farage's account was loss-making for the bank due to 'increased monitoring costs' applicable to PEPs or other high-risk customers.[223] The furore generated by the 'Farage farrago' led the FCA to set up an inquiry into the treatment of domestic PEPs in 2023.[224] In July 2024, the FCA reported,

[219] HL Deb 25 November 2021 Vol 816 Col 1001.

[220] HL Deb 25 November 2021 Vol 816 Col 1002.

[221] Sue E. Eckert, Kay Guinane and Andrea Hall, *Financial Access for U.S. Non-Profits*, February 2017, 28; interview with two international AML/CTF experts, 18 January 2024 (asking rhetorically whether smaller US banks truly understood the reasons for embassy debanking and could properly manage the risk).

[222] Kalyeena Makortoff, 'No Evidence Coutts Closed Accounts due to Political Views, Report Says', *The Guardian*, 15 December 2023.

[223] Travers Smith, 'Phase 1: Key Findings & Recommendations', 27 October 2023, para 2.10, www.natwestgroup.com/news-and-insights/news-room/press-releases/our-updates/2023/oct/key-findings-from-phase-1-of-travers-smith-review.html.

[224] FCA, 'Update on the FCA's Review of Treatment of Politically Exposed Persons', 19 June 2024, www.fca.org.uk/news/statements/update-fcas-review-treatment-politically-exposed-persons.

based on its analysis of a sample of only fifteen firms, that it was far more common for regulated businesses not to apply appropriate enhanced due diligence than it was for it to be excessive.[225]

There is a mildly comedic quality to the clarity of cross-party focus on the unintended consequences of AML rules that their application to MPs and peers has engendered, as opposed to the apathy with which the steady trickle of earlier debanking stories had been greeted. However, the issue of PEPs and derisking also has a serious side to it, especially in developing countries. If a government struggles to attract high-quality candidates to a career in public life, then the prospect of additional constraints on one's access to financial services can be a significant obstacle to the recruitment drive, especially if the PEP status attached to the individual long after he or she has left the position. The FATF does not prescribe for how long former senior public officials are to be treated as PEPs, and many regulated businesses adopt the clearcut 'once a PEP, always a PEP' rule.[226] This can be a sensible anti-corruption policy in light of the influence that former senior officials may continue to wield, but it also involves trade-offs in terms of dissuading engagement in public life.

By now, the issue of derisking writ large, PEP-related or not, has well and truly become a matter of recognised concern, but solutions to it are sorely wanting. The FATF's guidance on financial inclusion, published in 2011 and revised in 2013, states as follows:

> Promoting formal financial systems and services is (...) central to any effective and comprehensive AML/CFT regime. Financial inclusion and an effective AML/CFT regime can and should be complementary national policy objectives with mutually supportive policy goals.[227]

The statement that AML objectives and financial inclusion are complementary and mutually supportive is only partly convincing. On the one hand, it is true that, in order for financial surveillance of potentially criminal activities to be effective, regulated services need to be widely used. On the other hand, even leaving aside the costs of compliance when high-risk customers are involved, the imposition of criminal liability on regulated businesses for knowingly facilitating money laundering inevitably means that they will steer clear of certain categories of customers. In an ideal world, this would be a very narrow category of customers, such as those in relation to whom there are credible allegations of involvement in organised crime, but it would be unrealistic to expect for those measures to be so precise that no amount of derisking would take place whatsoever.

[225] FCA, *The Treatment of Politically Exposed Persons – Multi-Firm Review*, July 2024.

[226] The FATF notes that this approach is consistent with the Recommendations but not required: *PEP Guidance*, 12.

[227] FATF, *FATF Guidance: Anti-Money Laundering and Terrorist Financing Measures and Financial Inclusion*, February 2013, 15.

The better question, therefore, is what the right balance is between cutting off high-risk customers from access to the legitimate economy and ensuring financial inclusion. Like so many other questions at the heart of the financial crime regime, it ultimately comes down to a policy choice. In theory, one could imagine a society that prizes the integrity of the legitimate economy so much that excluding anyone holding the passport of a high-risk country is deemed an acceptable trade-off. On the other end of the spectrum is the pre-AML financial system. (It, too, had financial exclusion problems, but they mostly came down to people having no money at all to engage in any financial transactions, which still remains an issue!).

The disquiet that the FATF and domestic governments are exhibiting is indicative of the sense that, currently, there is too much AML-driven derisking.[228] Furthermore, one could argue that it is occurring for problematic reasons, driven as it is primarily by cost-cutting imperatives rather than an abundance of caution so as not to allow criminals to take advantage of the legitimate economy. Ultimately, however, this status quo is an inevitable consequence of placing upon the private sector the responsibility for deciding where the right balance between exclusion and surveillance should run.

Half-measures, such as permitting simplified due diligence, alleviate some of the drivers of derisking but do not significantly alter the incentive structures at play. A serious solution to derisking needs to involve the setting of clear parameters as to when regulated businesses must either allow access to their services or, conversely, deny them. There is likely to remain some grey zone and, therefore, some potential for derisking, but minimising its breadth is useful. Potential avenues for doing so are considered in Section 3.5.

3.4.4 *Displacement Effect*

Related to but distinct from derisking is the issue of the displacement effect of AML rules. Even if criminals were unable to invest or move the proceeds of crime via regulated sectors, they would still have those proceeds of crime to dispose of. That means that, in all likelihood, they would seek to invest or move proceeds of crime via other, unregulated sectors of the economy. Similar movement can also occur within regulated sectors, where customers offboarded by a certain business due to suspicions of money laundering can totter on to another, less vigilant business.[229] This set of issues is often referred to as the 'displacement effect': a phenomenon that is sometimes believed to cast doubt on the utility of the entire AML regulatory edifice.

[228] For a fairly representative expression of these views, see Noelle Acheson, 'Should Banks Be Crime Fighters? The Hidden (and Not So Hidden) Costs', *CoinDesk*, 12 June 2024, www.coindesk.com/opinion/2024/06/12/should-banks-be-crime-fighters-the-hidden-and-not-so-hidden-costs/.

[229] Attorney General's Department (Australia), *Report of the Statutory Review of the Anti-Money Laundering and Counter-Terrorism Financing Act 2006*, 2016, 102.

There is compelling and unambiguous evidence of the displacement effect in action. For instance, as discussed previously, the emergence of cryptocurrency was largely motivated by the perception in some quarters that a less regulated alternative to the traditional financial sector was desirable. This view stemmed from legitimate financial privacy concerns but was also shared by criminals, as borne out by their subsequent exploitation of cryptocurrency. Or, to take another example, once the UK started requiring the disclosure of beneficial ownership information for limited liability companies and partnerships, the rates of establishing Scottish limited partnerships, which were not covered by any such rules, increased dramatically.[230] More broadly, the entire history of the expansion of AML rules across various sectors of the economy, which began in the early 1990s and is still ongoing, reflects policymakers' perception that criminal activities move on to new industries.

The displacement effect is a grave threat to the effectiveness of the AML regime. Both the objective of excluding proceeds of crime from the legitimate economy and the objective of surveilling criminal activities are jeopardised if, instead of engaging with compliant regulated businesses, one can try one's luck with a less regulated sector. For instance, if an organised crime group engaged in drug trafficking cannot move funds overseas via the formal banking system, they might purchase some used cars or consumer electronics and ship those goods to be resold in another jurisdiction – a simple variation of trade-based money laundering.

Thinking about the displacement effect and its implications in a nuanced fashion requires considering carefully the objectives of exclusion and surveillance and how they manifest themselves depending on the situation. In the example of a domestic organised crime group engaged in drug trafficking, proceeds of crime are generated within the jurisdiction. Short of extremely unusual scenarios, such as bags stuffed with cash being dug into the ground and left to rot, as was the case with some Latin American gangs who had more money than they could launder, those proceeds are going to be used in some way, shape or form within that jurisdiction. Shutting them out of the financial sector makes some of their uses more difficult, but also comes at the cost of valuable financial intelligence, as discussed above. This is encapsulated in the words of a senior AML executive in a major UK bank, who would often say words to the effect of: 'I want criminals to bank with me, so I can report their activities'.

Still, shutting off access to the legitimate economy can be useful as a means of disrupting criminal activities, including by rendering money laundering more expensive and, therefore, making the criminal operation as a whole less profitable. So, while the purchase of used cars might enable the organised crime group to accomplish its purpose of moving value overseas, the lengths it has to go to in order to do so compares unfavourably, from the criminal's perspective, to pushing the button in a mobile

[230] Department for Business, Energy and Industrial Strategy (UK), 'Limited Partnerships: Reform of Limited Partnerships Law', 30 April 2018, 8.

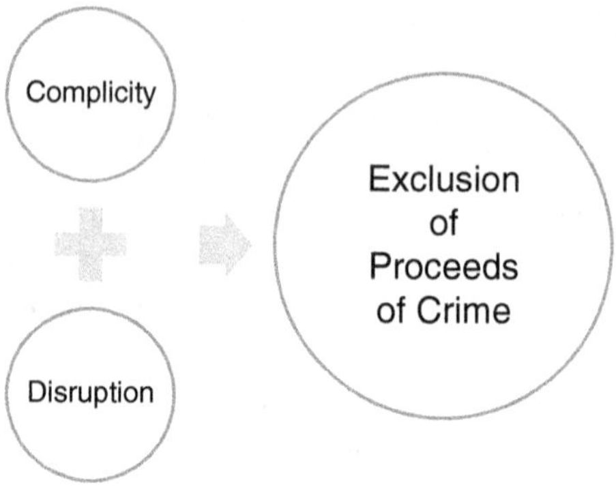

FIGURE 3.5 The two rationales behind the exclusion paradigm

banking app. This criminal-oriented rationale for excluding proceeds of crime from the legitimate economy is different from the regulated sector-oriented rationale of ensuring that legitimate businesses are not complicit in money laundering.

This suggests that, when discussing the exclusion paradigm, it is useful to distinguish between two underlying rationales. One is the complicity rationale, that is ensuring that the integrity of the legitimate economy is not tainted by criminal entanglements, as discussed previously. The other is the disruption rationale, that is, introducing friction into criminal operations by denying criminals access to the resources and services that they need to do their job. Both of these rationales need to be taken into account in deciding how valuable exclusion is in a given context, and how far it ought to be pursued. For instance, pushing domestic drug trafficking groups towards less accessible avenues for money laundering might either be a significant way of disrupting their operations or a minor irritant if those alternative options are effective and easily available. This is summarised in Figure 3.5.

Contrast the example of domestic drug trafficking with the case of a corrupt foreign official who might be eyeing the purchase of real estate in a particular jurisdiction. Here, displacement is a sensible and realistic objective. True, the official concerned may well be able to buy a villa in a less well-regulated country instead, but at least the first-mentioned jurisdiction will have avoided acting as a safe harbour to the proceeds of foreign crime. And, in contradistinction to the domestic drug trafficking example, little valuable purpose would be served by collecting financial intelligence about that official's activities if the domestic justice system of his or her state is suborned by corruption and not in a position to effectively prosecute high-level wrongdoing.

Therefore, different approaches can and should be taken to different criminal threats. Or, to put it in different terms, it is odd to maintain that the same AML response is always appropriate notwithstanding the nature of the predicate crime. That, however, is the default position under the current regime, which creates a set of blunt incentives that operate in the same fashion regardless of how well, or how poorly, that fits with the overall law enforcement strategy. That is the essence of the undirected deputisation of the private sector, which involves superficially sensible action that may or may not be aligned with the genuine needs of law enforcement agencies that the AML regime is meant to serve. How to solve this alignment challenge is the subject of Section 3.5.

3.5 POTENTIAL SOLUTIONS

In summary, AML regulation is based on reasonable instincts about what should be done in response to money laundering. However, its application is incoherent and untethered from the pursuit of any overarching objective. One could compare the operation of the AML regime to a restaurant whose chef, instead of coming up with a list of products he or she needs to make a dish, directs the staff to buy something tasty and healthy. The overall message is sound, but the likelihood of the staff delivering what the chef wants day in, day out is vanishingly small – especially if the staff have no clue whether taste or health is to be prioritised. Suppose, further, that the staff need to pay for those products out of their own salary: one can hardly expect for this to have no impact on their decisions. That is the key downside of the undirected deputisation that AML rules rest upon.

Some of the tensions at the heart of the AML regime implicate fundamental civil liberties, such as the tension between exclusion of proceeds of crime and the presumption of innocence or the tension between financial surveillance and financial privacy. They require open public discussion and a legislative framework reflecting a coherent vision of the presumption of innocence or financial privacy, rather than a hotchpotch of one-off solutions that differ across sectors.

By contrast, the question of whether exclusion or surveillance ought to be prioritised is unlikely to have a single answer. The choice depends on what best serves law enforcement needs in light of the criminal threat involved. This, in turn, requires the consideration of various potential solutions to the problem of aligning private sector action with law enforcement needs. This basic need for alignment has been long recognised. As early as in 1989, at a hearing before the US Senate Committee on Banking, Housing, and Urban Affairs, Chuck Morley said:

> Based upon my experience with all the work I've done with the Banking Associations, I can state that the banking industry in this country is cooperating to a phenomenal degree. Granted, they had to be brought to this point by cases like the Bank of Boston case. Nonetheless, I think it's time, as you say, Senator, to start dangling some carrots out here in front of the financial institutions. I think it is time that we give them all the tools they need to cooperate in this problem of identifying money launderers.[231]

[231] US Senate, Committee on Banking, Housing, and Urban Affairs, Subcommittee on Consumer and Regulatory Affairs, *Drug Money Laundering Control Efforts*, 1 November 1989, 84.

If one substitutes the Bank of Boston case for a more recent money laundering scandal, this is without exaggeration the point that one will hear at most of today's AML conferences. For the reasons discussed above, better operation of the AML regime requires a shared understanding of what the priority law enforcement threats are and how they are best detected and addressed. There are ways to generate this shared understanding short of a public–private partnership, but, as discussed below, they are limited and inefficient.

3.5.1 *Publication of Typologies and Priorities*

The traditional approach taken by the FATF and domestic governments is to educate the regulated sectors through the publication of money laundering typologies. Such typologies take the form of case studies or summaries, sanitised to remove any operationally sensitive details, which are meant to alert regulated businesses to the red flags they should look for. For instance, here is the FATF's typology of black market peso exchange, a form of trade-based money laundering used by Latin American drug traffickers to move drug cash from the US back to their home countries:

> In January 2020, the US Justice Department indicted six Colombian nationals, in co-operation with an Indian national, for their roles in an international money laundering scheme involving [trade-based money laundering] and the use of unlicensed money transmission business. The purpose of the scheme was to launder the proceeds of drug trafficking, primarily using a Black Market Peso Exchange-style process so the cash located in the United States was not physically transferred. The scheme was built around the Colombian nationals allegedly working as money brokers that receive criminal proceeds from couriers located throughout the United States, and the receipt of incoming international wire transfers. The physical cash was introduced into the U.S. financial system so as not to raise suspicion, before being transferred to the business bank account controlled by the Indian national, who was an alleged complicit merchant. The merchant exported consumer electronics to buyers throughout the world, including importers located in Colombia. The merchant exported roughly the equivalent value of consumer products to the importers in Colombia, who in turn arranged to pay for the products by delivering pesos to the money brokers in Colombia, who passed this to the drug trafficking organisation. This negated the need for the drug traffickers to attempt any movement of cash across borders, thus reducing their risk of detection.[232]

Depending on how a bank's compliance team operationalise this typology, they may, for example, ensure that the bank's transaction monitoring system flags up for review transactions involving the sale of consumer products to customers in

[232] FATF, *Trade-Based Money Laundering: Trends and Developments*, December 2020, 28.

Colombia by small or medium-sized US-based businesses wholly owned by non-US nationals. However, published typologies tend to be limited in terms of the level of granularity they provide as well as their timeliness.[233] Suppose that available intelligence indicates that most black market peso exchange schemes involve a particular kind of consumer electronics (e.g. mobile phones), a particular profile of complicit merchants (e.g. men from South-East Asia under the age of thirty who never before ran a business) and a particular location within the US (e.g. Los Angeles). All of that information may not be appropriate for wide dissemination, so as not to prompt criminal groups to alter their tactics, but would be extremely helpful in focusing banks' attention.

Equally, things change. It is entirely possible that, over the several years since the publication of the FATF's report in 2020, black market peso exchange has evolved to, say, primarily exploit the export of used cars to Mexico through businesses set up by US citizens. If that were the case, then our hypothetical bank's conclusions from the FATF's typology will have been overrun by events. Of course, the bank could try to exercise vigilance in relation to all flows of goods from the US to all Latin American countries, but that would most likely lead to over-reporting or, if the effort proves too expensive, ultimately result in offboarding the mostly legitimate customers who engage in those kinds of business.

The other, more novel, avenue for the dissemination of relevant information by governments to the regulated sector has been the publication of official AML priorities, so as to give a sense of the areas of criminal activity that law enforcement agencies are most concerned with detecting. In the US, the Anti-Money Laundering Act 2020 introduced amendments to the Bank Secrecy Act 1970 requiring FinCEN to publish a list of national AML priorities.[234] The preambular provisions in the relevant section of the Act refer expressly to the need to ensure that the private sector's compliance resources are spent efficiently and that undue derisking is minimised. FinCEN's first priorities list, published in 2021, included – 'in no particular order' – eight broad types of criminality, namely:

> (1) [C]orruption; (2) cybercrime, including relevant cybersecurity and virtual currency considerations; (3) foreign and domestic terrorist financing; (4) fraud; (5) transnational criminal organization activity; (6) drug trafficking organization activity; (7) human trafficking and human smuggling; and (8) proliferation financing.[235]

One can have sympathy for the dilemma that FinCEN faces since identifying some crime types as especially important means that other crime types are, correspondingly, less important. The inevitable consequence is that FinCEN's resulting list is

233 Interview with two UK law enforcement experts, 28 June 2024.
234 Section 6106 of the Anti-Money Laundering Act 2020 (US).
235 FinCEN, 'AML/CTF Priorities', 30 June 2021.

so broad as to be utterly meaningless, covering as it does all forms of organised criminality.[236] This conclusion is reinforced by FinCEN's accompanying statements for banks and DNFBPs, which expressly say that the priorities list does not affect any of the legal obligations under the US AML framework.[237] Despite this, in July 2024 FinCEN published an advance notice of proposed rule-making that would, among other things, require regulated businesses to take account of the national AML priorities in designing their compliance programmes – a requirement of limited import if everything is a priority![238]

Given these limitations of publishing typologies and priorities, other solutions are necessary to handle the alignment challenge. The most notable advance in tackling it has been the development of public–private partnerships, which bring together regulators, law enforcement agencies and regulated businesses to formulate a common set of AML priorities, identify typologies and, in some partnerships, share operational information. This development is discussed in Section 3.5.2.

3.5.2 *Public–Private Partnerships*

As we have seen, the need for public–private collaboration has been recognised in broad terms since at least 1989. Nonetheless, it took time for it to crystallise into the establishment of formal partnerships. One of the early steps in that direction was the adoption of the US's second-ever national money laundering strategy in 2000.[239] The strategy identified four high-level goals, one of which was 'enhancing regulatory and cooperative public–private efforts to prevent money laundering'.[240] However, specific proposals put forward under the strategy eschewed reference to any standing partnership or legislative pathways for two-way information-sharing, save for a commitment to providing greater feedback to regulated businesses on the utility or otherwise of submitted SAR.

Then, following the terrorist attacks of 9/11, the Patriot Act was adopted to strengthen the US response to money laundering and terrorist financing alike. The enactment of the Patriot Act in October 2001, a mere month after the attack, conceals the far longer gestation period of most of the ideas that were included in the

[236] Interview with two international AML/CTF experts, 18 January 2024; interview with a UK AML/CTF expert, 30 January 2024.

[237] FinCEN, 'Statement on the Issuance of the Anti-Money Laundering/Countering the Financing of Terrorism (AML/CFT) National Priorities', 30 June 2021.

[238] FinCEN, *Anti-Money Laundering and Countering the Financing of Terrorism Programs*, 89 FR 55428, 3 July 2024. See also FinCEN, Board of Governors of the Federal Reserve System, Federal Deposit Insurance Corporation, National Credit Union Administration and Office of the Comptroller of the Currency, 'Interagency Statement on the Issuance of the AML/CFT Program Notices of Proposed Rulemaking', 19 July 2024.

[239] US Treasury and DOJ, *The National Money Laundering Strategy for 2000*, March 2000, 26, 46.

[240] Ibid.

Act. There had been a great deal of dormant legislative proposals that, due to a lack of interest and urgency, had been overlooked prior to 9/11 but were then swiftly incorporated into the Patriot Act.[241] One of those provisions ultimately became Section 314(a) of the Patriot Act, which in relevant part provides as follows:

> (1) Regulations. Secretary shall, within 120 days after the date of enactment of this Act, adopt regulations to encourage further cooperation among financial institutions, their regulatory authorities, and law enforcement authorities, with the specific purpose of encouraging regulatory authorities and law enforcement authorities to share with financial institutions information regarding individuals, entities, and organizations engaged in or reasonably suspected based on credible evidence of engaging in terrorist acts or money laundering activities.

This and other provisions of Section 314(a) are complemented by Section 314(b), which provides for private-to-private information-sharing among financial institutions. For a long time, however, the implementation of these provisions did not benefit from any standing institutional structure, such as a formalised partnership. That changed in 2017 with the establishment of FinCEN Exchange, a public–private partnership largely based on the UK's Joint Money Laundering Intelligence Taskforce (JMLIT),[242] which marks a watershed in the development of public–private partnerships.[243]

The history of the JMLIT began in 2014 with the publication of the NCA's National Strategic Assessment of Serious and Organised Crime.[244] It was thought within the government at the time that quantifying the scale of money laundering in the UK would be useful to give a sense of how serious the problem is. Measuring it scientifically is next to impossible, and the NCA settled on the best available 'guesstimate' of several hundred billion pounds per year.[245] Coupled with London's regular involvement in money laundering scandals, this figure got widely reported on in the media, which consequently led government ministers to take the problem seriously.

That year, two 'business breakfasts' took place between senior officials and bank representatives, including then-Home Secretary Theresa May, the Governor of the Bank of England Mark Carney and the Director of the NCA Keith Bristow. The idea of setting up a JMLIT between the government and the banks was born then. Both government and bank representatives found the concept appealing, with HSBC acting as a strong proponent as part of its broader push to make up for its then-recent money laundering failings in Mexico.

241 Interview with a US lawyer specialising in AML/CTF (A), 14 November 2023.

242 Pronounced 'Jim-Lit'.

243 Nick J. Maxwell, 'Expanding the Capability of Financial Information-Sharing Partnerships', *RUSI Occasional Paper*, March 2019, 27.

244 The following account is largely based on an interview with two UK law enforcement experts, 28 June 2024.

245 NCA, *National Strategic Assessment of Serious and Organised Crime*, May 2014, 12.

The first meeting focused on the JMLIT's mission and overall concept, whereas at the second one practical details were discussed, including the legal basis for the taskforce. That basis was found in Section 7 of the Crime and Courts Act 2013, which authorised private individuals and organisations to disclose information to the NCA. It was believed that those provisions allowed setting up an information-sharing environment for law enforcement agencies and banks. JMLIT's concept was highly innovative but draw some inspiration from the existing idea of the Joint Fraud Taskforce, which involved government agencies and banks coming together for periodic meetings without the sharing of operational information.

As a team of NCA and Home Office experts began work on setting up the JMLIT, several key decisions were made. One was that the JMLIT would share operational information, and not merely typologies. The other was to launch a pilot, which commenced in early 2015. The JMLIT team also had to develop performance metrics that appealed to both law enforcement agencies, such as the numbers of arrests and amounts of criminal assets seized, and bank executives, with a focus on off-boarded customers and improved transaction monitoring rules. In essence, the message to banks was that the JMLIT would enable them to more efficiently carry out their AML regulatory obligations.

That raised a competition law concern. Since the JMLIT's membership was going to be limited to a select group of banks, the question emerged of whether their sharing of information to better detect money laundering could constitute anti-competitive behaviour. Following the NCA's discussions with the Competition and Markets Authority, the conclusion was reached that competition law did not preclude the JMLIT's establishment; however, typologies identified through its work would have to be shared openly with the entirety of the regulated sectors. Another key consideration was financial privacy. The NCA's legal advisors were of the view that the sharing of information within the JMLIT's framework was compatible with the Human Rights Act 1998 provided that all participants meaningfully and actively contributed to the JMLIT's operations. By contrast, if one of the banks were to passively consume information as a matter of course without making any contribution, then the sharing of information with that particular bank may prove not to be necessary or proportionate.

During the pilot in 2015, the JMLIT proved its value in helping investigate cases that had previously stalled due to the inability to effectively collect financial intelligence from various banks. This proof of concept led to the JMLIT's placement on a permanent footing in 2016, as well as widespread recognition of its value by law enforcement agencies from across the country, including regional organised crime units. The JMLIT's structure came to involve the Operations Group, which met in person weekly to discuss ongoing cases and share operational information, and several expert groups, such as those on corruption, terrorist financing or trade-based money laundering. Since the JMLIT's expert groups focus on trends and typologies, their discussions are less sensitive and, with time, representatives of non-governmental organisations and think tanks were invited to either take part in expert group meetings on a permanent basis or present their research to the group as and when the occasion arose. With only minor modifications, this JMLIT model established in 2016 continues to operate today. Furthermore, amendments introduced via the Criminal Finances Act 2017 expanded regulated businesses' capacity to engage in private-to-private information-sharing without the JMLIT's intermediation to file the so-called super-SARs drawing on information from multiple institutions.[246]

The JMLIT rapidly became known as a great success, with over fifty references to its activities found in the MER published by the FATF in 2019.[247] Drawing on consultations with UK authorities, multiple other countries have established their own, JMLIT-style public–private partnerships, including the Fintel Alliance in Australia, FinCEN Exchange in the US, Fraud and Money Laundering Intelligence Taskforce in Hong Kong, Anti-Money Laundering and Countering the Financing of Terrorism Industry Partnership in Singapore, the South African Anti-Money Laundering Integrated Taskforce in South Africa, the Swedish Anti-Money Laundering Intelligence Task Force in Sweden, the Canadian Major Reporters Forum, the Anti-Financial Crime Alliance in Germany and the Netherlands Terrorist Financing Taskforce.[248] Precise details of the operation of these groups vary. For instance, the Canadian and German partnerships only share typologies, rather than operational details.[249] Public–private partnerships are also provided for in Article 75 of the EU's Single Rulebook Regulation, with the EU banking sector currently exploring the opportunities this offers.[250]

The crucial limitation of, and challenge inherent in, the operation of public–private partnerships is their exclusivity. For instance, the JMLIT brings together approximately 40 banks out of over 300 banks operating in the UK.[251] The approach of the JMLIT's founders was to 'marry threats to participants', that is, ensure that the taskforce had sufficient coverage of key sectors of the economy, from retail banking to capital markets. Once that point was reached, the fact that not *all* banks were taking part was deemed to be an acceptable compromise. This is because the

[246] Section 339ZB of Proceeds of Crime Act 2002 (UK).

[247] FATF, *Anti-money Laundering and Counter-Terrorist Financing Measures: United Kingdom, Fourth Round Mutual Evaluation Report*, 2018.

[248] Nick J. Maxwell, 'Expanding the Capability of Financial Information-Sharing Partnerships', *RUSI Occasional Paper*, March 2019, 6–8.

[249] Reports by the Future of Financial Intelligence Sharing programme run by Nick Maxwell, one of which is referenced in the previous footnote, are an unrivalled source of information on the operation of public–private partnerships.

[250] Koos Couvée, 'New EU AML Regulation Could Supercharge Financial-Intelligence Sharing', *moneylaundering.com*, 27 June 2024.

[251] See Bank of England's list of banks operating in the UK as of 1 January 2023 available at www.bankofengland.co.uk/-/media/boe/files/prudential-regulation/authorisations/which-firms-does-the-pra-regulate/2023/list-of-banks/banks-list-2301.pdf.

Operations Group meetings take place in a close-knit, carefully vetted environment: a law enforcement briefing with the presenter 'lecturing to 400 people' would not produce the same effect.

The difficulty this entails is particularly acute in the non-banking context. Some sectors, especially non-financial ones such as real estate agents, accountants and legal professionals, primarily consist of small and medium-sized businesses in many jurisdictions. As a result, one cannot obtain the same coverage as one can in the banking sector by bringing together a small group of major players. This is a crucial limitation of public–private partnerships as a means of overcoming the challenge of aligning private-sector action with law enforcement priorities. One attempt to plug the information-sharing gaps in more fragmented sectors of the economy has been undertaken in the UK, with Intelligence Sharing Expert Working Groups (ISEWGs)[252] in the accountancy and legal sectors, respectively, bringing together law enforcement agencies and sectoral AML supervisors, without direct involvement of regulated businesses.[253] These arrangements are limited to the sharing of typologies, rather than operational information.

Still, some form of a public–private partnership is one of the best ways, if not the best one, of addressing the misalignment between law enforcement priorities and private-sector compliance efforts. In particular, one of the advantages of public–private partnerships such as the JMLIT is the sharing of detailed typology information in close to real time. So, to take the black market peso exchange example discussed previously, one would identify as high-risk mobile phone shops in Los Angeles operated by South-East Asian men under thirty years of age who had never held a job before – as opposed to some more vague and generic description, such as that referring to the trade of consumer products in the US. The speed with which such information would be shared with the regulated sectors would also differ dramatically from waiting until a vetted, sanitised report is written up and published for general consumption.

The model of a public–private partnership that takes the notion of real-time information-sharing the furthest is pooling multiple banks' customer data together and centralising their transaction monitoring efforts in a single entity. Since 2020, this model has been pioneered by a partnership established by five Dutch banks and known as Transactie Monitoring Nederland (TMNL).[254] Despite the FATF's and experts' cautious optimism about TMNL's early results,[255] in July 2024 it announced

[252] Pronounced 'easy wigs'.

[253] FCA, 'Legal Sector Intelligence Sharing Expert Working Group: Terms of Reference', www.fca.org.uk/publication/opbas/legal-sector-intelligence-sharing-expert-working-group-terms-of-reference.pdf; FCA, 'Accountancy Sector Intelligence Sharing Expert Working Group: Terms of Reference', www.fca.org.uk/publication/opbas/accountancy-sector-isewg-terms-of-reference.pdf.

[254] TMNL, 'About TMNL', https://tmnl.nl/en/about-tmnl/.

[255] FATF, *Anti-money Laundering and Counter-Terrorist Financing Measures – The Netherlands: Mutual Evaluation Report*, August 2022, 42; FATF, *Stocktake on Data Pooling, Collaborative Analytics and Data Protection*, July 2021, 18; Redhead, 'The Future of Transaction Monitoring', 15.

the winding down of its operations to assess the implications of Article 75 of the EU's Single Rulebook AML Regulation,[256] which prompted the Dutch FIU to describe TMNL's move as 'premature'.[257] In the meantime, following years of preparatory work, three UK banks launched a TMNL-style initiative coordinated by the NCA in May 2024.[258] A similar project went live in Singapore in April 2024, but its information-sharing is limited to customer data identified by the six participating banks as exhibiting 'red flags'.[259]

3.5.3 *'Keep Open' Regime*

A related issue, and one that is sometimes addressed via public–private partnerships, is the tendency of regulated businesses to discontinue relationships with customers of interest to law enforcement agencies. This practice is often observed in connection with bank accounts once banks receive production orders or similar requests for information from law enforcement agencies.[260] Many banks worldwide have internal 'three strikes and out' rules to the effect that, if a customer becomes the subject of a SAR on three occasions, the customer relationship will be dropped.[261] This is sometimes a product of implicit regulatory expectations. While regulators would never explicitly suggest that such a blunt rule be adopted, field examiners will quiz any bank that chooses to retain customers that recurrently become subject to law enforcement requests or internal suspicions.[262] Whether the decision to exit the relationship is motivated by limiting compliance costs or regulatory engagement, its upshot is that a potentially valuable source of financial intelligence is cut off.

If a law enforcement agency is aware of the bank's intention to exit the relationship, it may formally request the bank to keep the account open instead. Such requests are occasionally known as 'keep open requests' or 'hold harmless letters'. Despite their importance in AML investigations, such requests have no binding force in the UK, US, Australia, Canada or New Zealand. In the US, FinCEN

[256] TMNL, 'Transaction Monitoring Netherlands Adapts Its Working Method to New European Legislation', 1 July 2024, https://tmnl.nl/en/article/transaction-monitoring-netherlands-adapts-its-working-method-to-new-european-legislation/.

[257] Paul O'Donoghue, 'NEWS: Dutch FIU Laments 'Premature' Wind Down of TMNL; Highlights Money Laundering through Labour-Intensive Sub Contractors in CCMs', *AML Intelligence*, 13 July 2024, www.amlintelligence.com/2024/07/news-dutch-fiu-laments-premature-decision-by-dutch-banks-to-wind-down-aml-coalition-tmnl/.

[258] Kirstin Ridley and Sinead Cruise, 'LATEST: Staff From Seven UK Banks Seconded to Police in ML Crackdown; Data Sharing Project Has Already Identified Eight Crime Networks', *AML Intelligence*, 26 July 2024, www.amlintelligence.com/2024/07/news-staff-from-seven-uk-banks-seconded-to-police-in-ml-crackdown-project-has-already-identified-eight-crime-networks/.

[259] Monetary Authority of Singapore, 'COSMIC', www.mas.gov.sg/regulation/anti-money-laundering/cosmic.

[260] Maxwell, 'Expanding the Capability of Financial Information-Sharing Partnerships', 44–46.

[261] Interview with two UK law enforcement experts, 28 June 2024.

[262] Interview with two international AML/CTF experts, 18 January 2024.

published guidance on hold harmless letters in 2007 but emphasised their non-binding nature and that the decision whether to abide by the request remained with the bank.[263] That creates a paradoxical position where, despite a law enforcement agency's unambiguous indication of what the interests of the investigation require, a bank is free to frustrate those interests in the name of removing any risk of regulatory enforcement for keeping the account open, no matter how remote the risk is.

Public–private partnerships help redress this problem. For one thing, banks often do not treat requests received via a partnership or discussions that take place within a partnership's framework on the same footing as they do law enforcement agencies' production requests. In other words, if a bank shares information about a customer via a public–private partnership, this does not trigger the application of the bank's internal 'three strikes and out' rule.[264] More broadly, though, the collaborative ethos underpinning public–private partnerships engenders – ideally – a shared focus on achieving law enforcement outcomes rather than merely facilitating participants' AML compliance efforts. In the UK's JMLIT, this ethos was partly a reflection of the group's composition, which included multiple former senior law enforcement officers who went on to work for banks but, in the words of two interviewees, 'still wanted to be law enforcement officers'.[265]

All of that being said, public–private partnerships are not the only answer to the problem of accounts that present high law enforcement value being closed down. Formal 'keep open' laws can be adopted to require regulated businesses to maintain certain business relationships following a request from a law enforcement agency. Over the past several years, the value of such laws has gained increased recognition.

In Australia, the government consulted on incorporating 'keep open notices' in the country's AML rules, although the effect of a notice would be merely to shield regulated businesses from liability for continuing to provide services covered by the notice rather than *requiring* that they do so.[266] In Canada, the Commission of Inquiry into Money Laundering in British Columbia, chaired by the judge Austin Cullen and widely known as the Cullen Commission, proposed the introduction of a legally binding 'keep open' regime as one of the recommendations stemming from its sweeping review of British Columbia's AML measures, published in 2022.[267] In the EU, member states are now required to implement such a regime under Article 25 of 6MLD:

[263] FinCEN, *Requests by Law Enforcement for Financial Institutions to Maintain Accounts*, 13 June 2007.
[264] Interview with two UK law enforcement experts, 28 June 2024.
[265] Ibid.
[266] Attorney General's Department (Australia), *Reforming Australia's Anti-Money Laundering and Counter-Terrorism Financing Regime – Paper 5: Broader Reforms to Simplify, Clarify and Modernise the Regime*, May 2024, 26–28.
[267] Cullen Commission, *Final Report*, 1008–1009.

> Member States shall ensure that FIUs are empowered to instruct obliged entities to monitor, for a period to be specified by the FIU, the transactions or activities that are being carried out through one or more bank accounts or payment accounts or crypto-asset accounts or other business relationships managed by the obliged entity for persons who present a significant risk of money laundering, its predicate offences or terrorist financing. Member States shall also ensure that FIUs are empowered to instruct the obliged entity to report on the results of the monitoring. Member States shall ensure that FIUs are empowered to impose monitoring measures as referred to in this Article at the request of an FIU from another Member State.

In light of the clear need for such a regime, one may find it surprising that formal 'keep open' rules do not yet exist in other jurisdictions, or that law enforcement agencies do not agitate more actively for their introduction. A plausible, if somewhat cynical explanation for this state of affairs is that, if an account stays open due to a binding direction from a law enforcement agency, that agency will be politically (if not legally) responsible for the consequences. Few leaders of law enforcement agencies would wish to wake up to a newspaper headline reading something like *REVEALED: POLICE SAY BANKS MUST SERVE DRUG LORDS AND FRAUDSTERS*.

For now, therefore, in most jurisdictions decisions as to whether an account should remain open continue to be relegated to the level of regulated businesses. In talking about the ensuing dilemmas, near-ritualistic mention is often made of the need for those businesses to act in line with a 'risk-based approach' or consistent with their 'risk appetite'. What this means, and why this is not a plausible solution to any of the challenges involved, is considered in Section 3.5.4.

3.5.4 *Risk-Based Approach*

The FATF and domestic governments emphasise the 'risk-based approach' as a cornerstone of AML compliance. For instance, the FATF's Recommendation 1 requires that:

> [C]ountries should apply a risk-based approach (RBA) to ensure that measures to prevent or mitigate money laundering and terrorist financing are commensurate with the risks identified. This approach should be an essential foundation to efficient allocation of resources across the anti-money laundering and countering the financing of terrorism (AML/CFT) regime and the implementation of risk-based measures throughout the FATF Recommendations.

The term has emerged as vague, all-encompassing shorthand for the notion of purposive compliance, that is, the taking of compliance measures that are tailored towards a regulated business's circumstances and are aimed at pursuing socially useful outcomes. Unfortunately, the primary role that the risk-based approach plays in AML regulation is that of a rhetorical *deus ex machina*. Almost any systemic failing can be presented as incorrect implementation of the risk-based approach, despite the limited explanatory power that this assertion holds.

Derisking is a case in point, with the FATF presenting the risk-based approach as the opposite of derisking. The former involves thoughtful management of risk on a case-by-case basis; the latter is 'the wholesale cutting loose of entire classes of customer, without taking into account, seriously and comprehensively, their level of risk or risk mitigation measures for individual customers within a particular sector'.[268] Or, as the cliché goes, derisking is a failure to *manage* the risk – and banks, in particular, are in the business of managing risks.

This brings us back to a point made in Chapter 2, namely that the language of risk does not adequately reflect the *opportunities* that financial surveillance presents. The ability to identify and surveil criminal activities in the legitimate economy is a social good. Indeed, as we saw, this is one of the premises on which the development of the AML framework from the 1970s onwards rests. Yet not only does the AML regime fail to provide sufficient incentives to regulated businesses to harness those opportunities, but the language of the risk-based approach does not even adequately acknowledge them. This is a glaring omission at the heart of the regime because the very concept of a risk-based approach, which is meant to structure and clarify the thinking of all participants in the AML regime, is in fact confusing.

Insofar as risks are concerned, the primary AML risks that regulated businesses face are the legal, regulatory and reputational risks of complicity in money laundering.[269] These risks can either be minimised through derisking or managed through ongoing monitoring of high-risk customers, with the costs attendant on the latter option. The FATF's criticism of derisking is an acknowledgment of the other societal values and principles involved, such as financial surveillance and financial inclusion. Still, the FATF's proposed solution to the problem of derisking is *not* a requirement for countries to set up incentive structures that promote effective financial surveillance and financial inclusion – let alone any concrete indications of how that might be achieved.

Instead, the FATF suggests that regulated businesses should define and act within their 'risk appetite', or the level of their tolerance to AML risks.[270] Implicit in the criticism of derisking is the suggestion that risk appetite cannot be too low, lest

[268] FATF, 'FATF Clarifies Risk-Based Approach: Case-By-Case, Not Wholesale De-Risking', 23 October 2014, www.fatf-gafi.org/en/publications/Fatfgeneral/Rba-and-de-risking.html.

[269] The risk of enforcement action stemming from purely regulatory failings, rather than complicity in money laundering, does not appear to be relevant to the correct application of the risk-based approach but, in the thinking of financial institutions, may be difficult to isolate from the risk of complicity in money laundering: Louis de Koker and Doron Goldbarsht, 'FATF's Risk-Based Approach: Has the Pendulum Swung Too Far?' in Louis De Koker and Doron Goldbarsht (eds), *Financial Crime and the Law* (Springer, 2024).

[270] See, e.g., FATF, *Guidance for a Risk-Based Approach: The Banking Sector*, 2014, 15, 19. Similar statements are contained in the FATF's guidance on the risk-based approach for other sectors.

swathes of high-risk customers be excluded from regulated services, but otherwise it is up to regulated businesses to set their risk appetite. This is overwhelmingly a commercial decision.

The complex balancing of the paradigms financial exclusion (the risks of complicity) and financial surveillance (the opportunities of information-gathering), as well as of the competing values of financial privacy and the presumption of innocence, involves societal-level policy choices. The notion that they can be satisfactorily resolved by regulated businesses through defining their 'risk appetite' is nothing short of extraordinary. Equally unimpressive is the FATF's and governments' criticism of derisking when it is the most rational way for many businesses to deal with the AML risks that they hear so much about.

A far more clear and coherent approach would be to recognise explicitly that countries should seek to maximise the law enforcement value of financial intelligence from regulated sectors (the opportunity) while minimising the risks of regulated sectors' complicity in money laundering (the risk). Their competent authorities' regulatory and supervisory efforts should, therefore, be focused on guiding regulated businesses in achieving the right balance in light of relevant law enforcement priorities; supporting their compliance in maximising opportunities and minimising risks; and creating incentives for effective compliance in both those contexts. One must recognise, further, that for many businesses their risk appetite will militate towards derisking. This is where bespoke arrangements, such as public–private partnerships, may come in useful to mitigate against those derisking tendencies at least among major, systemic institutions. One can also consider a surveillance-oriented paradigm for certain basic services, as discussed in Section 3.5.5.

All of this is consistent with the spirit behind the risk-based approach. For all its limitations, it is useful to recall that the risk-based approach has evolved in AML regulation as an alternative to, and improvement upon, a rule-based approach that would have seen all regulated businesses comply with a certain set of rules admitting of little variation in light of a given business's circumstances. The use of the risk-based approach in the sense of focusing on things that matter, rather than trivial issues or risks, is wholly praiseworthy. The rhetorical invocations of risk may have also helped make AML regulation more palatable and relatable to financial institutions, whose core business involved managing various forms of financial risk. What is important is that this rhetoric should not obscure the substance of the issues involved, which concern striking a delicate balance between competing societal values and principles, rather than purely commercial risk management.

3.5.5 *Stratification of Regulated Services*

A concrete manifestation of tackling the conflict between competing values and principles head-on, rather than hiding behind the opaque language of the risk-based approach, concerns one of the proposals that have been floated to address derisking.

The proposal is to treat certain financial services, such as basic bank accounts, as a quasi-public utility that should be provided to the public at large on a non-discriminatory basis. For instance, one author writes in the US context:

> Congress could pass laws that would require banks to open and maintain accounts for businesses that were able to meet some standard of due diligence. This type of action would bring banks closer to the 'public utility' concept that they resist. But it would also lessen their regulatory burden to some extent by providing clear guidelines on the minimum standard firms have to achieve to open and maintain a business account with banks.[271]

The concept of public utility is cognate to that of common carrier, discussed in Chapter 2.[272] Among other things, the status of a public utility shields businesses from liability for the provision of their services to any particular customer. The argument in favour of requiring banks to provide customers with a basic bank account subject to certain threshold conditions draws on a rich tradition of thinking about various functions of commercial banks as so crucial to public life as to merit being treated, in some sense at least, as public utilities.[273]

The precise terminology used or its genesis is of secondary relevance for present purposes. What matters is the idea of exempting a category of AML-regulated services from the exclusion-oriented paradigm that AML regulation engenders. Not only will regulated businesses not be required to consider whether a customer should be dropped on account of potential involvement in money laundering, but there will be an affirmative obligation to provide basic services to customers satisfying the requisite threshold requirements. This would not affect any otherwise applicable record-keeping or reporting requirements, such as the obligation to file SARs.

This proposition may appear radical, but it does no more than query the assumption that all AML-regulated services must be regulated in the same fashion. It is perfectly plausible to suggest that the provision of some services should be subjected to surveillance, but nothing would be gained by driving would-be customers away. For instance, if a local drug trafficker is turned away by a bank, the proceeds of his or her crime do not magically dissolve into thin air. They will be invested elsewhere

[271] Amber D. Scott, 'If Banks Can't Solve the Derisking Dilemma, Maybe the Government Will' (2015) 60(1) *American Banker*.

[272] Cornell Law School, Legal Information Institute, 'Public Utility', www.law.cornell.edu/wex/public_utility. For an overview of the differences between public utilities and common carriers, see Eli M. Noam, 'Beyond Liberalization II: The Impending Doom of Common Carriage' (1994) 18(6) *Telecommunications Policy* 435, 436. Both stem from the historical development of 'public service companies' discussed in Charles K. Burdick, 'The Origin of the Peculiar Duties of Public Service Companies: Part I' (1911) 11(6) *Columbia LR* 514.

[273] See, e.g., Lev Menand and Morgan Ricks, 'Rebuilding Banking Law: Banks as Public Utilities' (2024) *Yale J Regulation*; Ryan Bernard and Ashton Smith, 'Central Banks as Utilities? (Summary of Private Roundtable Discussion)', *U Michigan Center on Finance, Law & Policy*, 28 January 2021. See also Stephen Anthony, 'Australia's Banks Have Lost Their Way. We Need to Rethink How to Regulate Them', *The Sydney Morning Herald*, 2 October 2017.

or otherwise moved or spent. For sure, access to a basic bank account would be convenient for this hypothetical drug trafficker, but it is not obvious that it would enable him or her to achieve anything truly qualitatively different from what hiding that cash under the mattress or entrusting it to a hawaladar would provide. Meanwhile, declining the unfortunate drug dealer's custom would mean that a potentially useful source of financial intelligence is foregone.

By contrast, other regulated services are highly specialised. They are only normally used by a narrow proportion of highly wealthy or sophisticated customers, and their availability can make a significant difference to the success of a large-scale money laundering scheme. In connection with those services, liability for money laundering can kick in at a lower threshold, such as if the regulated business suspects proceeds of crime are involved, so as to incentivise the exclusion of a broad range of potentially criminal transactions.

While this is a far-reaching approach, access to such services, such as 'mirror-trading' securities purchases effected by Deutsche Bank's Moscow office for a range of high-risk customers, is not essential to any plausible conception of human flourishing.[274] On the other hand, they can be used to facilitate large-scale and sophisticated money laundering that cannot be easily replicated without access to comparable, specialised services. Meanwhile, the human impact of derisking in connection with such services is inherently modest. One can rightly sympathise with Iranian doctors unable to set up a bank account in the UK solely on account of their nationality, but few would be outraged at the kind of 'derisking' whereby a customer is wrongly denied access to top-flight investment banking facilities. This is not to suggest that the latter state of affairs is desirable, but the adverse impact of getting things wrong is rather modest.

If one accepts this logic, it suggests a three-tier stratification of regulated services based on (a) whether or not they are essential to a fulfilling ordinary, day-to-day life in a modern economy and (b) whether or not they provide significant advantages for money laundering that cannot easily be replicated without access to those services. The three tiers include basic services, or public utilities, that are subject to financial surveillance but must be provided to the general public, subject only to minimal threshold requirements; general services, which remain subject to the kind of AML regulation we have today; and specialised services, to which suspicion-based liability for facilitating money laundering attaches. This tripartite division is summarised in Figure 3.6.

This stratification of regulated services into basic services, general services and specialised services requires drawing some lines that might be difficult to set. However, it will generate welcome additional clarity. It will also mark a step away from the one-size-fits-all approach that characterises AML regulation. There is absolutely no reason why basic banking or money transmission should be treated on the

[274] FCA, 'Final Notice: Deutsche Bank', 30 January 2017.

FIGURE 3.6 Regulatory objectives by the nature of the service

same footing as investment banking. Furthermore, existing incentive structures lead to perverse outcomes. Since those who seek access to basic services generally have less money to spend than those looking for specialised services, they are the most likely ones to be derisked, which leads to loss of access to potentially valuable financial intelligence with no tangible upside.

One challenge this approach might give rise to is the financial viability of providing basic services. Since reporting obligations will continue to be attached to the provision of such services if a suspicion of money laundering exists, regulated businesses will bear the costs of such reporting, which may or may not be economical in light of the revenue generated by the customer's activities. There may not be any easy, or at least any cost-free, solution to this conundrum, although one might hope that cost-efficient approaches could be identified. In any event, this approach is vastly preferable to existing derisking, which marginalises swathes of customers while depriving law enforcement agencies of the potentially high-value intelligence that the AML regime was set up to generate.

3.5.6 *Modified Reporting Regime*

Finally, the last major category of proposed solutions to the challenges of undirected deputisation is the departure from SAR filing and introduction of a modified reporting regime. As discussed previously, SARs fulfil the dual functions of alerting the FIU to suspicious activity and providing the FIU with information that it might not otherwise have had. However, one might wonder whether SARs justify their privileged position as the *only* form of AML reporting required by the FATF Recommendations, particularly in light of the challenges associated with defensive reporting that have become apparent since the idea of SARs was first internationalised.

The diversity of other possible approaches to reporting opens up ample opportunities for countries to experiment with various systems.[275] One area of particularly notable recent developments has been the attempts to put into operation the so-called privacy-enhancing (or privacy-preserving) technologies.[276] Despite some variation in what they entail and how they operate, the basic idea is enabling the FIU to query data held in the private sector so as to identify suspicious activity without that data being divulged in bulk to the government. One example is 'federated learning', or a system whereby algorithms developed by the FIU run on bank databases and only once a match occurs is the relevant information disclosed to the FIU.[277] The benefits of such a system include alleviating reliance on reporting by regulated businesses, especially insofar as subjective standards such as 'suspicion' are involved, while eschewing bulk transfer of data to the government.

The implications of privacy-enhancing technologies resemble those of introducing retail CBDCs. In either case, regulated businesses' – primarily, banks' – role as intermediaries who decide what information to report is diminished. From a law enforcement perspective, this is a positive development because it reduces the difficulty of aligning banks' incentives and priorities with law enforcement needs. The downside is that whatever limited role banks are now playing in safeguarding customers' financial privacy will be further eroded by vesting the government with greater powers to access the information it wants directly. This is yet another example of the trade-offs inherent in the AML regime.

3.6 LAWYERS: A DIFFICULT CASE

In his accounts of life at the criminal bar, Horace Rumpole, the fictional barrister created by John Mortimer QC, muses on his relationship to proceeds of crime through Rumpole's representation of the Timson family:

> [T]hat huge clan of South London villains whose selfless devotion to crime has kept the Rumpoles in such luxuries as Vim, Gumption, sliced bread and saucepan scourers over the years, not to mention the bare necessities of life, such as gin, tonic and cooking claret from Pommeroy's Wine Bar.[278]

As this passage makes abundantly clear, Rumpole is not prone to scruples over his retainers being paid from the proceeds of the Timsons' many crimes. Nor is there

[275] For proposals to that effect, see Helena Wood, David Artingstall, Haylea Campbell and Anton Moiseienko, 'Known Unknowns: Plugging the UK's Intelligence Gaps on Money Laundering Involving Professional Services Providers', *RUSI Occasional Paper*, 2018, 54–55.

[276] See Nick J. Maxwell, 'Innovation and Discussion Paper: Case Studies of the Use of Privacy Preserving Analysis to Tackle Financial Crime' (Version 1.3), *Future of Financial Intelligence Sharing (FFIS) Research Programme*, January 2021.

[277] Ibid, 40.

[278] Jonh Mortimer, *The First Rumpole Omnibus* (Penguin, 1983) 39.

any doubt, given his ironclad commitment to treating everyone as innocent unless proven otherwise, that he would not take kindly to any requirement to report his clients' suspicious activities. In short, it is fair to say that he would be unlikely to be a fan of AML regulation for lawyers.

Many real, flesh-and-blood legal professionals share Rumpole's inclinations. So far, this chapter has considered the challenges associated with excluding proceeds of crime from the legitimate economy and surveilling the financial activities of suspected criminals. In the legal profession sector, both the exclusionary and surveillance paradigm are particularly problematic and give rise to especially difficult dilemmas. The gist of them is encapsulated colourfully in this anonymous comment left under an article published in the UK's Law Society Gazette:

> Money Laundering Regulations and our responsibilities as lawyers in respect of them, are frankly a cancer on the underpinnings of our profession. If I am instructed to defend a client in criminal proceedings and he tells me that he committed multiple murders, I must not tell anyone. Yet, if he instructs me to buy a house and he tells me he saved for his deposit by selling bootleg CDs, I'm expected to snitch on my own client. How ridiculous.[279]

3.6.1 *Lawyers and Money Laundering*

The overarching issues arising in the context of the legal profession are the same as elsewhere: first, which services should be subject to AML regulation and which should not; and, secondly, how the precise regulatory requirements should be adjusted to the nature of the specific service. The FATF's current scheme is broadly structured around the divide between litigation work, which is not subject to AML regulation, and transactional work, which is.[280] While this is a sensible approach, one can question both the blanket exclusion of litigation services and the one-size-fits-all regulatory treatment of transactional services, as discussed below.

The FATF included 'lawyers, notaries, [and] other independent legal professionals' within the scope of its 40 Recommendations in 2003 along with other DNFBPs.[281] Legal representation in litigation, whether criminal or civil, does not fall within the scope of the FATF Recommendations. Instead, the Recommendations are limited to a range of activities that, broadly speaking, involve transactional work:

- buying and selling of real estate;
- managing of client money, securities or other assets;

[279] Anonymous comment to Jonathan Goldsmith, 'Who Decides Whether the Client Is Telling the Truth?', *The Law Society Gazette* (13 March 2024) www.lawgazette.co.uk/commentary-and-opinion/who-decides-whether-the-client-is-telling-the-truth/5119037.article.

[280] FATF, *International Standards on Combatting Money Laundering and the Financing of Terrorism & Proliferation*, Recommendation 22.

[281] FATF, *The Forty Recommendations*, 2003, Recommendation 12.

- management of bank, savings or securities accounts;
- organisation of contributions for the creation, operation or management of companies; and
- creation, operation or management of legal persons or arrangements, and buying and selling of business entities.[282]

The inclusion of lawyers within the ambit of the FATF Recommendations reflects a long-standing history of their complicity in money laundering. The trail of lawyers' involvement in financial crime reaches many decades back. For instance, one may recall that one of the questions foreshadowed by the Kefauver Committee in the US was that of lawyers' and accountants' responsibility for facilitating financial crime.[283] The IRS agent Robert Mazur encountered a complicit lawyer and accountant on his first undercover assignment.[284] Nathan Markowitz, a Los Angeles attorney, was mentioned as a driving force behind money laundering via Garfield Bank in *The Cash Connection*.[285] An example of those issues brought out into the public in the US was an undercover journalist sting organised by the investigative journalism outlet Global Witness and aired on CBS's *60 Minutes* TV show that involved purported representatives of a corrupt African minister asking thirteen New York lawyers, including then-president of the ABA, on advice for anonymous movement of funds into the US. Of all these lawyers, only one declined representation.[286]

There is plenty of evidence of the same issues arising in other jurisdictions. In the UK, solicitor Bhadresh Gohil was convicted of helping the Nigerian state governor James Ibori launder the proceeds of his crime to buy a private jet, as were Ibori's two financial advisors.[287] In Australia, eminent solicitors specialising in criminal law across multiple states were convicted based on money laundering allegations.[288] In Canada, a leaked report prepared by FINTRAC, the Canadian FIU, for the Federation of the

[282] FATF, *International Standards on Combatting Money Laundering and the Financing of Terrorism & Proliferation*, Recommendation 22.

[283] See Chapter 2.

[284] Robert Mazur, *The Infiltrator: Undercover in the World of Drug Barons and Dirty Banks* (Corgi Books, 2015) Ch 1.

[285] President's Commission on Organized Crime, *The Cash Connection: Organized Crime, Financial Institutions and Money Laundering*, 1984, 45.

[286] 'Undercover Investigation of American Lawyers Reveals Role of Overseas Territories in Moving Suspect Money into the United States', *Global Witness*, 12 February 2016, www.globalwitness.org/en/press-releases/undercover-investigation-american-lawyers-reveals-role-overseas-territories-moving-suspect-money-united-states/. This undercover experiment is discussed in detail in Chuck Collins, *The Wealth Hoarders: How Billionaires Pay Millions to Hide Trillions* (Polity Press, 2021).

[287] *R v Gohil* [2014] EWCA Crim 1393. See also *R v Preko* [2015] EWCA Crim 42; [2015] All ER (D) 50 (Feb) (concerning Ibori's banker) and *R v McCann* [2011] EWCA Crim 2038 (concerning Ibori's financial advisor).

[288] Australian Federal Police, 'Operation Elbrus Court Outcome Revealed: Lawyer Jailed for 12 Years', 21 March 2023, www.afp.gov.au/news-centre/media-release/operation-elbrus-court-outcome-revealed-lawyer-jailed-12-years; Benita Kolovos, 'Vic Solicitor Jailed for Laundering $400k', *Blue Mountains Gazette*, 11 February 2020, www.bluemountainsgazette.com.au/story/6624511/vic-solicitor-jailed-for-laundering-400k/.

Law Societies of Canada in 2022 lays out how Canadian lawyers have been 'implicated in a wide range of suspicious activity'.[289] The list goes on and on.

In some places, like the UK, the AML regulation of lawyers was accepted, comparatively speaking, without much demur. In other countries, especially Australia and the US, it has proven to be a major stumbling block. Despite the FATF's indications that both countries are non-compliant with the FATF Recommendations,[290] their governments have continued to postpone the implementation of FATF-required changes in the face of vigorous opposition from the legal profession. In the US, the Enablers Act, which would have extended AML regulation to DNFBPs, was considered in 2022 but shelved by Congress until further notice.[291] In Australia, the so-called Tranche 2, as the expansion of AML regulation to DNFBPs came to be known, was floated multiple times, with the latest governmental commitment to its implementation made in early 2024 and relevant legislation finally adopted in December 2024.[292]

One of the objections frequently raised by legal professional bodies, such as the Law Council of Australia, is that there is no evidence of systematic exploitation of legal services by criminals to invest or move the proceeds of their crime.[293] What we have, the argument goes, is mere anecdotes that are insufficient to justify the imposition of additional regulatory burdens on a profession that largely consists of small practices or solo practitioners.[294]

The plausibility of this argument is undermined by existing systematic studies of lawyers' involvement in money laundering, such as Katie Benson's groundbreaking monograph, which brought together a wealth of open-source studies and analysed various modes of lawyers' involvement in money laundering, ranging from unwitting involvement to wilful complicity.[295] Nor is the argument based on lawyers'

[289] Zak Vescera, 'Canadian Lawyers Play Key Role in Money Laundering, Says Financial Intelligence Report', *CTV News*, 27 June 2024. The original FINTRAC report is available at https://s3.documentcloud.org/documents/24778544/fintrac-2022-report.pdf.

[290] FATF, *Horizontal Review of Gatekeepers' Technical Compliance Related to Corruption*, July 2024.

[291] Will Fitzgibbon, 'US Senate Blocks Major Anti-Money Laundering Bill, the Enablers Act', *ICIJ*, 12 December 2022, www.icij.org/investigations/pandora-papers/us-senate-blocks-major-anti-money-laundering-bill-the-enablers-act/.

[292] AUSTRAC, *Money Laundering in Australia: National Risk Assessment*, July 2024, 15.

[293] Dr Jacoba Brasch QC, 'Opening Statement at the Senate References Committee on Legal and Constitutional Affairs Inquiry on the Adequacy and Efficacy of Australia's Anti-Money Laundering and Counter-Terrorism Financing (AML/CTF) Regime', *Law Council of Australia*, 10 November 2021, 3 ('[t]here is no evidence, much less credible evidence which supports a conclusion that the Australian legal profession is a high or moderate-risk sector').

[294] The concern about disproportionate regulatory burdens is the focus of much of the criticism of AML laws levelled by the ABA in the US. See ABA, 'Gatekeeper Regulations on Attorneys', www.americanbar.org/advocacy/governmental_legislative_work/priorities_policy/independence_of_the_legal_profession/bank_secrecy_act/ and the letters cited therein.

[295] Katie Benson, *Lawyers and the Proceeds of Crime: The Facilitation of Money Laundering and its Control* (Routledge, 2020). The book fills some of the research gaps previously identified in David Middleton and Michael Levi, 'Let Sleeping Lawyers Lie: Organized Crime, Lawyers and the Regulation of Legal Services' (2015) 55(4) *Brit J Criminology* 647.

supposed irrelevance to money laundering schemes tenable given the sheer regularity with which lawyers feature in major money laundering scandals, as discussed above. Despite the saying 'the plural of anecdotes is not data', sometimes the abundance of anecdotes is such that it must amount to data.

There is, however, another, more nuanced and substantive variation of the same concern. As with any other category of regulated professionals, complicit lawyers will not abide by AML regulation in any event. The appropriate legal tool to address their conduct is therefore not regulation but criminal liability. By contrast, AML regulation is most helpful as a means of inducing compliant businesses to put in place controls that exclude the proceeds of crime from the economy and provide law enforcement agencies with financial intelligence. This is where countervailing considerations, such as the value of universal access to legal services and the confidentiality of legal advice, become particularly prominent, with a number of areas apt to test our intuitions as to whether AML regulation should apply.

3.6.2 *Exclusion of Proceeds of Crime*

If one imagined AML regulation that prevented legal practitioners from accepting suspected proceeds of crime as remuneration for representing clients at criminal trials, the absurdity of that state of affairs would be easily apparent. While it would serve the purpose of preventing criminals from benefitting from the proceeds of their illegal activity, it would also undermine, if not obliterate, the right to defence in a criminal trial. The effects of such a requirement would be particularly profound since the legal practitioner would need to decide whether they accept the client's brief before any allegations against the client are tested in court. It is not surprising, therefore, and entirely appropriate that no AML regulatory rules apply to representation in criminal trials, even if this means that there is a category of legal practitioners who, quite literally, make a living out of the proceeds of crime.

Nor does AML regulation extend to representation in civil litigation. This is a less self-evident limitation. On the one hand, in principle the values of equal access to justice and legal representation have the same purchase in the civil context as they do in the criminal one. On the other hand, not all forms of civil litigation are equally essential to human flourishing, and one could argue that the ability to bring some kinds of claims can legitimately be subject to more controls than others. That is precisely the line of thinking that animates the ongoing discussions of the so-called strategic lawsuits against public participation (SLAPPs), which are typically understood as frivolous libel or privacy-related claims brought against civil society activists, journalists or publishers with a view to wasting their financial resources through litigation rather than prevailing on the merits.[296] If, as some propose, SLAPPs can

[296] Joanna Dawson, 'SLAPPs: Strategic Litigation against Public Participation', *House of Commons Library, Research Briefing* No 9962, February 2024.

be subject to a bespoke case management process, so as to filter out unmeritorious claims at an early stage in the proceedings,[297] so could lawyers be required to carry out CDD checks and report suspicions that a lawsuit is being funded through proceeds of crime. The real challenge, as with any SLAPP-related reform proposal, is distinguishing between SLAPPs and other, presumptively more innocuous forms of civil litigation.

Professional legal bodies sometimes point to lawyers' ethical duties as the insurmountable impediment to any extension of AML obligations to litigation work. It is, the argument goes, a lawyer's sacrosanct duty to accept any client seeking court representation and render one's services without fear or favour. It is not, therefore, the lawyer's province to pass a judgment on whether the client might be involved in crime, let alone to decline to act or report the client's activities on the government on that basis. While this argument is put forth with particular vigour in the context of litigation, some also extend the same reasoning to all legal work, including transactional services. For instance, as discussed previously, the ABA's Samuel Buffone raised Sixth Amendment concerns when opposing the proposed money laundering offence in his congressional testimony before the enactment of the Money Laundering Control Act 1986.[298] The Sixth Amendment to the US Constitution protects the right to counsel, which does not exist in English or Australian law.[299]

Such arguments are hyperbolic at their core. Even in jurisdictions where the 'cab rank rule' obliges barristers to take up any case irrespective of the client's identity, activities or beliefs, solicitors are not bound by that rule at all, despite the essential role that they, too, play in the conduct of litigation.[300] One may wonder how a rule can be at once indispensable to the rule of law and inapplicable to a large swathe of the legal profession. Furthermore, the cab rank rule does not exist in jurisdictions without a split legal profession, including the US, outside the narrow context of court-appointed lawyers.[301] In those jurisdictions where it does apply, such as the

297 In the UK, such a process has been introduced under Section 194 of the Economic Crime and Corporate Transparency Act 2023.

298 US Senate Subcommittee on Financial Institutions Supervision, Regulation, and Insurance, *Tax Evasion, Drug Trafficking, and Money Laundering as They Involve Financial Institutions* (US Government Printing Office, 1986) 972 (Samuel J. Buffone, White Collar Crime Committee, American Bar Association).

299 In *Dietrich v R* (1992) 177 CLR 292; [1992] HCA 57, the High Court of Australia highlighted that a criminal trial must be fair, but the attributes of a fair trial must be assessed holistically and do not necessarily entail legal representation.

300 For a comprehensive overview of the cab rank rule, see John Flood and Morten Hviid, *The Cab Rank Rule: Its Meaning and Purpose in the New Legal Services Market*, Report for the Legal Services Board, 2013.

301 Laurel S. Terry and José Carlos Llerena Robles, 'The Relevance of FATF's Recommendations and Fourth Round of Mutual Evaluations to the Legal Profession' (2018) 42(2) *Fordham Int'l LJ* 627, 686–687.

UK, any barrister can effortlessly evade its application by pleading lack of time, and no one has ever been sanctioned for the breach of the rule.[302]

All in all, the notion that requiring lawyers to screen for proceeds of crime in respect of clients seeking litigation representation is inimical to the rule of law, is grossly overstated. It is not appropriate when criminal representation is concerned, but otherwise the nature of the litigation involved needs to be considered. The historical origins of the cab rank rule are murky, but the best guess we have places its genesis in the eighteenth century, possibly with Lord Erskine's representation of Thomas Paine at his trial for seditious libel in connection with publishing the second part of the *Rights of Man*.[303] The rule that has thus emerged has little to do with the question of whether, say, an English barrister can legitimately be required to inquire into the sources of the client's wealth and funds if approached to represent an overseas billionaire in a libel claim, divorce proceedings or international commercial arbitration. Similar discussions have started to emerge in the context of how lawyers think about their provision of legal services to legal but arguably problematic industries, such as big tobacco or fossil fuel companies.[304]

So far, however, the legal profession's staunch opposition to *any* form of AML regulation in some jurisdictions has stymied any potential conversation about expanding the FATF's existing catalogue or regulated services. As for transactional work, there is little doubt that it is appropriately subject to AML regulation, even if it does on occasion lead to some individuals' or companies' inability to receive legal services that they would otherwise obtain. Even if one considers the kinds of services that could be deemed essential to one's ability to lead a fulfilling life, such as real estate conveyancing, the societal interest in ensuring that they are not used to enable the investment of proceeds of crime appears to be overwhelming, particularly in view of the extensive evidence of real estate being used as a vehicle for storing and amassing illegally obtained wealth. Other AML-regulated legal activities on the FATF's catalogue, such as the establishment of companies or management of business structures, encroach on the domain of broader advisory services, which are also provided by a slew of other regulated professionals, and do not raise remotely the same rule of law or access to justice concerns as litigation representation. There is, therefore, a strong case in favour of AML regulation applying in relation to such services.

302 Jonathan Goldsmith, 'Cab-Rank Rule: Yes or No?', *The Law Society Gazette*, 24 October 2023, www.lawgazette.co.uk/commentary-and-opinion/cab-rank-rule-yes-or-no/5117656.article.

303 Geoffrey Robertson, *The Tyrannicide Brief* (Random House, 2010) 314.

304 Steven Vaughan and Emma Oakley, '"Gorilla Exceptions" and the Ethically Apathetic Corporate Lawyer' (2016) 19(1) *Legal Ethics* 50, 66 (drawing on interviews with fifty-seven corporate finance lawyers in London, recounting in particular an interview with a self-proclaimed environment lover who said they 'might struggle a bit' with a client who says 'we've got this amazing mandate to build a something on the mountains of DRC that currently are home to 500 gorillas').

3.6.3 *Financial Surveillance*

While a lawyer may decide to turn down a client as a result of AML rules, as discussed previously, there is no legal requirement to do so unless the lawyer is sufficiently convinced that proceeds of crime are involved that to proceed with representation would expose that lawyer to a risk of criminal liability for money laundering. There is, however, an obligation to report the client's activities if a suspicion of money laundering arises.

The compatibility of this requirement with legal professional privilege and client confidentiality has been much discussed. The terminology and law differ across jurisdictions, but legal professional privilege – or attorney-client privilege – can be understood as the legally protected confidentiality of communications between the lawyer and the client. The privilege belongs to the client, not the lawyer, and can therefore only be waived by the client.[305] Client confidentiality is a broader principle of professional ethics that extends beyond privileged material and requires the lawyer to keep any information about the client or his or her affairs confidential so far as possible.[306]

Both of those concepts are in tension with suspicious activity reporting or, indeed, any other form of AML reporting that a particular jurisdiction may introduce. This is recognised by the FATF. In contrast to the treatment of bank secrecy, which has been effectively displaced since the earliest days of the FATF Recommendations,[307] legal professional privilege is preserved. According to the FATF, information about a client's affairs is only reportable insofar as it is not covered by legal professional privilege.[308]

This crucial concession to the age-old special treatment afforded to legal advice is susceptible of two interpretations. One school of thought holds that the conflict between suspicious activity reporting obligations and legal professional privilege is thereby resolved.[309] The other view is that the resulting landscape is so contradictory and fraught with difficulty that the AML regulation of lawyers cannot be meaningfully implemented. If suspicious activity reporting requirements and legal professional privilege cannot be observed at the same time, then either one of the two will be disregarded in practice, or arbitrary choices will be made by the practitioners as to which one to prioritise.[310]

305 International Bar Association, 'IBA Statement in Defence of the Principle of Lawyer-Client Confidentiality', 2022, 8.

306 *Scottish Legal Complaints Commission v Murray et al* [2022] CSIH 46, para 27. See also 'Scottish Court Clarifies the Distinction between Confidentiality and Legal Privilege', *Pinsent Masons*, 23 December 2022.

307 See Chapter 2.

308 FATF, *International Standards on Combatting Money Laundering and the Financing of Terrorism & Proliferation*, Interpretive Note to Recommendation 23, para 1.

309 Interview with Bruce Zagaris, 4 December 2023.

310 Interview with a US lawyer specialising in AML/CTF (B), 27 November 2023; interview with a US academic lawyer specialising in AML/CTF, 1 December 2023.

The treatment of this conundrum differs across jurisdictions. In the UK, where AML regulation of lawyers has been in place for over two decades, the Law Society has published detailed guidance as to the circumstances that are – or, correspondingly, are not – covered by legal professional privilege.[311] UK lawyers appear to have largely embraced the notion that SAR reporting and legal professional privilege can be reconciled.[312] For instance, Sarah Kebbell's insightful analysis of forty interviews with compliance experts from the UK's top fifty law firms notes that 'privilege was not a notable theme within the data':

> A number of participants simply noted that privilege was a factor to be considered when determining whether or not to make a SAR, but no further issues with privilege were evident from the interview data.[313]

Press reports disclose occasional instances of UK lawyers playing a valuable role in the detection of criminal activities as a result of SAR submissions. For example, *The Times* reported in March 2024 that a law enforcement inquiry into the property purchase of a fugitive cryptocurrency entrepreneur suspected of building a £3.4-billion cryptocurrency Ponzi scheme was triggered by an 'alarm' raised by a lawyer at a London law firm – presumably referring to the filing of a SAR.[314]

By contrast, the Canadian Supreme Court ruled in 2015 that the introduction of AML regulation in respect of lawyers was unconstitutional due to the incompatibility of SAR reporting obligations with the attorney-client privilege.[315] The Court implicitly rejected a UK-style view that the two could co-exist depending on whether the privilege applies but did this without any examination of comparative experience from other common law jurisdictions or any meaningful engagement with the FATF Recommendations.

In the US, the ABA has forcefully put forth a similar view.[316] The changes adopted to the ABA Model Rules in early 2024 require US lawyers to carry out limited CDD checks and retain relevant documentation but do not provide for any reporting obligations,[317] and the ABA's official position is to oppose any such obligations. The approach is similar to the voluntary due diligence arrangements that

[311] The Law Society, *Legal Sector Affinity Group Anti-Money Laundering Guidance for the Legal Sector*, March 2023.

[312] Interview with Dr Katie Benson, 1 July 2024.

[313] Kebbell, *Anti-Money Laundering Compliance and the Legal Profession*, Ch 6.

[314] David Brown, 'How Crypto Queen Built £3.4bn Empire and Dreamt of Buying a Country', *The Times*, 20 March 2024.

[315] *Canada (Attorney General) v Federation of Law Societies of Canada* [2015] 1 SCR 401.

[316] ABA, 'Gatekeeper Regulations on Attorneys'.

[317] Rule 1.16 of ABA Model Rules, www.americanbar.org/groups/professional_responsibility/publications/model_rules_of_professional_conduct/rule_1_16_declining_or_terminating_representation/. For commentary, see Monique D. Hayes, Susan A. Maslow, Shannon Arthur Singleton and James J. Wheaton, 'Has a New Day Dawned? The Corporate Transparency Act and Amended ABA Model Rule 1.16', ABA, 26 March 2024, www.americanbar.org/groups/business_law/resources/business-law-today/2024-march/corporate-transparency-act-amended-aba-model-rule-1–16.

the Swiss banking sector put in place in the 1970s, except that Swiss banks accepted governmental oversight of the quality of their CDD measures,[318] whereas the ABA considers that, too, to be an outrage upon the independence of the profession.

This severing of the link between CDD and SAR reporting raises the question of the purpose behind CDD. In the ABA's proposed model, lawyers are meant to use CDD to identify circumstances where they are used to facilitate a money laundering scheme, in which case they should refuse to act. One key limitation of the ABA Model Rules is that it does not specify the level of certainty, or state of mind, that the lawyer must form in order to refuse to act. Definitive knowledge that proceeds of crime are involved will hardly ever be achieved, even in the most suspicious of circumstances, yet it is not clear whether any state of mind short of that would trigger the ethical obligation to turn down the customer or discontinue the relationship. The lack of clarity around this obvious issue is yet another indication of the abiding lack of seriousness with which some legal professional associations continue to treat the issue of money laundering.

In summary, both exclusion and surveillance generate particular challenges in the legal profession. While no easy solution is apparent, one possible way forward is distinguishing with greater granularity between the AML/CTF obligations attaching to representation in criminal trials, certain types of civil litigation and transactional work, with only the former category of legal representation subject to a blanket exclusion from AML regulation. Meanwhile, drawing a satisfactory line between those circumstances that are covered by legal professional privilege and those where SARs can appropriately be filed will likely remain an acute challenge for the foreseeable future.

3.7 CONCLUSION

Chapter 2 traced the emergence of criminal and regulatory AML rules, which has been dominated by concerns about the witting or unwitting involvement of legitimate businesses in the investment or use of proceeds of crime. These concerns have resulted in a legal framework that vests regulated businesses with the responsibility to detect and report suspicious activities as well as avoiding the knowing facilitation of money laundering. These objectives of exclusion and surveillance are commendable on their own terms but involve multiple dilemmas and tensions that have never been satisfactorily resolved by policymakers, whether internationally or domestically.

This chapter has outlined those dilemmas and tensions in detail. In particular, it has demonstrated how the broad objective of excluding proceeds of crime from the legitimate economy can be thought about more granularly in terms of complicity, that is, concern that regulated businesses should not have their integrity

[318] See Chapter 2.

compromised by involvement in crime, and disruption, that is, concern with undermining criminal activities that rely on exploring regulated services. The practical implications of this important conceptual distinction are further explored in Chapter 4, which deals with terrorist financing and targeted financial sanctions.

For the most part, however, this chapter has focused on the dilemmas and tensions inherent in the existing model of undirected deputisation, where regulated businesses are placed under a set of blunt and contradictory incentives as they are expected to counteract money laundering. Exclusion of proceeds of crime from the legitimate economy and their surveillance point in the same direction insofar as they minimise the likelihood of money laundering going undetected, but they can also conflict with each other if swathes of the population lose access to regulated services. Furthermore, each of those objectives sits uneasily with other values and principles we hold dear as society, including the presumption of innocence, understood here in the broad sense of treating fellow citizens as presumptively innocent of criminal wrongdoing, and financial privacy.

These tensions are evident and long-standing, but the difficulty of prioritising one over the others is such that we have never had any coherent scheme for doing so. The ever-evolving renegotiation of boundaries between financial surveillance and financial privacy is a case in point. The global community has largely done away with bank secrecy vis-à-vis governments, but the ability to conceal one's property via corporate structures and trusts continues to be the norm, despite its genesis as an unintended consequence of corporate limited liability. The emergence of virtual assets and CBDCs further shed light on the absence of any coherent conception of the boundaries between surveillance and privacy.

4

Zero Tolerance

Terrorist Financing and Targeted Sanctions

4.1 INTRODUCTION

So far, this book's analysis has focused on money laundering: the crime of using, moving or hiding the proceeds of crime. The establishment of money laundering as a distinct criminal offence and the emergence of a regulatory infrastructure around it have proved to be momentous developments in the fight against organised crime, although whether the regime delivers value for money is as intensely controversial now as ever before. AML rules, however, are not the only component of today's global financial crime regime. This chapter focuses on two other key elements, namely CTF and targeted financial sanctions, and the challenges that they present.

The commonly used abbreviation AML/CTF speaks to the strong connection between AML and CTF in terms of legal and regulatory requirements, government infrastructure and compliance practices that underpin each of those regimes. The key difference is self-evident. While money laundering involves the use of proceeds of crime, terrorist financing can feature, and often does feature, legitimately acquired funds that are directed towards terrorist use. Some therefore describe terrorist financing as 'reverse money laundering' and question whether the amalgamation of AML and CTF rules into a single regulatory regime is appropriate.[1]

As this chapter discusses, a well-thought-through account of the CTF framework requires considering several differences compared to the AML regime. One of them relates to the reasons for excluding terrorist funds from the legitimate economy. In addition to preventing the complicity of legitimate businesses and terrorist financing and disrupting terrorist financing operations, the rationale of denying terrorists

[1] For example, R. T. Naylor writes of 'the USA's numismatic jihad' (financial warfare) aimed at making AML and CTF measures 'both tributary to the newly expanded national-security functions at home and abroad': R. T. Naylor, *Satanic Purses* (McGill-Queen's University Press, 2006) 52, 143–151. For a less colourful expression of similar arguments, see Nicholas Ryder, *The Financial War on Terrorism: A Review of Counter-Terrorist Financing Strategies since 2001* (Routledge, 2015) 5, 173–182.

access to funds comes into play. This gives rise to debates about whether such denial is realistic and how that might depend on the terrorist actor being targeted.

Another significant shift is the movement from excluding *criminal funds* towards excluding criminals, in this case terrorists, *themselves* from the legitimate economy. This is effected by means of targeted financial sanctions. Such sanctions are in and of themselves an important pillar of current responses to organised and economic crime. They have evolved originally in the context of tackling the activities of foreign governments, rebel groups and dictatorships, but have since then become a mainstay of measures against organised crime groups and terrorist actors. The advent of targeted sanctions involves a move from general exclusion, which is characterised by requiring regulated businesses to detect proceeds of crime, to targeted exclusion, which mandates all businesses to avoid any interactions with, and freeze the assets of, targeted persons. The challenges of targeted exclusion present a new array of considerations for policymakers and businesses alike.

This chapter first discusses the history of CTF measures and targeted sanctions. Then, it considers the challenges presented by targeted exclusion, which arise in the context of CTF as well as being inherent to the operation of targeted financial sanctions. Finally, this chapter parses out the difficult case of coerced payments, including criminal ransoms, terrorist ransoms and ransomware payouts.

4.2 COUNTERTERRORIST FINANCING AND SANCTIONS

As discussed in Chapter 2, the development of the AML regime can largely be traced across two tracks. The first one is the evolution of criminal law rules about money laundering, which with time came to classified as a distinct criminal offence separate from complicity in the predicate crime. The other track is the development of regulatory requirements binding upon certain sectors of the economy, such as those pertaining to the reporting of suspicious activities and CDD. The same is largely true in the context of terrorist financing. There is, however, another relevant source of influence that must be remarked upon. That is the law and policy surrounding the treatment of rebel and insurgency groups since that, for much of the history, has been the primary wellspring of sectarian conflict and therefore terrorism. While the current global focus on terrorism financing for most intents and purposes dates back to 9/11, CTF measures had been in place before then, too. That forms the natural starting point for an examination of the contemporary CTF framework.

4.2.1 *Counterterrorist Financing before 9/11*

Up until the modern era, most terrorist organisations were small, operated on a modest scale and therefore did not require – nor could they procure – significant injections of funds:

> [T]he terrorist movements of the nineteenth century were poor. Outside support was rare. The gift of a million francs from a wealthy Frenchwoman to her friend the Spanish anarchist Francisco Ferrer was atypical. The Irish Revolutionary Brotherhood was created in 1858 with an American donation of $400. Terrorists were often forced to turn to crime to fund their activities. In the early twentieth century, a group of Indian terrorists tried, and failed, to counterfeit banknotes, before turning to burglary. In France, the gang led by the anarchist Joseph Bonnot specialized in armed robberies before being apprehended by the police in 1912.[2]

As Jodi Vittori observes, some of the terrorist groups of that era may have been government-funded, including the Serbian nationalist group the Black Hand, which instigated the assassination of Archduke Franz Ferdinand in 1914.[3] Still, the point about the relatively modest scale of such groups' operations and correspondingly limited expenses stands, even if on some occasions – such as Franz Ferdinand's murder – the effects could hardly be overstated.

The closest modern progenitor of CTF measures is the raft of restrictions introduced by the British government against Irish nationalist terrorist groups from the 1970s onwards, most prominently the Irish Republican Army (IRA).[4] From the 1970s, the UK government has maintained a proscription regime, which penalises, among other things, the provision of financial support to a designated organisation. That presages a model of financial constriction that has since been applied internationally to many alleged terrorist organisations, including Al Qaeda and ISIS.

The heavy-handed nature of the British counterterrorism regime has not escaped the notice of commentators.[5] That said, the draconian effect of the provisions and the relative ease with which they could be put into effect have been sidelined by the pressing public interest in protection against acts of terrorism. The lynchpin of the UK's pre-9/11 counterterrorism regime was the Prevention of Terrorism (Temporary Provisions) Act 1974, enacted into law as a response to the bombings of two pubs in Birmingham, which left twenty-one people dead. As Clive Walker observed, writing in 1986, the law was widely presented as a swift and radical response to the bombings, but in reality, the bombings were a catalyst for the adoption of multiple provisions that had been developed in draft form over the preceding several years:

2 Gérard Chaliand and Arnaud Blin, *The History of Terrorism: From Antiquity to ISIS* (University of California Press, 2016) 182.

3 Jodi Vittori, *Terrorist Financing and Resourcing* (Palgrave Macmillan, 2011) 54.

4 Also known as the Provisional IRA or the 'Provos'. For more on the IRA, see Colin P. Clarke, *Terrorism, Inc.: The Financing of Terrorism, Insurgency, and Irregular Warfare* (Praeger Security International, 2015) Ch 2.

5 See Gerard Hogan and Clive Walker, *Political Violence and the Law in Ireland* (Manchester University Press, 1989) 138–143, noting criticism of the alleged unevenness in the application of proscription powers, focused almost exclusively on IRA rather than loyalist supporters in the 1980s, and of the potential impact of proscription on the democratic process in Northern Ireland.

> Indeed, it would have been surprising if the government had ignored the continuing mayhem [of escalating IRA attacks] and did not have counter-measures 'on the stocks' and ready to roll down the parliamentary slipway at the appropriate moment.[6]

The parallels with the enactment by the US of the Patriot Act in 2001 could not be any clearer.[7] The overpowering impulse towards cracking down on terrorism – if need be, at the expense of the safeguards that would otherwise be cherished – is further evident from the continued mischaracterisation of the British prescription regime as temporary, despite it becoming abundantly clear some years into its operation that this was a misnomer. Indeed, the proscription of the IRA remains in place up until now, expanded and augmented by the addition of multiple other entities to the list of proscribed organisations, including violent Islamic political groups and, since 2023, Russia's Wagner Group.[8]

Despite the seriousness with which the British have treated their homegrown terrorism, as well as similar measures and approaches taken across the rest of the Western world, up until 9/11 CTF measures had had a certain rudimentary quality to them. It may be recalled, for example, that in 1980 the Council of Europe issued a non-binding Recommendation calling for the matching of bank notes and a perfunctory form of CDD so as to prevent left-wing radical groups from capitalising on the proceeds of their robberies and kidnapping.[9] There is no evidence of the efficacy of those measures, and their non-binding nature ensured that there was no meaningful follow-up on their implementation.

For a long time, that was the extent of international norm-making in the domain of CTF. Disagreements as to what terrorism means, who is involved in it, or whether it can ever be justified – aptly encapsulated in the cliché 'one man's terrorist is another man's freedom fighter' – undermined cooperation even between otherwise close allies. For instance, the IRA, despite its proscription in the UK, could successfully raise funds in Boston and other North American cities through its charity arm NORAID until its gunrunning operations drew the ire of US law enforcement.[10]

Far-reaching international responses to terrorist financing did not begin to come into effect until 1999. That year, the UN General Assembly adopted the International Convention for the Suppression of the Financing of Terrorism.

6 Clive Walker, *The Prevention of Terrorism in British Law* (Manchester University Press, 1986) 23.

7 The Patriot Act likewise comprised a range of measures that had been 'oven-ready' for a while but lacked an impetus for their adoption: interview with a US lawyer specialising in AML/CTF (A), 14 November 2023.

8 See Home Office, 'Proscribed Terrorist Groups or Organisations', updated 26 April 2024, www.gov.uk/government/publications/proscribed-terror-groups-or-organisations--2/proscribed-terrorist-groups-or-organisations-accessible-version.

9 See Chapter 1.

10 For an excellent piece of contemporary journalism, see Linda Charlton, 'Fund-Raising by a Group in U.S. Called Vital to I.R.A. Operations', *The New York Times*, 24 September 1979, www.nytimes.com/1979/09/24/archives/fundraising-by-a-group-in-us-called-vital-to-ira-operations.html.

Similar to the criminal law rules against money laundering introduced in the mid 1980s, the Convention required states parties to treat terrorist financing as a distinct criminal offence. The convention was the product of a French-led G8 initiative that had identified terrorist financing as a new frontier of combatting terrorism.[11] France itself had struggled with a spate of terrorist attacks in 1996–1997.[12]

It was the French government's view that existing counterterrorism rules could not reach the financiers of terrorist activities. Despite their centrality to the carrying out of terrorist attacks, they continued to remain one step removed from the violent attack and therefore could not be easily processed by the criminal justice systems of the time. The proposal was not universally applauded. One concern raised in response was whether ordinary criminal law of complicity could not already be successfully brought to bear against terrorist financiers and, therefore, whether a distinct criminal offence was truly necessary.[13] This discussion is reminiscent of the trajectory that the offence of the handling of stolen goods and the offence of money laundering had undergone before that, as discussed in Chapter 2.

Ultimately, the French proposal was adopted, but the Convention was a pyrrhic victory at first. Since its adoption in 1999, only four states parties – Botswana, Sri Lanka, the UK and Uzbekistan – had ratified the Convention before 9/11.[14] It is fair to say, therefore, that the necessity of going after terrorist finances had not yet imprinted itself on the collective consciousness of the world's nations.

4.2.2 *Counterterrorist Financing after 9/11*

The state of affairs changed dramatically with the terrorist attacks of 9/11. The primary driving force of that change was to be found domestically within the US. Within weeks after the attacks, President George W. Bush vowed to 'starve the terrorists of funding'.[15] The issue of how the 9/11 attackers had managed to fund their activities became one of the central focal points for the 9/11 commission set up by the US government, which ultimately concluded that the attack had cost less than $500,000 and Al Qaeda's budget had been predominantly funded with diverted charity donations, rather than Osama bin Laden's personal fortune.[16]

[11] Clifton M. Johnson, 'International Convention for the Suppression of the Financing of Terrorism' (2000) 39(2) *Int'l Legal Materials* 268.

[12] Jeremy Shapiro and Bénédicte Suzan, 'The French Experience of Counter-Terrorism' (2003) 45(1) *Survival* 67.

[13] Anthony Aust, 'Counter-Terrorism – A New Approach: The International Convention for the Suppression of the Financing of Terrorism' (2001) 5(1) *Max Planck Yearbook of United Nations Law* 285, 288.

[14] UN Treaty Collection, 'International Convention for the Suppression of the Financing of Terrorism', https://treaties.un.org/pages/ViewDetails.aspx?src=TREATY&mtdsg_no=XVIII-11&chapter=18&clang=_en.

[15] The White House, 'President Freezes Terrorists' Assets', 24 September 2001.

[16] National Commission on Terrorist Attacks upon the United States, *The 9/11 Commission Report*, July 2004, 170–172.

In October 2021, the US Patriot Act was adopted, which contained a sweeping suite of reforms to the US AML/CTF framework, including the establishment of private-to-private and public-to-private information-sharing pathways,[17] as discussed in Chapter 3, and the expansion in the list of predicate offences for money laundering.[18] Despite the appearance of speed – and perhaps haste – that the Patriot Act conveys, the reality is that it was used as a convenient conduit for the adoption of a raft of legislative reforms that had been languishing in US Congress prior to that but did not enjoy the political will to ensure their expeditious passage.[19] The Patriot Act also amended existing provisions pertaining to the reporting of suspicious activities, including those potentially related to terrorism, and the criminalisation of material support for terrorism.[20]

In the aftermath of 9/11, international goodwill towards the US was soaring high, and so was the willingness of international organisations and groups, including the FATF, to assist the US in its newly proclaimed war on terror. In 2001, therefore, the FATF adopted nine Special Recommendations with a focus on terrorist financing.[21] The nine Special Recommendations required countries to criminalise terrorist financing, to collect information on wire transfers, which were believed to have been utilised by the 9/11 attackers, and to exercise effective oversight over non-profit organisations to ensure they were not complicit in terrorist financing, among other things.[22]

Overall, however, there is little difference between AML-oriented and CTF-oriented compliance requirements. That is to say, regulated businesses need to report suspicious activities whether they relate to money laundering or terrorist financing, and the entire spectrum of other AML/CTF obligations – such as CDD, enhanced due diligence or the wire transfer rule – are meant to equally serve the detection of money laundering or the detection of terrorist financing. Very often, a business that detects suspicious activity will not be able to tell whether it relates to potential money laundering, terrorist financing or sanctions evasion. Some commentators maintain that this regime, which has originated to combat money laundering, is not truly suitable to the pursuit of terrorist financing activities, which often tend to evolve smaller amounts of money not otherwise marked by any signs of criminality due to their legitimate origin.[23] The merits of this view are considered later on in this chapter.

Another key CTF development was the recourse to targeted financial sanctions in order to freeze the assets of suspected terrorists. The first individual ever sanctioned by the UN Security Council was Osama bin Laden.[24] That happened

[17] Sections 314(a) –(b) of the Patriot Act (US), Pub. L. 107-56.

[18] Section 315 of the Patriot Act (US).

[19] Interview with a US lawyer specialising in AML/CTF (A), 14 November 2023.

[20] Sections 358, 805–807 of the Patriot Act (US).

[21] For an overview of the FATF's CTF role, see Doron Goldbarsht, *Global Counter-Terrorist Financing and Soft Law: Multi-Layered Approaches* (Edward Elgar, 2020).

[22] FATF, *IX Special Recommendations*, October 2001.

[23] See footnote 1.

[24] Interview with a Swiss sanctions expert, 5 June 2024.

before 9/11, but the extent and pace of terrorism-related sanctions designations took off after 9/11 with the establishment of the so-called 1267 Sanctions Committee.[25] The Committee was tasked with administering the UN's counterterrorism sanctions regime, specifically deciding whom to place on the sanctions list. In the early days of such sanctions, designations were made with abandon, with almost all US requests being acquiesced to by the rest of the Committee members.[26] One of the ramifications of this practice was that, even in the absence of any international consensus as to the overarching definition of 'terrorism', the ability of states' to agree on whether a particular person was an alleged terrorist rendered definitional debates moot.[27]

This laissez-faire regime underwent significant changes as due process challenges began to emerge across domestic legal systems and, especially, in the EU. The pivotal case is that of Muslim financier Yassin Kadi, who challenged the sanctions that the EU imposed upon him in implementation of the relevant UN Security Council designation. Kadi's first challenge in the CJEU's then-Court of First Instance[28] failed on the basis that the EU had no choice but to follow the UN Security Council's requirements.[29] On appeal, the Court of Justice ruled that it was in fact necessary to inquire into whether the EU's implementation of UN sanctions, as distinct from the UN sanctions themselves, contravened the EU's fundamental rights.[30] The second instalment of *Kadi* litigation before the CJEU – known as *Kadi II* – led to the conclusion that Kadi's rights had, indeed, been violated.[31]

Despite the CJEU's conceit that its review of the validity of the EU's implementation of UN sanctions did not amount to pronouncing on the lawfulness of the UN sanctions themselves, the dualist reasoning employed by the CJEU created an evident conflict between the EU's legal order and obligations under the UN Charter.[32] The legal course charted by the CJEU was controversial, but its political ramification was that the Security Council for the first time faced a genuine incentive to inject due process into its decision-making.

Compelling research by Gavin Sullivan of the University of Edinburgh suggests that this external push towards greater due process was welcomed by some members

[25] Set up under UN Security Council Resolution 1267 (1999).

[26] Interview with a Swiss sanctions expert, 5 June 2024.

[27] Gavin Sullivan, *The Law of the List: UN Counterterrorism Sanctions and the Politics of Global Security Law* (Cambridge University Press, 2020) 67–74.

[28] Now, the General Court.

[29] *Kadi v Council and Commission*, Court of First Instance, Judgment of 21 September 2005 in Case T-315/01.

[30] *Kadi and Al Barakaat v Council and Commission*, European Court of Justice, Judgment of 3 September 2008 in Joined Cases C-402/05 P and C-415/05 P.

[31] *Kadi v Commission and Council*, General Court, Judgment of 30 September 2010 in Case T-85/09; *Council and Commission v Kadi*, Court of Justice, Judgment of 18 July 2013 in Joined Cases C-584/10 P, C-593/10 P and C-595/10 P.

[32] See Juliane Kokott and Christoph Sobotta, 'The Kadi Case – Constitutional Core Values and International Law – Finding the Balance?' (2012) 23(4) *EJIL* 1015.

of the 1267 Committee.[33] Whatever the formal legal position, the Committee had to work with UN member states in order to secure the effective implementation of sanctions, and requiring states to act upon designations that rested upon a flimsy listing process was an increasingly unattractive proposition. The ensuing reform of UN sanctions first involved the establishment of the Focal Point for De-Listing, which forwarded any delisting requests to the relevant Sanctions Committee to consider and communicated with the petitioner.[34] The Focal Point has been convincingly described as hardly more than 'a glorified postbox' with no powers of review and a correspondently limited contribution to due process.[35]

A true change came to pass with creation by the Security Council of the Office of the Ombudsperson as in independent agency authorised to review the Security Council's listing decisions.[36] The Ombudsperson's decisions are not technically binding, but they are virtually invariably followed in practice. The procedure of 'reverse consensus' employed by the Security Council means that the Ombudsperson's decisions are going to be acted upon unless the Security Council chooses to oppose it by consensus.[37] That has never happened, and therefore the Ombudsperson's decisions do provide a significant degree of protection to sanctioned persons.

The mandate of the Office of the Ombudsperson only extends to a number of counterterrorist sanctions programmes and does not encompass the entirety of UN sanctions regimes, for example, targeted financial sanctions related to North Korea. This is a significant limitation since, as discussed in Sections 4.2.3 and 4.2.4, terrorism-related sanctions do not exhaust the panoply of UN sanctions, let alone sanctions imposed by states unilaterally outside the UN framework. As a result, Malta and the US co-sponsored the UN Security Council Resolution 2744 (2024) that is intended to streamline the Focal Point's working processes, including by requiring it to produce 'comprehensive reports' on petitioners' delisting submissions, as well as establishing an informal working group to discuss improvements to all UN sanctions regimes.[38] The Resolution was adopted unanimously in July 2024, with its practical effects remaining to be seen.[39]

33 Sullivan, *The Law of the List*, 155–163.

34 Thomas Biersteker and Sue Eckert, 'Addressing Challenges to Targeted Sanctions: An Update of the "Watson Report"', *Watson Institute for International Studies*, 2009, 12–14.

35 Devika Hovell, *The Power of Process: The Value of Due Process in Security Council Sanctions Decision-Making* (Oxford University Press, 2016) 21.

36 Office of the Ombudsperson of the UN Security Council's 1267 Committee, 'Approach and Standard', https://main.un.org/securitycouncil/en/ombudsperson/approach-and-standard.

37 This change was introduced in response to the CJEU's criticism of the Ombudsperson system in *Kadi II*: Kokott and Sobotta, 'The Kadi Case', 1021.

38 'Sanctions: Vote on a Draft Resolution on the Focal Point for Delisting and Informal Working Group on UN Sanctions', *Security Council Report*, 17 July 2024, www.securitycouncilreport.org/whatsinblue/2024/07/sanctions-vote-on-a-draft-resolution-on-the-focal-point-for-delisting-and-informal-working-group-on-un-sanctions.php.

39 UN, 'Security Council Bolsters Mandate of Focal Point for Delisting to Receive Requests from UN Sanctions Regimes, Unanimously Adopting Resolution 2744 (2024)', 19 July 2024, https://press.un.org/en/2024/sc15770.doc.htm.

4.2.3 *UN Sanctions and Proliferation*

The UN Security Council's power to impose sanctions resides in Chapter VII of the UN Charter, which deals with threats to international peace and security. It is up to the Security Council to decide what constitutes a threat to international peace and security. There are therefore multiple sanctions regimes operated by the UN, of which terrorism-related ones are only a sliver. One crucial category of UN sanctions is those put in place to tackle the proliferation of weapons of mass destruction as well as their financing, known as proliferation financing.[40] The UN Security Council resolutions that establish such sanctions complement the relevant non-proliferation treaties that cover nuclear, chemical and biological weapons.[41] This can be seen as one of the many manifestations of the growing overlap between financial crime and national security.[42]

There have historically been three prongs to the UN's counter-proliferation sanctions: those addressing proliferation by non-state actors (since 2004); by North Korea (since 2006); and by Iran (also since 2006).[43] This sustained focus on proliferation from the mid 2000s onwards was in response to revelations about a nuclear proliferation network set up by the Swiss-trained Pakistani nuclear physicist A. Q. Khan, who first helped Pakistan procure military nuclear technologies and then went on to sell them to countries including Iran and North Korea,[44] as well as offering them to others, including Iraq and Libya.[45] Khan confessed to his activities in an interview on Pakistani TV and later died under house arrest, but the concern about proliferation never abated since then and was compounded with time because of the political tensions between the US, on the one hand, and North Korea and Iran on the other hand.

Resolution 1540 (2004), which requires UN member states to take action against proliferation activities by non-state actors, exemplifies the essence of the measures required under such non-proliferation resolutions:

40 For a general overview, see Togzhan Kassenova and Bryan R. Early, 'Countering the Challenges of Proliferation Financing', *The Center for Policy Research, University at Albany*, July 2023.

41 These include the Treaty on the Non-Proliferation of Nuclear Weapons (commonly known as the Non-Proliferation Treaty); the Convention on the Prohibition of the Development, Production, Stockpiling and Use of Chemical Weapons and on their Destruction; and the Convention on the Prohibition of the Development, Production and Stockpiling of Bacteriological (Biological) and Toxin Weapons and on their Destruction.

42 See Martin Navias, *Finance and Security: Global Vulnerabilities, Threats, and Responses* (Hurst Publishers, 2020) Ch 1.

43 For a concise overview, see Emil Dall, Andrea Berger and Tom Keatinge, 'Out of Sight, Out of Mind? A Review of Efforts to Counter Proliferation Finance', *RUSI Whitehall Report*, June 2016, 3–7.

44 Michael Laufer, 'A. Q. Khan Nuclear Chronology', *Carnegie Endowment for International Peace*, 7 September 2005, https://carnegieendowment.org/research/2005/09/a-q-khan-nuclear-chronology?lang=en.

45 A recent book documents A. Q. Khan's abortive involvement in the Irani and Libyan nuclear programmes: Målfrid Braut-Hegghammer, *Unclear Physics: Why Iraq and Libya Failed to Build Nuclear Weapons* (Cornell University Press, 2016) 120 (on Iraq), 187 (on Libya).

> [A]ll States, in accordance with their national procedures, shall adopt and enforce appropriate effective laws which prohibit any non-State actor to manufacture, acquire, possess, develop, transport, transfer or use nuclear, chemical or biological weapons and their means of delivery, in particular for terrorist purposes, as well as attempts to engage in any of the foregoing activities, participate in them as an accomplice, assist or **finance** them.[46]

This and other counter-proliferation Resolutions distinguish between nuclear, chemical or biological weapons themselves; their means of delivery (e.g. missiles) and other 'related materials'. The latter is a broad category encompassing multiple dual-use goods. For instance, the definition of 'related materials' in Resolution 1540 is as follows:

> [M]aterials, equipment and technology covered by relevant multilateral treaties and arrangements, or included on national control lists, which could be used for the design, development, production or use of nuclear, chemical and biological weapons and their means of delivery.[47]

This can include a truly vast array of equipment ranging from vacuum pumps to gyroscopes.[48] This presents substantial challenges for governments, private-sector manufacturers and financial institutions alike.[49] All of them are vested with responsibility for distinguishing between innocuous, legitimate transactions involving dual-use goods and transactions related to proliferation. This focus on identifying proliferation-related activity is often described as 'activity-based' counter-proliferation financing (CPF) controls.[50]

The other component of the contemporary CPF landscape is targeted financial sanctions. Like terrorism-related sanctions, they involve the freezing of the assets of, and the prohibition of any transactions with, designated individuals or entities.[51] Multiple such individuals or entities were designated by the UN Security Council on account of alleged involvement in proliferation under North Korea- and Iran-related resolutions, although no such measures have been put in place

46 Para 2 (emphasis added).

47 Footnote to UN Security Council Resolution 1540 (2004).

48 A useful table of dual-use goods drawn up by the Swedish Security Service is reproduced in FATF, *Proliferation Financing Report*, June 2008, 7.

49 For excellent overviews of the challenges involved in implementing CPF measures, see Louis de Koker, 'The FATF's Combating of Financing of Proliferation Standards: Private Sector Implementation Challenges' in Doron Goldbarsht and Louis de Koker (eds), *Financial Crime and the Law: Identifying and Mitigating Risks* (Springer, 2024); Noémi També and Fatima Busra Alsancak, 'Challenges for Counter-Proliferation Finance and Sanctions Control in Banking', *RUSI Special Resource*, May 2024.

50 De Koker, 'The FATF's Combating of Financing of Proliferation Standards', 130.

51 See Anton Moiseienko, *Corruption and Targeted Sanctions* (Brill, 2019). Targeted financial sanctions are a subsection of targeted sanctions, as distinct from targeted immigration sanctions (i.e. visa denials and entry bans).

under Resolution 1540.[52] Following the adoption of the Joint Comprehensive Plan of Action (JCPOA), an international agreement aimed to ease tensions between Iran and the proverbial 'collective West', the UN lifted all targeted sanctions against Iranian persons from 2018 onwards.[53] As a result, post-JCPOA, the UN only maintains proliferation-related targeted sanctions in relation to North Korean targets, although the US chose to reinstate most of its sanctions against Iran in 2018.[54]

The expansion of the corpus of international CPF rules, as well as sustained international focus on Iran and North Korea, combined to prompt the addition of CPF measures to the FATF's mandate in 2012.[55] However, the FATF only focuses on CPF-related targeted sanctions, rather than activity-based CPF controls.[56] This reflects the lack of consensus as to whether a more substantial engagement with proliferation-related concerns, including screening for dual-use goods, would be feasible for regulated businesses.[57]

This choice remains controversial among experts due to the fragmentation it creates in the global CPF regime, with only a segment of binding Security Council requirements underpinned by the FATF Recommendations. This is particularly important because, despite UN sanctions being binding on all UN member states by virtue of the Charter, the UN does not really have any significant machinery at its disposal to ensure their effective implementation.[58] That task is de facto carried out by the FATF. Therefore, the same peer review mechanism that underpins the implementation of the FATF Recommendations overall serves to ensure compliance with the UN financial sanctions.

In substance, the FATF's rules relating to CPF sanctions are the same as those pertaining to CTF sanctions, namely that they must be implemented effectively

52 UN Security Council, '1718 Sanctions List', https://main.un.org/securitycouncil/en/sanctions/1718/materials (on current North Korea sanctions). For the termination of Iran-related sanctions, see UN Security Council Resolution 2231 (2015).

53 'Joint Comprehensive Plan of Action (JCPoA) Transition Day: UK statement', *UK Government*, 18 October 2023, www.gov.uk/government/news/uk-statement-on-joint-comprehensive-plan-of-action-jcpoa-transition-day.

54 The White House, 'Remarks by President Trump on the Joint Comprehensive Plan of Action', 8 May 2018, https://trumpwhitehouse.archives.gov/briefings-statements/remarks-president-trump-joint-comprehensive-plan-action/.

55 De Koker, 'The FATF's Combating of Financing of Proliferation Standards', 129–130; Dall, Berger and Keatinge, 'Out of Sight, Out of Mind', 8.

56 See FATF, *International Standards on Combatting Money Laundering and the Financing of Terrorism & Proliferation*, updated November 2023, updated November 2023, Interpretive Notes to Recommendations 1, 2 and 7.

57 Dall, Berger and Keatinge, 'Out of Sight, Out of Mind', 8. An extensive list of CPF case studies intended to support private-sector efforts is available in Jonathan Brewer, 'Study of Typologies of Financing of WMD Proliferation', *Project Alpha, King's College London*, October 2017.

58 This explains, for example, why the UN Security Council's 1267 Committee engaged with the International Civil Aviation Organisation to ensure the effective implementation of UN travel bans against suspected terrorists through shaping airport security practices: Sullivan, *The Law of the List*, 124–127.

and without delay, and that their breaches must be subject to effective, prompt and dissuasive penalties.[59] This might appear to be a relatively straightforward regime to put in place – and, compared to the complexities of activity-based sanctions, such an assessment is arguably not too far off the mark – but, as discussed in Section 4.3, it, too, presents formidable challenges.

The absence of FATF-level enabling infrastructure for the implementation of activity-based sanctions has not been entirely unaddressed. Between 2009 and 2024, a Security Council-appointed Panel of Experts was operational that produced regular and meticulous reports on the state of implementation of North Korean sanctions.[60] The Panel of Experts' mandate expired in April 2024 when Russia blocked its periodic extension, shortly prior to the Russian president Vladimir Putin's meeting with the North Korean leader Kim Jong Un.[61] The resulting dearth of monitoring insofar as activity-based sanctions are concerned further accentuates the disparity in the institutional machinery available for the implementation of targeted financial sanctions on the one hand and the broader suite of North Korean sanctions on the other hand.

4.2.4 *Unilateral Sanctions and Crime*

Besides UN sanctions, there are multiple sanctions regimes that are put in place by states independently of the UN. Such sanctions are commonly known as 'unilateral' or 'autonomous'.[62] Unilateral sanctions regimes span a wide gamut of reasons, from the purely political to distinctly criminal. Of particular relevance for present purposes are sanctions predicated on allegations of serious criminality, including corruption, money laundering, cybercrime or other transnational organised crime activities.[63] For decades, the US has been the frontrunner in the use of such sanctions. Their genesis reaches back into the enactment in the 1970s of the International Emergency Economic Powers Act 1977 (IEEPA), which was meant to codify the government's powers to impose sanctions in peacetime, as distinct from

59 FATF, *International Standards on Combatting Money Laundering and the Financing of Terrorism & Proliferation*, Recommendation 7 (CPF sanctions) and Recommendation 6 (CTF sanctions).

60 The Panel of Experts' final report is available at UN Security Council, 'Final Report of the Panel of Experts Submitted Pursuant to Resolution 2680 (2023)', S/2024/215, 7 March 2024. See also Aaron Arnold, 'Russia Just Gutted the UN Panel of Experts on North Korea – What Now?', *RUSI Commentary*, 3 April 2024, https://rusi.org/explore-our-research/publications/commentary/russia-just-gutted-un-panel-experts-north-korea-what-now.

61 'Security Council Fails to Extend Mandate for Expert Panel Assisting Sanctions Committee on Democratic People's Republic of Korea Text Rejected on Account of Veto Cast by Russian Federation', *UN Press*, 28 March 2024, https://press.un.org/en/2024/sc15648.doc.htm. See also Tessa Wong, 'Putin and Kim Pledge Mutual Help against "Aggression"', *BBC News*, 20 June 2024.

62 See Tom Ruys and Cedric Ryngaert, 'Secondary Sanctions: A Weapon Out of Control? The International Legality of, and European Responses to, US Secondary Sanctions' (2020) *BYBIL* 1.

63 For in-depth analysis, see Anton Moiseienko, 'Crime and Sanctions: Beyond Sanctions as a Foreign Policy Tool' (2024) 25(1) *German LJ* 17.

the operation of the Trading with the Enemy Act 1917 during times of war.[64] The IEEPA enables the US President or his delegates, most often the State Secretary or Treasury Secretary, to proclaim an economic emergency and impose a broad array of sanctions to address it.[65]

The primary use of such powers involves sanctions against a foreign state or its government. In 1995, the Clinton administration first resorted to such sanctions in order to address a criminal justice threat, specifically the operations of Latin American drug cartels.[66] That action concerned Colombian drug cartels and was credited with bringing down the Cali cartel by constricting its access to US financial institutions.[67] Similar measures have been put in place since then against a range of drug traffickers under the Foreign Narcotics Kingpin Designation Act 1999.[68] The subsequent history of US sanctions is one of constant expansion of both the programmes in place and the numbers of people sanctioned under them. One of the more recent developments is the introduction since 2012 of so-called Magnitsky sanctions against foreigners suspected of corruption or human rights abuse.[69] The commodious nature of the concepts of corruption and human rights abuse means that they can be used, and have been used extensively, to address a diverse array of forms of economic crime and violent crime that might not have otherwise fit within the scope of any other available sanctions programme.[70]

The relatively recent vintage of 'crime-based' sanctions belies the long history of the thinking giving rise to them, traceable all the way back to the Chicago Crime Commission's publication of the list of 'public enemies' and banks' voluntary commitment to deny service to them and their affiliates.[71] The formalisation of such sanctions over the past several decades raises a number of special challenges, which have only recently started to become a subject of sustained study. One of them is the question of whom to sanction: in a world with a nearly limitless supply of corruption, human rights and cybercrime cases, it can be difficult to decide which to prioritise and on what basis.[72] This opens up opportunities for questioning the fairness and consistency of sanctions programmes, with potentially detrimental effects for their credibility.

64 The origins of sanctions as tools of interstate coercion are discussed in detail in Nicholas Mulder, *The Economic Weapon: The Rise of Sanctions as a Tool of Modern War* (Yale University Press, 2022).

65 For an overview of the US sanctions framework, see Kern Alexander, *Economic Sanctions: Law and Public Policy* (Palgrave Macmillan, 2009).

66 Executive Order 12978, 60 FR 54579 (21 October 1995).

67 Cathy Haenlein, Sasha Erskine, Elijah Glantz and Tom Keatinge, 'Targeted Sanctions and Organised Crime: Impact and Lessons for Future Sanctions', *RUSI Occasional Paper*, March 2022, 27–35.

68 21 USC § 1901.

69 Moiseienko, *Corruption and Targeted Sanctions*, Ch 2.

70 For example, a Pakistani surgeon allegedly involved in organ harvesting was sanctioned under the human rights prong of the US Global Magnitsky programme: US Department of the Treasury, 'United States Sanctions Human Rights Abusers and Corrupt Actors Across the Globe', 21 December 2017, https://home.treasury.gov/news/press-releases/sm0243.

71 See Chapter 2.

72 Moiseienko, 'Crime and Sanctions'.

So far, governments have been slow to set out any clear criteria for the application of crime-based sanctions, preferring instead to secure for themselves the maximum available room for manoeuvre. This is understandable but comes at a cost in terms of credibility and predictability. One exception is the promulgation by the UK government of a set of criteria that govern the imposition of corruption and human rights sanctions.[73] The US government has also published some observations on its approach to cybercrime sanctions. In particular, it has committed to continuing using sanctions in conjunction with criminal prosecutions, which has been its practice in connection with certain ransomware outfits and North Korea cyber-activities.[74] While the rationale for this approach has not been expressly articulated, in many instances of cybercrime the alleged perpetrators are overseas and cannot be easily brought within the reach of the US justice system.[75] Therefore sanctions, rather than criminal indictments, are the tool that produces the most tangible immediate effects by requiring everyone within the US jurisdiction to forego interactions with sanctioned persons.

One noteworthy crime-based sanctions programme is the measures imposed under Section 311 of the US Patriot Act. They can be imposed on countries, entities or transactions of 'primary money laundering concern'.[76] If an entity is targeted under Section 311, this does not necessarily mean that its assets in the US are frozen or that US persons are prohibited from transacting with it. Section 311 measures may only entail additional record-keeping requirements. However, even if that is the case, the mere fact of a Section 311 designation is likely to render US businesses extremely wary of engaging with the designated entity, thereby being essentially equivalent to outright sanctions.[77] These consequences are particularly severe for foreign banks that need to maintain dollar clearance facilities in the US and therefore rely on correspondent banking relationships with US banks. Given this impact of Section 311 designations, parallels may be drawn between them and FATF blacklisting, which may or may not involve an explicit call for countermeasures, but in any event undermines the appeal of doing business with the blacklisted jurisdiction.

73 UK Foreign, Commonwealth & Development Office, 'Global Anti-Corruption Sanctions: Consideration of Designations', 26 April 2021, www.gov.uk/government/publications/global-anti-corruption-sanctions-factors-in-designating-people-involved-in-serious-corruption/global-anti-corruption-sanctions-consideration-of-designations; UK Foreign, Commonwealth & Development Office, 'Global Human Rights Sanctions: Consideration of Designations', 6 July 2020, www.gov.uk/government/publications/global-human-rights-sanctions-factors-in-designating-people-involved-in-human-rights-violations/global-human-rights-sanctions-consideration-of-targets.

74 US Department of Justice, *Report of the Attorney General's Cyber Digital Task Force*, July 2018, 74.

75 Moiseienko, 'Crime and Sanctions'.

76 A list of Section 311 measures taken by FinCEN can be found at: www.fincen.gov/resources/statutes-and-regulations/311-and-9714-special-measures.

77 This flexibility was one of the reasons why the Task Force on Terrorist Financing convened by the Council on Foreign Relations in 2002 called for the use of Section 311 sanctions: 'Terrorist Financing: Report of an Independent Task Force Sponsored by the Council on Foreign Relations', *Council on Foreign Relations*, October 2002, 26.

The variety of uses to which sanctions are put contradicts the notion of them being ring-fenced from AML/CTF or, indeed, criminal justice writ large. The origin of sanctions as a means of economic competition or diplomatic pressure has tended to result in simplistic references to sanctions being a 'foreign policy tool'. This description of sanctions is outdated and ultimately meaningless because it tells us nothing about how they are utilised, or should be utilised, across multiple domains of criminal justice, ranging from drug trafficking to cybercrime to money laundering to terrorist financing.

The best way to think about sanctions is by reference to their effect – the exclusion of specific, identified persons and groups from the sanctioning state's legitimate economy – rather than any particular field of application, such as foreign policy, terrorist financing, proliferation financing, and so on. As discussed below, this can be conceptualised as a form of *targeted exclusion*, that is, the exclusion of specific persons from the legitimate economy, as distinct from the *general exclusion* enacted through AML/CTF measures, that is, the exclusion of suspected proceeds of crime or terrorist funds. This paradigm of exclusion gives rise to novel and complex questions that have rarely if ever been properly considered.

4.3 TARGETED EXCLUSION

As discussed in Chapter 2, AML rules prohibit knowingly dealing *in proceeds of crime*, rather than dealing *with criminals*. So, one does nothing wrong by buying a painting from a convicted murderer or even purchasing a house from a drug trafficker, provided only that the house does not stem from the proceeds of drug trafficking.[78] One way of expressing this is by saying that the AML framework is offence-based, not offender-based.[79]

In the CTF context, this distinction between an offence-based and offender-based framework begins to evaporate. On the one hand, one can plausibly say of the CTF rules under the 1999 Convention and the FATF Recommendations that they, too, enact an offence-based framework. It is a crime to provide funds or other resources to anyone knowing that they will be used to commit an act of terrorism, but it is not a crime to buy a coffee for someone who is involved in a terrorist plot – so long as the coffee is not connected to the plot!

On the other hand, terrorist proscription and sanctions regimes alter that. Once one is sanctioned, or belongs to a sanctioned group, no provision of resources for the benefit of that person or group is legal. This applies to terrorist proscriptions and other sanctions designations alike. Such targeted exclusion involves the shutting out

[78] See Chapter 1.

[79] Michael Levi, 'Pecunia Non Olet: Cleansing the Money-Launderers from the Temple' (1991) 16(3) *Crime, Law and Social Change* 217, 236.

TABLE 4.1 *General versus targeted exclusion*

General exclusion	Targeted exclusion
Focused on proceeds of crime	Focused on criminal actors
Requires identifying a class of (suspicious) activities	Requires identifying the assets of a specific person or group
Operates based on general rules	Operates based on blacklists
Imposes obligations on the regulated sectors	Imposes obligations on everyone
Indirectly implicates due process	Directly implicates due process

of a particular person or group from the legitimate economy and is qualitatively different from the general exclusion that characterises AML regulation.

Targeted exclusion is person-oriented; general exclusion is activity-oriented. Targeted exclusion rules bind all persons within the sanctioning state's jurisdiction; general exclusion rules only apply to regulated businesses. Targeted exclusion directly and obviously implicates due process concerns; general exclusion operates in a more oblique fashion and therefore does not trigger those concerns in the same way. These differences are summarised in Table 4.1 and explained in greater detail in the text that follows.

At first blush, one might expect targeted exclusion to be easier for regulated businesses to implement and for governments to supervise. The private sector is relieved of the need to make difficult judgement calls that the undirected deputisation inherent in the conventional AML regime requires. That, however, is only partly true. Targeted exclusion presents range of conceptual and practical difficulties and trade-offs, the first of which is the question of when it should be pursued and to what end.

4.3.1 *Complicity, Disruption and Denial*

One of the significant differences between AML on the one hand and CTF and sanctions on the other hand is that the latter are much more geared towards preventing their targets from acquiring funds to begin with. In the context of AML, the availability of the proceeds of crime is a given. AML measures are meant to prevent, or at least impede, the movement, storage or use of those proceeds; there is no realistic expectation that criminals will stop amassing criminal wealth due to AML regulation alone. The objective of divesting them of the proceeds of crime has to be fulfilled by a distinct body of rules, namely the proceeds of crime law, which enables criminal or civil confiscation of the proceeds of crime.

By contrast, much of the policy discourse around CTF and sanctions has gravitated towards the question whether the targets of those measures are successfully denied the ability to generate the financial resources that they require for

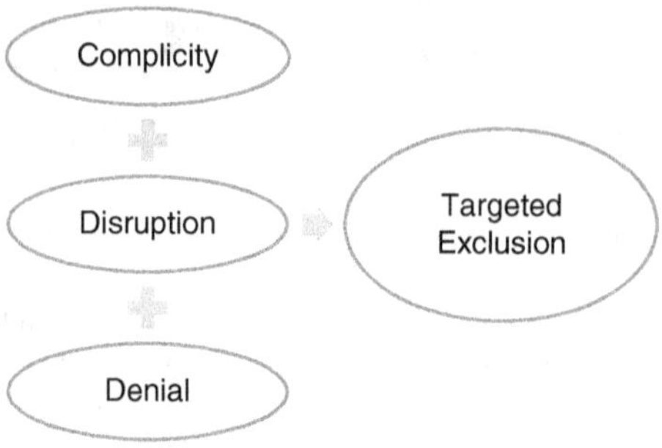

FIGURE 4.1 The three rationales behind the targeted exclusion

their malign activities.[80] A prime example of that is the rhetoric used by President George W. Bush in the days following 9/11.[81] Experts and practitioners who took 'starving' terrorists of resources to be the benchmark for the effectiveness of CTF measures later observed that, by that standard, most CTF efforts have failed spectacularly – after all, terrorists continue to be able to generate the funds they require to mount acts of terror.[82] One might also query whether CTF measures can ever succeed in that sense given that acts of terror generally require modest amount of funds that can be easily raised through legitimate means, such as wages or unemployment benefits, even in the absence of any significant sources of wealth.

The substance of this discussion betrays the emergence of another, additional rationale behind the targeted exclusion that characterises CTF efforts. Besides avoiding the legitimate economy's complicity in terrorist financing and disrupting terrorist financing activities, the more far-reaching objective of *denying* terrorists access to the resources they need comes into play, as summarised in Figure 4.1.

The denial rationale can be seen as either a self-standing objective of targeted exclusion or a more far-reaching, radical version of disruption. Whichever classification one opts for, the language of denial conveys a more uncompromising stance towards terrorist financing than we display towards money laundering, perhaps in reflection of the higher stakes involved in the commission of terrorist acts. Still, the utility and validity of that objective has been fraught with uncertainty.

Some of the more constructive contributions to the debate highlight the differing ways in which terrorist groups raise funds depending on their nature, operations and local environment. This determines, in large part, whether the objective

80 An excellent discussion of this objective and its limitations is available in Tom Keatinge and Florence Keen, 'A Sharper Image: Advancing a Risk-Based Response to Terrorist Financing', *RUSI Occasional Paper*, March 2020.

81 The White House, 'President Freezes Terrorists' Assets'.

82 Peter R. Neumann, 'Don't Follow the Money: The Problem with the War on Terrorist Financing' (2017) 96(4) *Foreign Affairs* 93.

of 'starving' them of resources is ever going to be realistic. The point is aptly put by Timothy Wittig:

> [A]ctivities typically represented as 'terrorist financing' (for example, donations, criminal activities, weapons procurement, and so on) ought to be understood in terms of how 'terrorists' – as socio-political actors – access and interact with particular – and often legitimate – political economic communities; rather than as elements of some vast, mysterious, and entirely illicit financial edifice supposedly underpinning global terrorism.[83]

This idea is further expanded upon in RUSI's sweeping overview of CTF history and practice, which argues that the objectives of CTF measures need to be tailored to the type of the terrorist actor at hand. For example, corporatised terrorist groups such as the Hezbollah might rely significantly on their ability to transact and move funds internationally, often through otherwise legitimate means of commerce, in a fashion similar to a legitimate enterprise.[84] So, the friction introduced by CTF regulatory rules and the spotlight shone onto terrorist operations by sanctions can be a significant enough interference with the Hezbollah's modus operandi to deny it access to the resources that it would otherwise be able to raise.

Compare that to the position of a territory-controlling terrorist group, such as ISIS at the height of its expansion or Al-Shabaab in certain parts of Somalia. The bulk of those groups' resources come from taxation, extortion and the clandestine sale of natural resources in the territories they control. Therefore, CTF efforts of the kind that have been put in place to target the likes of Al Qaeda are likely to be of marginal utility in terms of denying those groups the funds or resources they need to sustain their operations. On the other hand, this is not to deny the usefulness of CTF surveillance measures in identifying and tracking the activities of ISIS or Al-Shabaab operatives overseas.

Indeed, the occasional corrective to the discussion has involved contributions that focus on the financial surveillance component of CTF efforts.[85] Whether or not they cut off the access of terrorists to the resources they need, the ability to trace financial networks and identify movement of funds can contain useful clues for financial investigations. There is limited if any available evidence of those financial investigations helping foil terrorist attacks, but there is little doubt that they often prove valuable in the immediate aftermath of terrorist incidents, for instance, to establish whether the terrorist actor was acting on his own or was part of a larger network.[86] Here is one author's comment that captures the mixed indications that

83 Timothy Wittig, *Understanding Terrorist Finance* (Palgrave Macmillan, 2011) 188–189.

84 Keatinge and Keen, 'A Sharper Image', 46–47. On the Hezbollah, see Matthew Levitt, *Hezbollah: The Global Footprint of Lebanon's Party of God* (Georgetown University Press, 2013).

85 Matthew Levitt and Katherine Bauer, 'Can Bankers Fight Terrorism? What You Get When You Follow the Money' (2017) 96(6) *Foreign Affairs* 144.

86 Keatinge and Keen, 'A Sharper Image', 14, 45.

publicly available information gives about the efficacy of terrorism-related financial surveillance:

> The provision of information on existing targets should be much easier than identifying new suspects, but even this is not always so straightforward. For example, in 2011 the UN monitoring team declared it knew of: 'virtually no cases where suspicious transaction reports have led to prosecutions or even investigations of Al-Qaida or Taliban related criminality' (although this did not stop it insisting 'customer due diligence measures have yielded some positive results in dissuading Al-Qa'ida and Taliban financiers from abusing the financial systems').[87]

Crucially, the financial surveillance apparatus set up for that purpose is exactly the same as that serving AML objectives, relying primarily on SARs and other forms of reporting as well as retention of wire transfer information. This is appropriate and, as discussed here and in Chapter 2, consistent with the history of AML/CTF measures, which has often been intertwined. By and large, the operation of the ensuing financial surveillance machinery is crime-agnostic and equally suited to detecting predicate offences, money laundering, terrorist financing, proliferation financing or sanctions evasion. This reality is often overlooked in the criticism of the supposedly mindless extension of AML surveillance measures to other contexts, which, despite its gloss of seeming sophistication, hardly ever explains what precisely is wrong with such an expansion.

The same question of the balance between complicity, disruption and denial manifests itself with full force in connection with targeted financial sanctions writ large, whether or not terrorism-related. For instance, in the aftermath of large-scale Western sanctions imposed on Russia and its regime-affiliated individuals and companies following the full-scale invasion of Ukraine in February 2022, discussions swiftly emerged as to whether those sanctions are successful in undermining Russia capacity to wage war or changing its behaviour.[88] Most of those debates have focused on broader economic, financial and trade sanctions, rather than targeted financial sanctions. However, even if one only considers the latter, there is no consensus as to the objectives that such sanctions aim to achieve. Arguably the best way to understand them is as a tool of preventing the complicity of Western businesses in the continued enrichment of Russian oligarchs. Whatever the practical impetus behind their imposition, the overarching moral instinct of avoiding complicity in unpalatable behaviour is an arguably powerful rationale behind the adoption. In that sense, targeted sanctions are not too dissimilar from the AML measures discussed in Chapter 2.

87 Peter Sproat, 'The Global System of Counter-Terrorist Finance: What Has It Achieved; What Can It Achieve?' in Genevieve Lennon and Clive Walker (eds), *Routledge Handbook of Law and Terrorism* (Routledge, 2015) 245.

88 See Anton Moiseienko, 'The Future of EU Sanctions against Russia: Objectives, Frozen Assets, and Humanitarian Impact' (2022) (2) *EUCrim* 130.

This can be contrasted to CPF sanctions related to North Korea, which pursue an ambitious overall objective of preventing the North Korean government from raising the funds for its proliferation programme. The difficulties associated with such a sanctions regime are manifold. For example, undermining North Korea's ability to raise revenue for proliferation also deprives it of the resources it could theoretically spend for the benefit of its population. This gives rise to a truly intractable humanitarian issue that the Panel of Experts has repeatedly commented upon without purporting to resolve.[89] Notably, in Australia's only prosecution for the evasion of North Korea-related sanctions, Adamson J accepted that the defendant – a South Korean-born Australian citizen – had been genuinely 'shocked by the effects of the famine, for which he blamed the international community for imposing sanctions'. Still, the judge ruled in sentencing that the defendant was *not* 'solely motivated by his desire to help North Korea since he was also motivated to earn income for himself'.[90]

There is little doubt that the ultimate moral and political responsibility for any adverse impact on the North Korean population lies with the country's totalitarian regime. Still, nations imposing sanctions against North Korea – and, indeed, the UN – face a genuine dilemma in whether they wish to push sanctions to the extreme so as to constrict the North Korean ability to raise revenue or make concessions that could benefit the innocent population while also opening up opportunities for nuclear proliferation. These are the kinds of dilemmas associated with denial as a self-standing objective of CTF controls, CPF measures and many instances of targeted financial sanctions. These issues also surface in the difficult case of coerced payments, such as ransoms paid to criminal groups, terrorist organisations or cybercriminal groups, as discussed later in this chapter.

4.3.2 *Due Process*

One of the cardinal characteristics of contemporary sanctions laws is that, bluntly put, if a government wants to sanction a foreigner, it can.[91] The position of the sanctioning state's own citizens is somewhat more complicated, as discussed below. But, insofar as foreigners are concerned, several features of sanctions laws conspire to make the imposition of sanctions easy, and challenges to them correspondingly difficult. Such is the position in the UK, US, EU, Australia and Canada, with only small discrepancies, which are remarked upon as appropriate.

To begin with, governments are essentially free to define the criteria for imposing sanctions. The typical legislative scheme provides for a very broad range of

89 See, e.g., UN Security Council, 'Letter dated 25 February 2022 from the Panel of Experts established pursuant to resolution 1874 (2009) addressed to the President of the Security Council', UN Doc S/2022/132, 80–83.

90 *R v Choi (No 10)* [2021] NSWSC 891.

91 See Anton Moiseienko, 'Due Process and Unilateral Targeted Sanctions' in Charlotte Beaucillon (ed), *Research Handbook on Unilateral and Extraterritorial Sanctions* (Edward Elgar, 2021).

objectives in pursuit of which the government is authorised to lay out sanctions regulations. For instance, this could be done in pursuit of international peace and security, domestic foreign policy objectives or human rights protection. Some sanctions laws explicitly state that such objectives must have some connection to foreign policy: that is, sanctions regulations cannot be promulgated for purely domestic policy reasons.[92] Subject to that limitation, virtually any legitimate policy objective can form the basis for the establishment of a sanctions regime. This general authorisation to create sanctions regimes is normally found in an overarching sanctions law, such as the UK's Sanctions and Anti-Money Laundering Act 2018 (SAMLA), the IEEPA in the US or the EU's treaty framework.

Provided that the legal basis exists for establishing a new sanctions regime, this is done by means of a sanctions regulation (in the UK and Australia), presidential Executive Order (in the US) or some other comparable subsidiary instrument. This is where governments' extraordinarily broad sanctions powers first become apparent. It is wholly up to them to decide upon the exact criteria for imposing sanctions. For instance, as of July 2024, the EU's Syria sanctions regulation authorises sanctions against the following categories of persons:

(a) leading businesspersons operating in Syria;
(b) members of the Assad or Makhlouf families;
(c) Syrian Government Ministers in power after May 2011;
(d) members of the Syrian Armed Forces of the rank of 'colonel' and the equivalent or higher in post after May 2011;
(e) members of the Syrian security and intelligence services in post after May 2011;
(f) members of regime-affiliated militias; or
(g) persons operating in the chemical weapons proliferation sector, and persons associated with them.[93]

As we can see from this example, sanctions criteria are often expressed by reference to someone's status, for example, being a member of a certain government or parliament, a leading businessman in an overseas country or even a member of someone's family. Such 'status-based' sanctions are occasionally contrasted with 'activity-based' sanctions, for instance, those predicated on alleged involvement in corruption or human rights abuse.[94]

On a philosophical level, the difference is elusive because having a certain status, such as being a member of the Syrian government post-2011, is inextricably associated with certain activities, such as involvement in violent repression. Therefore,

[92] See, e.g., Section 10(2) of the Autonomous Sanctions Act 2011 (Cth).
[93] Article 27(2) of the Council Decision 2013/255/CFSP of 31 May 2013 Concerning Restrictive Measures in View of the Situation in Syria [2013] OJ L 147 (consolidated version of 22 January 2024).
[94] European Union Committee, *The Legality of EU Sanctions*, HL 2016–17, 102, para 39.

status-based sanctions are essentially a shortcut to activity-based sanctions. On a practical level, however, it is far more difficult to challenge status-based sanctions. So long as the targeted person answers to the requisite description, sanctions are lawful. Status-based sanctions therefore leave no room to investigate actual involvement in the underlying undesirable activity. It is also possible that some of the targeted persons, while falling within the scope of sanctions criteria, are not engaged in any undesirable conduct at all: for instance, this may be the case with family-member sanctions. There is therefore some force in the suggestion by the leading sanctions barrister Maya Lester KC that status-based sanctions can elevate presumptions at the expense of evidence.[95] (If one took a criminal law theorist's approach to sanctions, one might also wonder if something akin to the 'fair labelling' principle ought to apply such that the reasons for listing fairly reflect the gravamen of the alleged wrongdoing!)

Regardless of the sanctions criteria utilised – status-based or activity-based – once sanctions are imposed, it tends to be extraordinarily difficult to challenge them in court. In common law jurisdictions, the rules of judicial review ordinarily only allow the striking down of sanctions decisions that are not merely wrong, but palpably so. For example, the *Wednesbury* principles of judicial review in the UK permit the striking down of a decision that was not just wrong but 'was either based on no evidence or was irrational'.[96] Substantively similar provisions are in place in the US under the Administrative Procedure Act 1946.[97] High standards of judicial review, combined with the vast discretion vested in governments, render the judicial striking down of sanctions difficult to achieve.[98]

One exception to that is the EU's experience. The CJEU's stance is more interventionist as it seeks to assess whether each sanctions designation before it is based on a 'sufficiently solid factual basis'.[99] This affords greater due process protection to sanctioned persons than they would enjoy in the UK, the US or Australia. Yet one must recall that this protection extends to establishing whether the targeted person fulfils the listing criteria that the EU itself decides upon at will. The almost illusory nature of this bulwark against arbitrary listing is made evident by the widely used practice of relisting on new grounds individuals who win sanctions cases against the Commission. Such relisting has been criticised by some,

95 Ibid, para 41.

96 *LLC Synesis* v *Secretary of State for Foreign, Commonwealth and Development Affairs* [2023] EWHC 541 (Admin), paras 81–82.

97 Section 706(2).

98 Rachel Barnes, 'United States Sanctions: Delisting Applications, Judicial Review and Secret Evidence' in Matthew Happold and Paul Eden (eds), *Economic Sanctions and International Law* (Hart Publishing, 2016) 678–684; Christina Eckes, 'EU Restrictive Measures against Natural and Legal Persons: From Counterterrorist to Third Country Sanctions' (2014) 51(3) *Common Market LR* 896, 897.

99 *Al Aqsa* v *Council and Netherlands* v *Al-Aqsa*, Joined Cases of Joined Cases C-539/10 P and C-550/10 P, Judgment of 15 November 2012, para 68.

including Maya Lester KC in testimony to the UK's House of Lords, but continues to be widely utilised within the EU.[100]

These limitations of available due process protections mean that the caricature of well-heeled oligarchs outgunning governments in sanctions litigation bears little resemblance to reality.[101] This is not to suggest that all sanctioned persons meekly accept their fate and cease any attempt to challenge sanctions. It is much more likely that those efforts are displaced towards the lobbying of, and representations made before, agencies administering sanctions, such as the Office of Foreign Assets Control (OFAC) in the US or the Office of Financial Sanctions Implementation (OFSI) in the UK.[102] The manual control over what is or is not legitimate economic activity that governments exercise under sanctions laws is not limited only to decisions as to whom to sanction. It also extends to the granting of licenses, permits or exemptions that authorise operations that would otherwise be in contravention of sanctions laws.

General licences authorise entire categories of transactions, for example, continued US and EU trade in Russian energy supplies in the course of the Russo-Ukrainian war that would otherwise have contravened sanctions.[103] Special licences can be granted to specific individuals or companies, for instance, to allow those under sanctions to fund their and their families' ordinary living expenses. The operation of these regimes has been a subject of some controversy, especially as it emerged that sanctioned Russian oligarchs had been granted allowances of many dozens of thousands of pounds per month for their living expenses in the UK.[104] In the US, the initial grant and subsequent revocation of a special licence to the sanctioned Israeli businessman Dan Gertler has likewise caused disquiet among anti-corruption NGOs.[105] Regardless of the merits of any particular licence or exemption, the operation of the regime as a whole supplies an unmissable indication of the evermore far-reaching control that governments exert over deciding what commercial activities are or are not lawful.

One constraint on the application of sanctions is that they only tend to target foreigners. This is not to say that they can never be directed against the sanctioning

[100] EU Committee, *The Legality of EU Sanctions*, paras 48–53.

[101] Anton Moiseienko, 'The Strange Game of Oligarchs Challenging Sanctions', *RUSI Commentary*, 22 May 2024, www.rusi.org/explore-our-research/publications/commentary/strange-game-oligarchs-challenging-sanctions.

[102] For an attempt to chart out the amount of sanctions-related lobbying in the EU, see Katharina Meissner, 'Lobbying Sanctions: Data from the European Union' (2024) 20(1) *Foreign Policy Analysis* 1.

[103] See the list of Russia-related General Licences at OFAC, 'Russian Harmful Foreign Activities Sanctions', https://ofac.treasury.gov/sanctions-programs-and-country-information/russian-harmful-foreign-activities-sanctions.

[104] Danielle Sheridan, 'UK Lets Sanctioned Oligarch Pay for 19 Staff Including Private Chefs', *The Telegraph*, 31 July 2023.

[105] US Department of State, 'Revocation of License Granted for Dan Gertler', 8 March 2021, www.state.gov/revocation-of-license-granted-for-dan-gertler/.

state's own citizens. For instance, under US law, US dual citizens fall within the definition of a 'foreign person' and can lawfully be sanctioned.[106] This has occasionally happened in relation to US dual citizens beyond the reach of US law enforcement, such as foreign terrorist fighters.[107] In Australia, despite a parliamentary recommendation to the effect that sanctions should never be used against Australian citizens, the government successfully opposed including such a proviso in Australian legislation.[108] In the UK, too, there is no bar on the use of sanctions against UK nationals.[109] All of that being said, all of the above-listed governments have been restrained in largely avoiding the use of sanctions against their own citizens. If such use became more widespread, the profound civil liberties and human rights implications of these measures would no doubt cause lasting legal and political controversy, potentially with drastic consequences for the use of sanctions altogether.

Besides litigating sanctions within the legislative schemes outlined above, one big-picture, systemic due process concern that has been litigated on multiple occasions is whether sanctions predicated on an allegation of criminal wrongdoing, such as terrorist financing or corruption, engage the presumption of innocence or other criminal trial guarantees. If they did, this would have seismic repercussions for the imposition of sanctions, at least crime-based ones, and almost inevitably stymie their use. With that in mind, it is unsurprising that both the UN Human Rights Committee and courts around the world have invariably rejected the contention.[110] While some may dispute this conclusion based on reasoning from first principles, revisiting those decisions would trigger such profound consequences for sanctions around the world, both at the UN level and domestically, that such a development remains unlikely.

The abiding significance of those challenges lies arguably not so much in the competing interpretations of international human rights law that they espouse, but in the overarching concerns they embody. With the evolution of targeted sanctions since the 1990s, governments now have extraordinary leeway in singling out individuals and companies, albeit primarily foreign ones, as beyond the pale of ordinary commercial interactions. This is not something many could have imagined to anywhere the same extent before the rise of sanctions. The occasional invocations of due process to impugn not just a particular listing but the whole notion of sanctions is best understood as an embodiment of a pre-1990s legal sensibility characterised

[106] Sections 1701–1708 of the International Emergency Economic Powers Act (US).

[107] Moiseienko, 'Crime and Sanctions', 29.

[108] Australian Government, Australian Government Response to the Joint Standing Committee on Foreign Affairs, *Defence and Trade Human Rights Subcommittee Report: 'Criminality, Corruption and Impunity: Should Australia Join the Global Magnitsky Movement?*, August 2021, 8, www.aph.gov.au/Parliamentary_Business/Committees/Joint/Foreign_Affairs_Defence_and_Trade/MagnitskyAct/Government_Response.

[109] *Shvidler v Foreign Secretary* [2023] EWHC 2121 (Admin).

[110] *Sayadi and Vinck v Belgium*, Human Rights Committee, Comm No 1472/2006, Views of 22 October 2008, para 10.11. See also Moiseienko, 'Crime and Sanctions', 177–203.

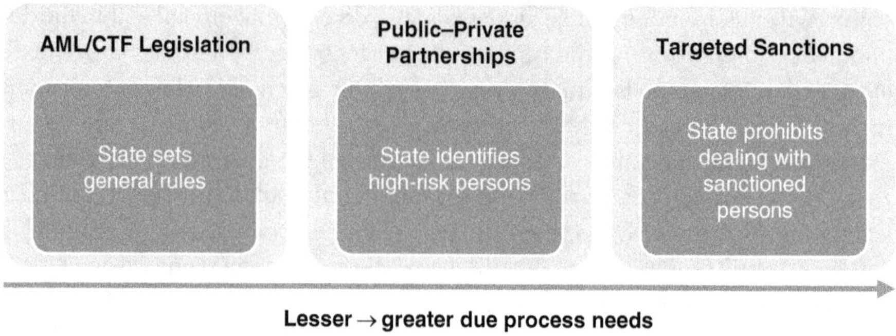

FIGURE 4.2 Due process continuum

by the dichotomy between criminal liability, proven beyond reasonable doubt in a court of law, and innocence.

With the emergence of AML, CTF and targeted sanctions, we are now well and truly into the world of greater gradation and more complicated shades of nuance. The targeted exclusion imposed through sanctions can be seen as a far end of the spectrum on which AML/CTF measures also lie. For instance, Benjamin Vogel and Maxime Lassalle query whether 'stronger legal scrutiny' is necessary of the derisking of customers identified as high-risk because of information exchanged via public–private partnerships:

> [W]hen obliged entities' CDD is increasingly based (in part) on information that the authorities provide to the obliged entities, de-risking and other measures detrimental to customers will often be effectively attributable to the authorities and thereby impact the legality of the authorities' interaction with the obliged entities.[111]

The implication is that, while derisking occurs anyway because of the incentives created by AML/CTF rules, the proactive provision by government of information about high-risk customers may create a greater need for due process protections. Targeted sanctions take this a step further by involving an explicit and binding direction to all persons within the sanctioning state's jurisdiction to avoid commercial interactions with the sanctioned person. This due process continuum is summarised in Figure 4.2.

As we have seen, although most would agree with the need for due process in the imposition of targeted sanctions, the extent of available due process protection tends to be modest. One might expect this to mean that sanctions offer a convenient and easy-to-use tool for governments to shut those they do not like out of the legitimate economy. However, as discussed in Section 4.3.3, that is only true to an extent.

[111] Benjamin Vogel and Maxime Lassalle, 'Developing Public-Private Information Sharing to Strengthen the Fight against Money Laundering and Terrorism Financing' [2023] (4) *EUCrim* 384, 386. As discussed in Chapter 3, many would argue that public–private partnerships help minimise derisking, which speaks to the complexity of this area!

4.3.3 *Identification of Sanctioned Persons*

The simplicity of the basic idea behind targeted sanctions may create the misleading impression of this whole area of law and practice being straightforward. After all, one only needs to sever commercial relations with, or in the case of a bank freeze the assets of, the sanctioned person. In truth, there are multiple challenges involved, both conceptual and practical. For ease of analysis, it is convenient to being with the practical ones.

In a straightforward case, it is true that the obligations involved are not at all difficult to understand or implement. So, if a UK bank holds an account that belongs to the UK-sanctioned Vladimir Putin, an obligation exists under UK sanctions laws to freeze that account. But it is commonly known that high-net worth individuals, especially those whose activities expose them to heightened likelihood of being targeted by foreign sanctions, rarely hold a significant amount of property in their own names. Even if they do, it is overwhelmingly likely they will also have vast amount of wealth hidden behind corporate structures, trust arrangements or nominee owners and directors.[112]

The identification of property that is indirectly controlled by sanctioned persons presents a major challenge that, despite its obviousness, cannot be overestimated. It bears resemblance to the problems that US prosecutors faced in the 1920s as, in the aftermath of the Supreme Court's *Sullivan* judgment, they began to assemble evidence of large-scale tax evasion by organised crime figures.[113] It quickly became apparent that major mobsters used networks of proxies to hold their property in a way that could not be easily connected to them or their activities. Unorthodox techniques such as handwriting analysis had to be employed to demonstrate that certain checks had in fact been issued by figures such as Al Capone or Waxey Gordon and therefore came from the accounts they controlled.

In today's world of sanctions, similar issues of indirect, de facto control arise. To understand how they play out, one must consider the practicalities of sanctions implementation. A sanctions list published by the government is just that: a list containing the sanctioned person's identification information, such as full name, date of birth, address and other identifying features for individuals; and name, incorporation number, registered office and other such details for companies. It is then up to the private sector to match the details on the sanctions list to those found in each business's customer or counterparty database. For large-scale businesses, including banks, the process has to be automated.[114]

The automatic process used for such matching is known as sanctions screening. Sanctions screening is used not only to identify existing customers that are subject to sanctions but also to screen outgoing payments to sanctioned persons or, indeed,

[112] Daniel Nielson and J. C. Sharman, *Signatures for Sale: How Nominee Services for Shell Companies Are Abused to Conceal Beneficial Owners*, Stolen Asset Recovery Initiative, 2022.

[113] See Chapter 2.

[114] Interview with a Swiss sanctions expert, 5 June 2024.

incoming payments from such persons. Sanctions screening is different from AML transaction monitoring discussed in Chapter 3 in that sanctions screening tends to happen in real time so as to prevent transactions with sanctioned counterparties from coming through. There are multiple commercial suppliers of sanctions screening software, some of which are widely used around the world.

One major limitation of any sanctions screening system is that, ultimately, it relies on the information published by the government in sanctions designations. A corollary of that is that sanctions screening systems can only identify direct matches between the sanctioned person and the business's customers or counterparties. They *cannot* detect indirect exposure, such as having a corporate customer that is ultimately owned or controlled by a sanctioned person, let alone people or companies acting on behalf of sanctioned parties as proxies.[115]

Identifying such indirect exposure, while critical to any meaningful sanctions implementation regime, requires a degree of investigation. Such an investigation would inevitably entail an expenditure of time and resources. Smaller companies might not have those at their disposal. Larger companies might have the resources but would also have a correspondently larger number of customers and counterparties in relation to whom sanctions due diligence ought to be performed. That requires a system of triage or prioritisation whereby high-risk situations are dealt with first. The development of such a system should, in turn, be shaped by legal and regulatory requirements. Otherwise, private-sector companies are overwhelmingly likely to consider their job done once sanctions screening is undertaken, despite the essentially rudimentary nature of such checks.

The extent of the difficulty can hardly be overstated, and it manifests itself across different contexts. For example, consider the implementation of targeted financial sanctions related to North Korea's nuclear proliferation. With North Korea being effectively cut off from the legitimate economy, its government has engaged in a sustained campaign of trying to raise funds through a variety of commercial activities including ship-to-ship oil transfers, the illegal wildlife trade and cybercrime.[116] One element of those activities is what would otherwise be legitimate trade with commercial counterparties had it not been carried out by sanctioned North Korean entities. In order to get around those restrictions, North Korea utilises the work of intermediaries, often including companies incorporated in jurisdictions such as Hong Kong or Singapore.[117] Therefore, a legitimate company anywhere in the world

115 Anton Moiseienko, Megan Musni and Eva Van Der Merwe, *A Journey of 20: An Empirical Study of the Impact of Magnitsky Sanctions on the Earliest Corruption Designees*, International Lawyers Project, June 2023, 24.

116 Final Report of the Panel of Experts; Daniel Salsbury, 'Shopping for Mass Destruction: North Korea's Illicit Procurement Networks', *RUSI Occasional Paper*, August 2024.

117 See RUSI, 'DPRK Reports', https://dprk-reports.org/. This database brings together information from the UN Panel of Experts' reports in an easily searchable format. For instance, a query for a particular jurisdiction will return a list of companies incorporated in it implicated in the Panel of Experts' reports.

might have to ask itself whether it is truly transacting with innocuous Hong Kong or Singaporean shipping company or, as a matter of fact, doing business with the North Korean regime. The exact same problem arises in connection with the implementation of any other targeted financial sanctions regime, including those against Russia, Iran and so on.

So far, governments have been slow to postulate detailed sanctions compliance requirements beyond sanctions screening, no doubt recognising the challenge of ensuring effective identification of sanctioned persons while not subjecting businesses to stifling administrative burdens. Documents such as AUSTRAC's national proliferation financing risk assessment give an indication of the range of additional techniques that can be employed by banks, such as using customer data to conduct network analysis and identify individuals and companies that may be involved in illicit procurement networks.[118]

This opens up opportunities that sophisticated businesses, such as banks, can use. Still, even they are struggling with the expansion of sanctions regimes, no matter how well-meaning and appropriate this expansion is. Furthermore, the implications of sanctions being binding on *all* persons within the sanctioning state's jurisdiction, no matter how big or small, have never been adequately thought through. The nascence of policy thinking in this area and sanctions implementation techniques puts into context the role of targeted sanctions as a supposedly swiftly and easily deployed foreign policy, national security and criminal justice tool, despite the undoubted importance that they came to hold.

4.3.4 *The Sanctions Penumbra*

One might think of the challenge of identifying sanctioned persons as a purely practical difficulty, albeit an extraordinarily complicated one. In reality, there is also a conceptual component to it, which is essential to understanding some of the most contentious issues surrounding sanctions design and implementation.

In his classic work, *The Concept of Law*, the English legal theorist H. L. A. Hart wrote about the 'penumbra of uncertainty' involved in the interpretation of legal texts.[119] Words often have a core meaning that will be uncontroversial, but there may also be a penumbra of other meanings that could be ascribed to them in a certain context. So, if the byelaws of a park prohibit vehicles in the park, there is little doubt one must not drive a car there. On the other hand, whether the prohibition extends to rikshaws or electric scooters is less clear. This category of problems involves challenges of legal interpretation, but also trade-offs in legislative drafting – there is

[118] AUSTRAC, *Proliferation Financing in Australia: National Risk Assessment*, 2022, 24. For more background on network analysis in law enforcement and criminological study, see Saskia Hufnagel and Anton Moiseienko (eds), *Criminal Networks and Law Enforcement* (Routledge, 2019).

[119] H. L. A. Hart, *The Concept of Law* (2nd edn, Oxford University Press, 1994) 12, 123.

a tension between the law's precision and its capacity to regulate unanticipated situations.

Sanctions, too, involve a penumbra of uncertainty, albeit of a different nature. As discussed above, it is clear that the assets directly belonging to a sanctioned person are subject to freezing. There are, nevertheless, three further questions that need to be considered for a holistic view of the effect of targeted sanctions:

- What does the sanctioned person control?
- Who acts on behalf of the sanctioned person?
- Who benefits from the sanctioned person's activities?

The practical challenges of identifying indirect control have been already discussed, but there is also the logically prior question of what control means in any event. Most sanctioning states try to get around the problem of indirect ownership by postulating that a particular property or company is subject to sanctions if a certain threshold of ownership by a sanctioned party is met. For instance, the US and EU extend sanctions to companies that are at least 50 per cent owned by a sanctioned party.[120] While the US government recognises that control can also be exercised through other means and reserves its ability to sanction companies that are controlled by a sanctioned party in the absence of a 50 per cent ownership stake,[121] the automatic extension of sanctions to companies 50 per cent owned by sanctioned persons is a key feature of the US sanctions regime.

Its implications have manifested themselves on multiple occasions in connection with the ongoing sanctions against Russian oligarchs. In 2023, the US government accepted that the major Russian aluminium company Rusal was no longer subject to US sanctions after its sanction shareholder Oleg Deripaska dropped his shareholding to 44.95 per cent.[122] This stands in contrast to what happened in Australia when a subsidiary of Rio Tinto refused to honour its contract for supply of aluminium to Rusal's subsidiary for fear of violating Australian sanctions by conferring a benefit, indirectly, on Rusal's sanctioned shareholders, Oleg Deripaska and Victor Vekselberg, despite their holdings being 25.58 and 12.58 per cent, respectively.[123] Unlike in the US, Australia does not specify any particular threshold that determines control. The Federal Court sided with Rio Tinto and decided that going ahead with the supplies would affect have contravened Australian sanctions laws. To use the Hart-inspired metaphor above, this indicates that the sanctions penumbra in Australia extends further than it does in the US, but it is not clear how far exactly.

[120] Council of the EU, 'Restrictive Measures (Sanctions) – Update of the EU Best Practices for the Effective Implementation of Restrictive Measures', Doc No 11623/24, 3 July 2024, para 63.

[121] OFAC, 'Entities Owned by Blocked Persons (50% Rule)', https://ofac.treasury.gov/faqs/topic/1521.

[122] Polina Devitt and Arshad Mohammed, 'Questions Linger over Deripaska's Rusal Influence after U.S. Deal', *Reuters*, 4 February 2019.

[123] *Alumina & Bauxite Co Ltd v QAL* [2024] FCA 43. See also Anton Moiseienko, 'Testing the Metal: An Extraordinary Sanctions Judgment from Australia' (2025) 133 *WorldECR* 28.

Here, too, the same tension emerges between clarity and predictability on the one hand and flexibility on the other hand.

The issue of control has confounded the courts in the UK, where a spate of conflicting judgments speak to the difficulties involved. In the case of *Mints*, a unanimous Court of Appeal held, obiter, that all businesses in Russia could be deemed to be controlled by a sanctioned person, that is, Russia's president Putin.[124] The Court recognised that the consequence of its holding are 'absurd' but suggested that they flow not from the Court's own interpretation of 'control' but from 'the subsequent designation by the Government of Mr Putin, without having thought through the consequences that, as [one of the counsel] put it, Mr Putin is at the apex of a command economy'.[125] The problem with the judgment is not so much the implication that all Russian companies are *ipso facto* subject to UK sanctions, but the suggestion that such a momentous step could have been taken accidentally, without the government realising what it was doing.

As of this writing, *Mints* is under appeal to the UK Supreme Court, which granted leave to appeal in January 2024.[126] In the meantime, the holding in *Mints* appears to be on shaky grounds. A mere several months after the Court of Appeal's judgment, in *Litasco*, Foxton J refused to follow its *obiter* and drew a contrast between latent control that a company could be brought under and existing de facto control.[127] Then, in *Hellard*, Thompsell J sought to reconcile *Mints* and *Litasco* and, in so doing, distinguished between four types of control:

i) de jure control: this exists where there is an absolute legal right to exercise control embedded, for example in the constitution of a company or a body;
ii) actual present de facto control: this exists where the putative controller is manifestly 'calling the shots' (to adopt the language used in *Mints*) with no legal right to do so;
iii) potential future de jure control (…). This would exist where, although the designated person enjoyed no current legal right of ownership or control, the designated person had the legal means to obtain ownership or control. The most obvious example of this, would be where the designated person had an option or a forward contract to acquire a majority shareholding in a company; and
iv) potential future de facto control. This would exist where although there was no evidence that the putative controller was currently exercising de facto control, there is some good reason to believe that the putative controller could, if he or she wished, exercise control in some manner.[128]

124 *Mints & Ors v PJSC National Bank Trust & Anor* [2023] EWCA Civ 1132, para 233.
125 Ibid.
126 UK Supreme Court, 'Permission to Appeal – January 2024', www.supremecourt.uk/pta/permission-to-appeal-2024–01.html.
127 *Litasco SA v Der Mond Oil and Gas Africa SA & Anor* [2023] EWHC 2866 (Comm), paras 66–71.
128 *Hellard & Ors v OJSC Rossiysky Kredit Bank & Ors* [2024] EWHC 1783 (Ch) (10 July 2024), para 76.

Thompsell J also provided further comments on what each of those forms of control properly entailed. Despite seeking to accommodate earlier judgments, that inevitably meant reading down the suggestion in *Mints* that all companies in an authoritarian state are treated, for sanctions law purposes, as controlled by the head of that state. Of greater relevance for present purposes, though, is the complexity that the concept of control may entail, as amply demonstrated in *Hellard*. It can be further compounded by the diversity of contexts within which the issue arises, from regulatory ones to sanctions-related civil or criminal litigation.[129]

Moving beyond corporate ownership or other similar arrangements, another related matter is whether sanctions should be extended to individuals acting on behalf of sanctioned persons. As mentioned previously, the use of nominee directors, shareholders or other proxies is commonplace in financial crime.[130] This can include regulated professionals, such as lawyers or financial advisors.[131] Sometimes, governments recognise these realities by explicitly sanctioning individuals and companies because they facilitate someone else's sanctions evasion by acting as a proxy. That in itself is not controversial, but difficulties arise once one asks whether certain categories of people should be *presumed* to be acting on behalf of sanctioned persons.

The issue has been acute in connection with sanctions imposed on family members of primary targets, such as dictators, oligarchs or suspected criminals. The treatment of family-member sanctions lacks consistency not only across countries but also across sanctions programmes within countries. For instance, US sanctions programmes are roughly equally divided between those that authorise family-member sanctions[132]

[129] For example, in May 2024 Cockerill J held that a sanctions evasion offence in the UK could only be committed if one dealt with a company that was in fact controlled by a sanctioned person, as opposed to a company reasonably suspected of being so controlled: *Vneshprombank LLC v Bedzhamov* [2024] EWHC 1048 (Ch).

[130] Nielson and Sharman, *Signatures for Sale*.

[131] See Justyna Gudzowska, Eliza Lockhart and Tom Keatinge, 'Disabling the Enablers of Sanctions Circumvention', *RUSI Policy Brief*, May 2024.

[132] Executive Order 13405: Blocking Property of Certain Persons Undermining Democratic Processes or Institutions in Belarus, 71 FR 35485 (16 June 2006), s 1(a)(ii)(C); Executive Order 14046: Imposing Sanctions on Certain Persons with Respect to the Humanitarian and Human Rights Crisis in Ethiopia, 86 FR 52389 (17 September 2021), s1(e); Executive Order 13936: Executive Order on Hong Kong Normalization, 85 FR 43413 (14 July 2020), ss 4 and 7; Executive Order 13315: Blocking Property of the Former Iraqi Regime, Its Senior Officials and Their Family Members, and Taking Certain Other Actions, 68 FR 52315 (28 August 2003), s 1(b)(i); Executive Order 13553: Blocking Property of Certain Persons with Respect to Serious Human Rights Abuses by the Government of Iran and Taking Certain Other Actions, 75 FR 60567 (28 September 2010), s 1(a)(ii)(A); Executive Order 13441: Blocking Property of Persons Undermining the Sovereignty of Lebanon or Its Democratic Processes and Institutions, 72 FR 43499 (1 August 2007), s 1(a)(i)(C); Executive Order 13566: Blocking Property and Prohibiting Certain Transactions Related to Libya, 76 FR 11315 (25 February 2011), s 1(b)(vi); Executive Order 14014: Blocking Property with Respect to the Situation in Burma, 86 FR 9429 (10 February 2021), s 1(a)(v); Executive Order 13894: Blocking Property and Suspending Entry of Certain Persons Contributing to the Situation in Syria, 84 FR 55851 (14 October 2019), s 2(a)(ii); Executive

and those that do not.[133] How best to deal with family members of sanctioned persons has been debated by experts since at least 1998–1999 when the wife of Raoul Cédras, the US-sanctioned then-president of Haiti, was photographed using a credit card in Miami.[134] Despite the longevity of this dilemma and the ever-growing amount of litigation stemming from family-member sanctions, this area of sanctions law and practice has not been the subject of any sustained public discussion by policymakers, and it is only very recently that the first detailed academic study of it emerged.[135]

In a nutshell, the conflicting intuitions involved in this discussion are easy to summarise. On the one hand, fairness counsels against imposing sanctions on someone based solely on their familial connections. On the other hand, omitting to enable sanctions at least against close family members of primary targets opens up obvious opportunities for sanctions evasion since they are especially likely to act on behalf of sanctioned individuals. This has been the EU's rationale for extending its Russia-related sanctions programme to family members of leading Russian businessmen.[136] In another notable EU sanctions programme, namely the one against Bashar Al-Assad's Syrian government, similar provisions were adopted with a safety valve that requires for family-member sanctions to be lifted if their target proves he or she does not support, nor benefits from, their family members' activities.[137]

This raises the question of whether sanctions can or should also be extended to those who, while not involved in facilitating sanctions evasion or acting on behalf of sanctioned persons, nonetheless benefit from their activities. On proper analysis, a substantial chunk of family-member sanctions, which do not feature any credible

Order 14098: Imposing Sanctions on Certain Persons Destabilizing Sudan and Undermining the Goal of a Democratic Transition, 88 FR 29529 (4 May 2023), s 1(a)(iii); Executive Order 13850: Blocking Property of Additional Persons Contributing to the Situation in Venezuela, 83 FR 55243 (1 November 2018), s 1(a)(ii); Executive Order 13391: Blocking Property of Additional Persons Undermining Democratic Processes or Institutions in Zimbabwe, 70 FR 71201 (22 November 2005).

133 Executive Order 14088: Taking Additional Steps to Address the National Emergency with Respect to the Situation in Nicaragua, 87 FR 64685 (24 October 2022); Executive Order 13851: Blocking Property of Certain Persons Contributing to the Situation in Nicaragua, 83 FR 61505 (27 November 2018); Executive Order 13536: Blocking Property of Certain Persons Contributing to the Conflict in Somalia, 75 FR 19869 (12 April 2010); Executive Order 13664: Blocking Property of Certain Persons with Respect to South Sudan, 79 FR 19283 (3 April 2014); Executive Order 13611: Blocking Property of Persons Threatening the Peace, Security, or Stability of Yemen, 77 FR 29533 (16 May 2012). The executive orders on North Korea can be found at https://ofac.treasury.gov/sanctions-programs-and-country-information/north-korea-sanctions.

134 Interview with a Swiss sanctions expert, 5 June 2024.

135 Anton Moiseienko, 'The Sins of the Fathers: Targeted Sanctions against Family Members of Primary Targets' (2024) 87(4) *Modern LR* 926. For EU-focused analysis, see Graham Butler, 'Of Rulers, Relatives, and Businesspersons: The Imposition of EU Restrictive Measures through Sanctions on Family Members' (2023) 50(4) *Legal Issues of European Integration* 367. For useful comments on family-member sanctions in the context of sanctions evasion, see Francesca Finelli, 'Countering Circumvention of Restrictive Measures: The EU Response' (2023) 60(3) *Common Market LR* 733.

136 Preamble 5 to Council Decision (CFSP) 2023/1094 of 5 June 2023.

137 Council Regulation (EU) No 204/2011, as amended by Regulation (EU) 2015/1828 of 12 October 2015, Article 1b.

allegations of sanctions evasion on the part of family members yet involve them benefitting from the primary target's alleged misconduct, is likely to fall within this category.[138] Here, too, governments have been non-committal. This is yet another example of how the superficial simplicity of sanctions conceals an emerging legal regime of great complexity and uncertainty.

4.4 COERCED PAYMENTS: A DIFFICULT CASE

If one considers the balance between exclusion and surveillance, then targeted financial sanctions are almost entirely exclusion-oriented.[139] The same is also true of the criminalisation of terrorist financing. All those measures are aimed at severing any connections between the legitimate economy, of the sanctioning state and terrorist or sanctioned actors. This uncompromising stance gives rise to complications in the case of coerced payments, such as ransom demand by terrorist organisations, cybercriminals or other criminal groups. The dilemmas that are created by the CTF and sanctions legislation in those instances require serious consideration.

4.4.1 *Terrorist 'Taxation'*

It is convenient to begin by exploring the position of companies or individuals that face terrorist taxation or extortion demands. Consider the case of Lafarge, a cement construction company that operated a plant in Syria prior to the emergence of ISIS. Having constructed its flagship plant in Syria for US$680 million shortly before the ISIS insurgency, Lafarge was keen to preserve the operation of the plant as well as the livelihoods of the people who worked there. In order to do so, Lafarge acceded to the taxation demands made by ISIS. As a result, the plant was allowed to continue to operate in an area under ISIS's control. Lafarge made millions of dollars in payments and, instead of consulting with any governmental authorities on the best course of action, sought to conceal those payments. In due course, that led to Lafarge being prosecuted for and pleading guilty to terrorist financing in the US.[140]

138 Moiseienko, 'The Sins of the Fathers'.

139 Note, however, initiatives such as H.R. 6370, or the proposed 'OFAC Licensure for Investigators Act', which would authorise certain US persons to 'conduct very limited financial transactions with and through sanctioned entities, enabling OFAC to investigate leads that would otherwise be prohibited under US sanctions laws': 'Ranking Member Waters Announces Passage of Bipartisan Legislation to Protect U.S. National Security During Full Committee Markup', *US House Committee on Financial Services: Democrats*, 14 November 2023, https://democrats-financialservices.house.gov/news/documentsingle.aspx?DocumentID=410988.

140 US Department of Justice, 'Lafarge Pleads Guilty to Conspiring to Provide Material Support to Foreign Terrorist Organizations', 18 October 2022, www.justice.gov/opa/pr/lafarge-pleads-guilty-conspiring-provide-material-support-foreign-terrorist-organizations.

In France, Lafarge and several of its executives are under criminal investigation for (financial) complicity in crimes against humanity.[141]

The moral and policy intuitions that such cases engender might pull in different directions. On the one hand, CTF and sanctions laws are intended precisely to ensure that terrorist or sanctioned organisations cannot continue to derive financial advantages from their interactions with legitimate companies, including through the kind of taxation that this case involved. On the other hand, one need not be oblivious to the profound human consequences that the closure of the plant would have had on the lives of those who worked there and their families. It is not necessarily self-evident that a complete cessation of all commercial activity in terrorist-controlled territory best serves the interests of the population that has to remain there.

A similar dilemma manifests itself in connection with charity activities that provide support to vulnerable populations in conflict-riven or terrorist-controlled areas. Their operations are complicated because of, among other things, the risks of liability for terrorist financing ad sanctions evasion if donations end up diverted to the hands of malicious actors. Even if a particular charity were prepared to undergo such a risk, chances are that financial institutions involved, such as banks, would not allow those operations to continue due to the risks that they themselves would face.[142]

4.4.2 *Terrorist Ransom*

The most stark and heartbreaking manifestation of the dilemmas borne out of an uncompromising prohibition on payment to terrorists arises in cases of families being faced with terrorist ransom demands. Kidnappings carried out by ISIS provide some of the best-known and tragic examples, such as the abduction and murder of the American journalist James Foley.[143]

In principle, neither the 1999 Convention nor the relevant Security Council Resolutions[144] allow for any exceptions to its overarching prohibition on the provision of financial resources to terrorists. The payment of a terrorist ransom should therefore prima facie be a criminal offence. Multiple governments, including those of the US and the UK, take precisely that view and vow zero tolerance towards such payments. Although most other governments around the world embrace the same position in their rhetoric, speculation abounds that for a long period of time some

[141] 'Lafarge Loses Latest Appeal over Crimes against Humanity Charges', *Reuters*, 19 May 2022.

[142] See Clive Walker, 'Terrorism Financing and the Policing of Charities: Who Pays the Price?' in Colin King and Clive Walker (eds), *Dirty Assets: Emerging Issues in the Regulation of Criminal and Terrorist Assets* (Ashgate, 2014). See also Clive Walker's written evidence to the UK House of Commons' Home Affairs Committee in 2013 available at https://committees.parliament.uk/writtenevidence/47679/html/.

[143] See 'Remembering James Foley Nine Years after His Death', *The National Press Club*, 25 August 2023, www.press.org/newsroom/remembering-james-foley-nine-years-after-his-death.

[144] Such as UN Security Council Resolution 2133 (2014).

states may not have been practising what they preach. That reportedly accounts for the returns of some hostages from the hands of terrorist organisations such as ISIS. In a paper surveying the status quo, Anja Shortland and Tom Keatinge write as follows:

> Governments know that engaging with, and offering large concessions to, designated terrorists creates greater insecurity for others, who may be targeted in the future. Yet, despite the signing of communiqués and the passing of UN Security Council Resolutions, de facto political commitment to implementing the blanket ban on concessions varies across countries. For example, after UN Security Council Resolution 2133 – which calls on states to prevent ransom payments and political concessions from benefiting terrorists – was passed in 2014, Argentina's representative noted that the response to kidnapping must take the specific circumstances of each incident into account. The diplomat added that such measures should not undermine the potential payment of ransoms for hostages. This statement aptly illustrates the gap between the aspiration to prevent substantial concessions (including the payment of ransoms) to designated terrorist groups and the reality of the actions of many nations when faced with hostage situations.[145]

The questions that arise in connection with terrorist ransom can be best understood by separating out the three rationales behind the exclusion of terrorists from the legitimate economy. As discussed in Section 4.3.1, those can be described in shorthand as complicity, disruption and denial. In the case of a territory-controlling terrorist organisation, such as ISIS, while ransom can be a not insubstantial source of revenue, it would be foolhardy to suggest that depriving the group of that income can meaningfully starve it of the resources it needs. The nature of a territory-controlling group is such that multiple other sources of income are available, not least the taxation of the population under its control, as well as clandestine sales of natural resources, such as ISIS's oil.

On the other hand, the complicity rationale is worthy of serious consideration. No one would seriously blame the family of a hostage for being morally complicit in terrorist acts if they acceded to a ransom demand and made the payout to free their loved one. To the best of my knowledge, no prosecutions have been brought in recent memory based on such a set of circumstances.[146] If they were, then criminal law defences such as of duress or necessity would present considerable obstacles to the prosecution case. Importantly, however, the payment of ransom often relies on intermediaries, such as professional kidnapping negotiating companies, who are

[145] Anja Shortland and Tom Keatinge, 'Closing the Gap: Assessing Responses to Terrorist-Related Kidnap-for-Ransom', *RUSI Occasional Paper*, September 2017, 1.

[146] As distinct from prosecutions of people sending money to their family members who travel to become foreign terrorist fighters: see 'Sally Lane and John Letts Sentenced for Sending Money to Daesh Supporting Son', Crown Prosecution Service, 2019, www.cps.gov.uk/cps/news/sally-lane-and-john-letts-sentenced-sending-money-daesh-supporting-son.

likely to be risk averse when faced with potential liability for terrorist financing.[147] Seen in that light, the primary import of the laws against terrorist ransom payments is not to enable the prosecution of understandably desperate families[148] but to prevent professional intermediaries from forming a market similar to that which exists for negotiations with Somali pirates.[149]

Whether or not preventing the establishment of such a market is worth the tragic consequences that follow a refusal to pay is a question that is inherently not susceptible to a clearcut answer. For now, despite the appearance of an international consensus, governments continue to take divergent views in practice on whether refusing to pay ransom in individual cases is outweighed by the broader systemic benefits of doing so.

4.4.3 *Ransomware*

A dramatically different situation that nonetheless implicates a somewhat similar array of considerations involves payouts in response to ransomware attacks,[150] which involve encrypting the victim's computer files and demanding payment in exchange for description. A more recent variation involves threatening the publication of stolen files, including confidential documents, on the Internet should the ransom not be forthcoming. That latter type of extortion is aimed at companies that otherwise may be impervious to ransomware demands because their files are appropriately backed up.

The arguments canvassed in the ransomware context bear resemblance to those that have surfaced in connection with terrorist ransom debates. On the one hand, there is little doubt that the availability of payments incentivises ransomware groups to carry on. On the other hand, there are other significant considerations, such as the harm that would eventuate from not paying or, in cases of attacks against critical services, the societal ramifications of not having certain services available for period of time due to a ransomware attack.[151]

147 On the economy of kidnap-for-ransom negotiations, see Anja Shortland, *Kidnap: Inside the Ransom Business* (Oxford University Press, 2019).

148 However, James Foley's mother, Diane, details in her book how she and her family 'were threatened on three different occasions [by the US government] with criminal prosecution if we tried to raise ransom money for Jim's release and were clearly told that there would be no attempted rescue or negotiation through a third party': Colum McCann and Diane Foley, *American Mother* (Bloomsbury Publishing, 2024) Book 2, Ch 4.

149 For examples of ransom negotiations related to Somali pirate hostage-taking, see Shortland, *Kidnap*, 107–130.

150 Ransomware is a portmanteau word comprising 'ransom' and 'malware', itself short for 'malicious software'.

151 For ransomware victims' perspectives and experiences, see Pia Hüsch, Gareth Mott and Jamie MacColl, with Jason R. C. Nurse, James Sullivan, Sarah Turner and Nandita Pattnaik, '"Your Data Is Stolen and Encrypted": The Ransomware Victim Experience', *RUSI Occasional Paper*, July 2024.

Empirical research conducted by the Tech Policy Design Centre at ANU demonstrates that intuitions about the propriety of ransomware payments differ widely depending on the situation.[152] Overall, there is no greater consensus as to the right course of action in the context of ransomware than there is for terrorist ransom. But the practical consequences of this uncertainty have been dramatically different. Unlike in connection with terrorism, in which context ransom payments are prohibited by virtue of the 1999 Convention and FATF Recommendations, as discussed above, ransomware payments are generally legal across the world.

This tracks the general common law position that, subject to specific exceptions in some jurisdictions,[153] ransom payments to criminals are not illegal – as distinct from, say, laundering their proceeds. Despite varying initiatives aimed at either criminalising ransom payments or imposing disclosure requirements, most of those initiatives remain nascent and have not yet been adopted.[154] The tentative nature of the ongoing discussions is evident from the multilateral Counter Ransomware Initiative (CRI), which brings together 50 states. In 2023, the CRI adopted a joint statement declaring that 'member governments should not pay ransoms', as well as committing to an array of measures to increase private-sector resilience to ransomware.[155]

Still, participating governments take differing positions on what that means. For instance, the Australian government has promulgated multiple documents suggesting that it 'strongly discourage[s] anyone from paying a ransomware demand'[156] and 'does not condone ransom payments being made to cybercriminals'[157] – despite there being no legislative prohibition on such payments in place in Australia. By contrast, the UK's official position is that the 'decision whether or not to pay the ransom is ultimately a matter for the individual or organisations concerned'.[158] In July 2024, the UK's new Labour government outlined in the King's Speech its plans to introduce a Cyber Security and Resilience Bill that would, among other things, require mandatory ransomware reporting.[159]

[152] Johanna Weaver, Tanvi Nair and Leah Lafferty, 'Combatting Ransomware: Policy Paper', *Tech Policy Design Centre*, August 2023.

[153] For example, in Nigeria the payment of ransom to criminal groups was criminalised in 2022: Priya Sippi, 'Nigeria's Kidnap Crisis: Inside Story of a Ransom Negotiator', *BBC*, 21 March 2024, www.bbc.com/news/world-africa-68612958.

[154] For example, the Australian Ransomware Payments Bill 2021 (No. 2) (Cth), which would have introduced mandatory ransomware reporting requirements, lapsed at the end of Parliament in July 2022.

[155] The White House, 'International Counter Ransomware Initiative 2023 Joint Statement', 1 November 2023.

[156] Commonwealth of Australia, *2023–2030 Australian Cyber Security Strategy*, 2023, 23.

[157] Commonwealth of Australia, *2021 Ransomware Action Plan*, 2021, 1, 5, 8.

[158] UK House of Commons, Joint Committee on the National Security Strategy, *Inquiry into Ransomware*, Written Evidence Submitted by His Majesty's Government, para 24, https://committees.parliament.uk/writtenevidence/114408/html/.

[159] Stuart Davey, 'King's Speech: New Cyber Resilience Laws Planned in the UK', *Pinsent Masons*, 17 July 2024, www.pinsentmasons.com/out-law/news/king-speech-uk-nis2-trailed-cyber-resilience-law-announced.

The overtones of exclusion and surveillance in the ongoing debates about optimal ransomware regulation are unmistakable. Much of the conversation revolves around the incentives created by potential ban on ransom payments. The principal concern is that imposing such a ban will not do much to change the underlying incentive structure. The pressure to pay in order to restore operations, eject the attacker from one's system or prevent the publication of confidential files may be overwhelming. If that is so, then a blanket ban on ransomware payouts will merely push them underground, thereby reducing law enforcement agencies' visibility into the ransom economy. Some, however, are sceptical of the argument. Ciaran Martin, the former head of the UK's National Cyber Security Centre, writes as follows:

> Terrible arguments have been made against a ban. One is that 'it will drive the problem underground'. Will company directors really knowingly break the criminal law? Other reasons are falling apart. When the Australian health insurer Medibank was hacked, the data of more than a third of the population was at risk. When the criminals released the data, however, it was suppressed by law enforcement and the media and no harm was done.[160]

Regardless of the view one gravitates towards, this is yet another manifestation of the tensions between exclusion and surveillance latent throughout the law of financial crime. Equally, given the potentially dire consequences of not paying, the question of whether ransom payments can be properly seen as a form of complicity in enabling the ransomware economy is a complicated one. Like with terrorist ransoms, the victim's position is dramatically different from that of a bank dealing proceeds of crime, who can well and truly be thought of as morally complicit in the predicate offence.

One significant difference between CTF rules and ransomware payments is that the discussions surrounding the appropriate regulation of ransomware have started from clean slate. By contrast, terrorist financing is the subject of a Convention in place since 1999, as discussed above, as well as the FATF Recommendations. The strictures of these international requirements mean that the pressure towards criminalisation of ransom payments is much greater in the CTF context. Whether that truly results in better, fairer and more socially beneficial regulation of the problem of terrorist ransoms is open to debate. It is entirely possible that the zero-tolerance stance taken by many governments vis-à-vis such payments is optimal, but one could also make the argument that it would benefit from an open discussion that is not beholden to the status quo.

All that said, there is one tool that governments have used in order to criminalise transactions with certain ransomware groups, namely targeted sanctions. Some ransomware outfits, as well as individual cybercriminals, have been designated under sanctions laws, with the effect that no person in the sanctioning state's jurisdiction is

[160] Ciaran Martin, 'Cyber Ransoms Are Too Profitable: Let's Make Paying Illegal', *The Times*, 4 March 2024.

allowed to pay them.[161] This gives rise to a two-tier hierarchy of ransomware actors: those who can be paid, problematic though such payments might be, and those who cannot be paid at all, under any circumstances, on pain of criminal prosecution. Being in that latter category is obviously undesirable from the vantage point of a ransomware group because the designation is liable to reduce victims' willingness to pay ransom.

This stratification of the ransomware economy raises novel questions for governments that resort to sanctions, namely how to decide when a particular ransomware group should be sanctioned. One possible approach is to reserve sanctions designations to the worst offenders that engage in activities that truly put them beyond the pale, such as attacks on critical national infrastructure. This would create a curious but arguably desirable state of affairs wherein certain ground rules may be recognised by most participants in the ransomware ecosystem, with sanctions reserved for the most renegade outfits.

One must of course be careful not to overstate the importance of sanctions, and others have argued compellingly that a whole-of-government approach is warranted to the worse ransomware incidents, including offensive cyber-operations and intensified efforts at bringing cyber criminals to justice.[162] Likewise, alternatives such as the licencing of ransomware payments or even their taxation have been floated by experts.[163] The overarching point is that the agile and responsive approach to ransomware through, among other things, designating the worst offenders might indeed be the way forward in this challenging area.

4.5 CONCLUSION

In Chapters 2 and 3, we encountered the manifold challenges arising from the undirected deputisation inherent in AML laws and regulations, which require regulated

[161] The first sanctions designation of a ransomware group is detailed in US Department of the Treasury, 'Treasury Sanctions Cyber Actors Backed by Iranian Intelligence Ministry', 17 September 2020, adopted based on Executive Order 13553 75 FR 60567 (2010). Later actions include US Department of the Treasury, 'Treasury Sanctions Evil Corp, the Russia-Based Cybercriminal Group behind Dridex Malware', 5 December 2019; US Department of the Treasury, 'United States and United Kingdom Sanction Members of Russia-Based Trickbot Cybercrime Gang', 9 February 2023; US Department of the Treasury, 'United States and United Kingdom Sanction Additional Members of the Russia-Based Trickbot Cybercrime Gang', 7 September 2023. The most recent such designation as of this writing is the joint US, UK and Australian designation detailed in NCA, 'LockBit Leader Unmasked and Sanctioned', 7 May 2024; www.nationalcrimeagency.gov.uk/news/lockbit-leader-unmasked-and-sanctioned.

[162] See Alvaro Marañon and Stephanie Pell, 'Countering the Ransomware Threat: A Whole-of-Government Effort', *Lawfare*, 22 November 2021, www.lawfaremedia.org/article/countering-ransomware-threat-whole-government-effort.

[163] Stewart Baker, 'The Cyberlaw Podcast: Serious Threats, Unserious Responses', 6 February 2024, www.lawfaremedia.org/article/the-cyberlaw-podcast-serious-threats-unserious-responses (arguing for taxation of ransomware payments).

businesses to report suspicious activities while avoiding knowing involvement in money laundering. As we saw, tensions between exclusion and surveillance produce difficult policy dilemmas that governments do not resolve, while other competing values and principles – such as the presumption of innocence and financial privacy – further complicate the picture.

CTF rules give rise to similar dilemmas. Here, too, commentators occasionally overlook or minimise the value of financial surveillance, which becomes especially apparent in the aftermath of terrorist attacks. This often leads to suggestions that AML and CTF efforts are so distinct in their focus that supporting them through what is effectively an amalgamated regulatory regime is a folly. These arguments overstate the differences between these two bodies of rules and underplay the importance that the same instruments of financial surveillance can legitimately play in both those domains.

As regards the exclusion of terrorist actors from the legitimate economy, the language of denying terrorists access to the resources they need features prominently in governments' rhetoric. One can think of this as an additional rationale ('denial') behind the exclusion paradigm that we discussed in connection with AML laws. Whether such denial is realistic depends heavily on the nature of the terrorist actor involved, for instance, whether it holds control over territory that it can exploit at will.

One essential component of today's CTF efforts has been the use of targeted sanctions to prohibit the provision of any resources to, and freeze the assets of, designated terrorists. The same measures have recently been adopted by some governments across vast swathes of criminal justice, including to address corruption, human rights abuse, drug trafficking, cybercrime and other transnational organised crime activities. Furthermore, the UN Security Council maintains a sanctions list of North Korean nuclear proliferators. Such sanctions involve a shift towards a different mode of financial exclusion: from the 'general' exclusion achieved through AML/CTF rules that place upon regulated businesses the burden of identifying suspicious or criminal activities to the 'targeted' exclusion by governments of specific person or groups, which *everyone* within the sanctioning state's jurisdiction must abide by.

Despite the lesser ambiguity that targeted exclusion entails, there remain significant conceptual and practical challenges. It is clear that the bank accounts of someone subject to sanctions must be frozen, but one might rightly ask what happens to the companies, trusts or property that person indirectly controls (and what does indirect control even mean?); other individuals acting on behalf of that person or even individuals benefitting from that person's alleged malign activities. All of those issues have caused genuine difficulties in the implementation of sanctions and, for ease of reference, all of them can be thought of as a 'sanctions penumbra' – a shade, long or short depending on the applicable legal framework, that the sanctions designations cast.

Furthermore, the expansion in sanctions regimes is hardly matched by the sophistication of their enforcement. It continues to rely significantly on sanctions screening, that is, the matching of customer or counterparty details with those on a sanctions list, which is only suited to identifying direct hits, rather than detecting any companies or properties indirectly controlled by sanctioned persons. All of that demonstrates how targeted exclusion, too, comes with its challenges.

Finally, one common feature of the criminalisation of terrorist financing and the prohibition of transacting with sanctioned persons is their all-or-nothing, zero-tolerance nature. Subject to government-issued sanctions licences, payments caught by sanctions are not allowed under any circumstances. This raises exceptionally difficult legal, moral and practical dilemmas insofar as coerced payments are concerned, such as terrorist 'taxation', terrorist ransom demands or ransomware attacks. From among those situations, ransomware is the only one that falls outside the ambit of any binding international instruments or the FATF Recommendations, and it is notable how cautiously governments around the world have moved in *not* enacting any ransomware payment-specific legislation. For now, this caution appears commendable.

5

Conclusion

A Call for Recalibration

5.1 INTRODUCTION

Every banking transaction you or I ever undertake, from using a debit card to buy a coffee to servicing a mortgage, is subject to automatic checks performed by the bank's transaction monitoring system.[1] Signs of suspicious activity, such as transfers to or from high-risk jurisdictions or anomalously large amounts involved, are known as 'red flags' and are likely to trigger manual review by an analyst. If ultimately deemed suspicious, the transaction will be reported to the government via a SAR, which may or may not lead to further law enforcement action – and, in any event, will form part of a database of SARs that law enforcement agencies may draw upon in the future. Customers that trigger 'red flags' too often or otherwise present costly due diligence requirements, for example, because of their nationality, may find themselves 'offboarded' as a client. And, of course, if they are in fact involved in money laundering or terrorist financing, they are liable to criminal prosecution. So, too, would be the bank if it knowingly facilitated money laundering or terrorist financing.

These controls that operate underneath the surface of everyday financial interactions are meant to counteract financial crime, including money laundering, terrorist financing and sanctions evasion. Despite their quotidian, technocratic nature, they raise a host of big-picture issues that define the relationship between the individual (or a business) and the state. First, who can be legitimately excluded from everyday commercial interactions? Second, and relatedly, are there any categories of such commercial interactions that *everyone* is entitled to? Third, what are the limits of financial privacy?

These questions go to the heart of the problem with financial crime regulation. We, collectively as society, are trying to do two worthwhile things at the same time. On the one hand, we are seeking to exclude criminal actors from the legitimate

[1] For simplicity, this example is framed in terms of a bank but, as explained in Chapter 2, a spate of regulated businesses are subject to the same requirements.

economy. On the other hand, we are attempting to surveil their financial activities. There is little clarity as to which of those objectives predominates. Some of the time, they point in the same direction in terms of the practical measures that need to be taken; at other times, they are mutually contradictory.

Furthermore, in relation to both those objectives, there is no certainty as to how far they should go, and how they ought to be weighed against other, countervailing values. As relates to exclusion, we do not ordinarily seek to isolate criminal actors from commercial interactions at any cost. Considerations such as the presumption of innocence (understood broadly, as a societal value, rather than narrowly as a criminal trial safeguard) and financial inclusion play a role. Therefore, there is a profound and abiding uncertainty as to who should be treated as a potential criminal in the absence of a criminal conviction; what the commercial interactions are from which that person can or cannot be excluded (for example, should the provision of basic banking services always be accessible to all?); and how the scope of exclusionary rules can be calibrated such that innocent third parties are not swept up in the same net.

The boundaries of financial privacy also remain strikingly indeterminate. They keep being relitigated anew in novel contexts. We accept that numbered bank accounts are not permissible, but whether anonymous corporate ownership should be countenanced remains controversial. Debates continue to unfold as to whether anonymity-enhancing cryptocurrencies or mixing technologies are a legitimate tool of protecting privacy or merely a means of concealing crime, and in the meantime some jurisdictions are contemplating a complete redefinition of financial privacy through the introduction of retail CBDCs.

These unresolved tensions at the core of the financial crime regime, which are highlighted in Table 5.1, have profound implications for debates around its effectiveness. Whatever benchmark we choose, our current framework can never be totally effective. It is not fully effective in shutting out criminal actors from the legitimate economy because it is not entirely geared towards that objective. By the same token, it is also not completely effective in surveilling the financial activities of suspected criminals: once again, this is not the sole, overarching objective of the regime.

Not only do the principal objectives of exclusion and surveillance come into tension with each other, but they are further diluted by other values and principles that we hold dear. In theory, it is possible to imagine a world where some of the trade-offs that we are grappling with would simply not arise. For example, suppose we accepted that the exclusion of suspected criminals from interactions with the legitimate economy was a worthwhile objective regardless of its collateral consequences. The issue of financial exclusion would remain but would no longer be considered a problem because we would accept it as a cost we are prepared to pay. Equally, if total financial surveillance by the government were desirable, then discussions around the optimal reporting models, such as whether they should be suspicion-based or rest on objective criteria, would become obsolete.

TABLE 5.1 *Exclusion and surveillance in financial crime regulation*

AML	The base case of the tensions that the financial crime regime engenders. AML regulation pursues the objectives of exclusion and surveillance, which are generally compatible but can come into conflict. Furthermore, both those objectives are in tension with other values and principles, such as the presumption of innocence (in the case of exclusion) and financial privacy (in the case of surveillance). These tensions give rise to complex question of principle that remain unresolved and surface repeatedly in different contexts. They give rise to an *alignment challenge* where these difficult tensions are left for the private sector to resolve in a manner that is untethered from law enforcement needs or priorities.
CTF	The exclusion objective frequently manifests itself in the CTF context as the (often unrealistic) objective of *denying* terrorist actors all access to funds. Taken to an extreme, it exacerbates financial exclusion concerns given the nature of businesses or individuals often affected by CTF rules, such as charities or foreign citizens from conflict-affected countries.
Sanctions	Sanctions present a different form of exclusion. Unlike 'general' exclusion focused on keeping the proceeds of crime or terrorist funds out of the legitimate economy, 'targeted' exclusion involves a blanket ban on commercial interactions with the sanctioned person, regardless of whether the proceeds of crime or terrorist funds are involved. Targeted exclusion gives rise to distinct policy, implementation and humanitarian challenges, including the question of who should be treated as being controlled by, or associated with, the targeted person.

The reason we continue to fumble away through a set of hard policy choices is precisely because we have no answers to those big-picture, conceptual conundrums. Nor should we have any easy solutions: those are genuinely difficult issues to address. We cannot jettison the presumption of innocence or financial inclusion because doing so would spare us the headache of thinking through their implications. Nor is it advisable to drop the twin projects of excluding criminals from the legitimate economy and surveilling their financial activities: for all the imperfections of implementation, those are worthy objectives.

In this state of uncertainty, one implication is that a great deal of responsibility is delegated to financial institutions and other regulated businesses. Suppose, for example, a bank needs to settle on an approach it will take to customers from a certain high-risk jurisdiction. The considerations of preventing financial crime, such as money laundering or sanctions evasion, might point in the direction of large-scale derisking, that is dropping a swathe of customers as clients on the basis of the risk that they present. Conversely, the imperatives of financial inclusion would militate the other way. This weighing of policy considerations should not be left in the hands of a private organisation; instead, clear, coherent and consistent governmental regulation needs to be issued.

So far, the favoured response of governments to such situations has been a non-response: instead of providing definitive guidance, preferably binding in law, financial regulators are likely to exhort the institution to act consistent with its own 'risk appetite'. That is industry jargon for weighing the risk of penalties for regulatory non-compliance against the benefits to be realised from continuing to do business with certain customers. This answer abdicates the governmental responsibility for setting out its policy; nor is it truly amenable to giving expression to a broader range of societal goals, such as financial inclusion, which have nothing to do with the regulated business's risk/reward calculus.

Any regulated business's rational behaviour would be to ensure punctilious compliance with applicable rules at the lowest possible cost without regard to whether or not such compliance achieves any valuable social goal: the so-called tick-box compliance. Suppose, however, that a given business wishes to move beyond this and achieve purposive compliance that truly advances the objectives of financial crime rules. That simply brings us back to what, precisely, those objectives are and how they are to be weighed against other competing values and principles.

5.2 CONTOURS OF A FUNCTIONAL FINANCIAL CRIME REGIME

What, then, is the cure to the challenges that continue to afflict financial crime regulation? There does not appear to be a single set of solutions, but, as a thought experiment, one can work through a range of possible parameters within which a financial crime regulatory regime could operate.

1. **Exclusion-oriented regime.** One could conceive of a system that is overwhelmingly exclusion-oriented in requiring regulated businesses to forego commercial engagements if they as much as suspect that proceeds of crime are involved. Such a regime would exact a significant cost in terms of financial exclusion of segments of the population, but it is an intellectually coherent response to the imperative of excluding the proceeds of crime from the legitimate economy. While this approach is radical, in some jurisdictions it would present a less dramatic departure from the law as it currently stands than one might have expected. For instance, Australian federal law criminalises dealing in the proceeds of crime if the person is reckless as to property constituting proceeds of crime, and recklessness involves a mere awareness of the *possibility* of that property being proceeds of crime. Of course, as ever with legal rules, for the exclusion approach to realise its effect it needs to be credibly enforced. Besides financial exclusion, it is virtually inevitable that, if effectively implemented, this approach would lead to the displacement of proceeds of crime into non-regulated sectors. Depending on whether one takes a complicity-oriented or disruption-oriented view of the value of exclusion, this can either be a desirable result or an unintended consequence.

2. **Surveillance-oriented regime**. Alternatively, one could imagine a system that prioritises financial surveillance. Its most far-reaching manifestation would be a regime wherein all financial transactions are freely accessible to law enforcement agencies. In such a system, finer details of reporting thresholds, such as whether reporting should be suspicion-based or predicated on objective criteria such as the nature or amount of the transaction, simply do not arise. While there is no precedent of a modern liberal democracy with comparable levels of financial surveillance, the introduction of retail CBDCs could give rise precisely to such a financial environment. In those circumstances, the FATF's existing suspicious activity reporting requirements would be rendered moot. Short of such a recalibration of our financial system towards total access to transactions for government and law enforcement agencies, our conceptions of financial privacy will continue influencing choices about the categories of transactions or other activities that should be reported: suspicious ones, unusual ones, cross-border ones, those in excess of a certain threshold, all of the above – or, perhaps, if one were to repudiate the surveillance-oriented regime entirely and return to the pre-AML/CTF world, none of the above.

One's instinctual response to the options laid out above is likely to be the Solomonic intuition that neither an entirely exclusion-oriented regime nor an entirely surveillance-oriented one is desirable, and charting out a middle course of some description must be preferable. That is partially true, but the compromise that the current AML/CTF framework rests upon merely delegates difficult choices to the regulated businesses.

In essence, this compromise is embodied in the FATF-mandated formula that suspicious activities must be reported while knowing involvement in money laundering must be criminalised. This is a sensible enough answer to the question of 'What is the right thing for a regulated business to do?'. However, the incentives it creates come with a raft of well-documented unintended consequences:

- To avoid the regulatory penalties and reputational consequences associated with under-reporting, regulated businesses engage in defensive filing, which diminishes the intelligence value of their reports and stretches the government's analytical resources.
- Once suspicious activity is detected and reported, they cut their ties with the customer in question, which causes the customer to decamp to another regulated business (which might or might not be equally diligent in compliance) or displace their activities to an unregulated sector of the economy altogether, depriving the government of further insight into that customer's activities.
- Some categories of customers that are presumptively treated as posing a higher financial crime risk – and therefore presenting a higher compliance cost – struggle to obtain access to regulated services at all, which undermines their access to essential services, such as bank accounts, while foregoing the availability of valuable financial intelligence in those cases where genuine suspicions could exist.

Not only are these consequences unintended, but they are also entirely divorced from governmental or law enforcement priorities at any given moment in time. For example, a police agency might be keen to obtain intelligence on financial flows associated with suspected human trafficking operations involving a specific third country's nationals. However, unless expanded and refined in domestic law, the reporting obligations stemming from the FATF Recommendations are not designed to be in any way responsive to the government's changing needs.

While much of the academic critique of the contemporary AML/CTF regime has focused on the deputisation of the private sector to carry out essentially governmental functions, from the effectiveness standpoint the problem is not so much that of deputisation as it is of *undirected* deputisation. Regulated businesses operate within the broad parameters of the incentives created for them, which are too blunt to be reflective of the law enforcement requirements of the day.

As mentioned previously, one might compare this state of affairs to being asked to do food shopping armed not with a shopping list, but with a general injunction to buy something healthy and tasty. The two requirements are not directly in contradiction, and with a modicum of common sense one can do a reasonable job in finding something that is generally healthy and generally tasty, but the probability of one's choice matching the cook's preferences on any given day is rather low. Like the hapless food shopper, regulated businesses operate under a set of incentives that says remarkably little of what a healthy and tasty financial crime regime is – or, in other words, what customers are best kept out from accessing their services and what valuable reporting looks like.

5.2.1 *Distinguishing between Regulated Activities*

There are multiple ways of imparting a greater sense of direction to the regulated sectors, all of which require revisiting elements of the existing regime. First, one can reconsider the implicit assumption that all regulated activities should attract the same AML/CTF regulation. Consider a basic bank account. Generally speaking, having access to one is a prerequisite to receiving salary, paying rent and handling other financial necessities of everyday life. The exclusionary effect of not having one is particularly pernicious and likely to affect the least protected strata of the society, including refugees and people living below the poverty line. There may also be some marginal benefits to forestalling criminal actors from accessing basic bank accounts, but the extent to which this is valuable must be in doubt. Proceeds of crime do not vanish into thin air simply because they cannot be invested or moved via the banking system, and money could still be moved in cash or via trade transactions, including internationally. The lack of access to bank accounts would create friction in a criminal enterprise, but there is a compelling argument that this benefit is outweighed by the risks of financial exclusion.

Contrast this to access to high-end investment banking services, such as those involved in the 'mirror trade' scheme designed by Deutsche Bank to move billions of dollars out of Russia and into the UK that subsequently led to a £163 million dollar fine by the FCA. The know-how involved in such services can amplify the sophistication of money laundering schemes, while the negative social consequences of excluding any particular individual or company from the ability to access such services are likely to be modest and limited to foregoing some economic efficiency gains. The range of persons who would seek such services is limited to begin with. Furthermore, the risks of unjustified exclusion are mitigated by the fact that the lucrative nature of those services creates an incentive to provide them. In short, there may be a segment of sophisticated, high-end services in relation to which a low liability threshold could be appropriate: for example, criminal or civil liability if those services are provided in connection with *suspected* proceeds of crime.

If this logic is accepted, then three categories of regulated services can be discerned:

- For certain basic services, which can also be described as public utilities, reporting requirements should be specified that enable government and law enforcement agencies to identify illegal activity but no liability should attach to the provision of those services to anyone at all, including criminal actors, so long as those reporting obligations are met.
- For the majority of regulated services, some compromise position that encompasses both exclusion and surveillance, similar to the duality of objectives embodied in the current FATF-mandated regime, can be maintained. However, as discussed below, governments and law enforcement agencies should have mechanisms available to them to focus the attention of the regulated businesses on specific organised crime threats whenever appropriate.
- For a small minority of highly specialised services with the potential to significantly increase the sophistication and scale of financial crime, the exclusion of proceeds of crime may be an appropriate overarching objective. This means that liability can be triggered by the provision of such services in connection with *suspected* proceeds of crime or be predicated on some other such low threshold.

The point being made here is not that governments should necessarily undertake a classification exercise to group all regulated services into one of those three categories, but that countries should be able to deviate from the FATF-mandated middle ground and prioritise either surveillance or exclusion in respect of certain regulated services if doing so best comports with their efforts against financial crime. For example, services whose potential for criminal exploitation is matched by their relative inaccessibility to vast swathes of the population are prime candidates for the exclusion paradigm: think of the storage of art in freeports, which is subject to the EU's AML/CTF rules.

The proposal to distinguish between various categories of regulated services in this manner might provoke the instinctual response that doing so would introduce a further layer of complexity to a regime that requires no such thing. In reality, though, this complexity would be limited to policymaking: that is, it would be incumbent on governments to think with greater clarity about what they hope to achieve from the regulation of a particular activity. In terms of compliance efforts, the ability to focus them on exclusion or surveillance depending on the nature of the regulated activity would be a source of greater ease, not additional difficulty.

Up until now, there have only been tentative steps towards this nuanced regulatory approach. They have mostly involved discussions of potential universal access to basic bank accounts, as well as the fact that representation of clients in litigation is not regulated under the FATF Recommendations, unlike transactional legal work. The inchoate state of debate in this area is regrettable, and the legal profession offers a particularly compelling example of a professional sector where sharper lines between the treatment of various regulated services would be helpful.

For instance, there is a strong argument in favour of maintaining the absolute confidentiality of lawyer–client discussions in criminal litigation; likewise, it would be inimical to the rule of law to require lawyers to forego criminal representation if they knew or suspected the client was guilty. Whether the same uncompromising approach should be taken to all categories of civil litigation is open to question. Not only can reporting obligations be contemplated, but one could also conceive of a requirement not to undertake certain categories of civil litigation work if a lawyer suspected that he or she would be paid from the proceeds of crime. The same point applies with greater force to transactional work, especially high-end advisory services.

These precepts, if accepted, would merely provide a general framework for the AML/CTF regulation of the legal profession. One would need to articulate the precise obligations that would attach to various legal services and, in doing so, consider the balance between the objectives of exclusion and surveillance. For instance, in the context of ongoing debates surrounding SLAPP lawsuits, one could require lawyers to reject such work if a suspicion arose that the client's wealth in general, or the money used to pay the lawyer specifically, was the proceeds of crime. In relation to transactional services, reporting obligations could be imposed without any such exclusion-oriented requirements being necessary.

As mentioned previously, this is but one example of a plausible regulatory scheme. It represents one of a range of possible options. Still, as mentioned earlier, most regulated services will continue to be characterised by some combination of exclusion- and surveillance-driven objectives. This does not mean that there are no alternatives to the undirected deputisation of today. That leads us to the second way of focusing the regulatory regime, namely recognising that law enforcement priorities are not static and that the financial crime regulatory regime should be capable of supporting those changing priorities.

5.2.2 *Aligning Compliance Efforts with Law Enforcement Priorities*

Suppose Australian law enforcement agencies decided that shutting drug trafficking groups out of the country's legitimate economy was essential to undermining their profitability. If effectively transmitted to the private sector, this law enforcement priority could inform both the thematic allocation of efforts, with a focus on transactions bearing hallmarks of drug trafficking, for example, cross-border transactions involving known high-risk jurisdictions, and their nature, with a bias towards the termination of customer relationships suspected of association with the drug trade. To achieve their desired effect, those measures would also require a degree of information-sharing among regulated businesses to ensure that terminated customers cannot literally or metaphorically walk down the street to bring their custom elsewhere. Conversely, if an Al-Shabaab fundraising cell operated in Australia, the benefits of tracing its financial activities might outweigh the modest rewards of shutting down its fundraising operations or driving it out into the unregulated financial sector, such as underground hawala transactions.

From a law enforcement perspective, therefore, whether exclusion or surveillance should be prioritised, can differ depending on the threat (e.g. the type of criminal activity); its source (domestic vs. foreign); and the nature of the country's exposure to that threat (e.g. an investment destination vs. corporate services hub). Such prioritisation choices can be difficult, but the crucial points are that, first, they have to be made; and, second, the financial crime regime need not be divorced from those priorities, as happens all too often.

There are multiple avenues that countries have pursued to align the efforts made by regulated businesses with the law enforcement priorities of the day. These include, most notably, public–private partnerships, whose entire ethos is that of collaboration in identifying and addressing criminal threats. So far, the greatest challenge that limits the reach and impact of public–private partnerships is the trade-off between expanding their scope to a greater number of regulated businesses and preserving the trusted environment that makes such partnerships worthwhile. Other options for ensuring such alignment include targeted reporting regimes, such as GTOs, a formal 'keep open' regime or even the simple issuance of appropriately focused regulatory guidance.

Save for public–private partnerships, none of these solutions have been attempted on a scale that could turn them into a plausible systemic remedy for the alignment challenge inherent in the undirected nature of the AML/CTF regime, but they represent promising concepts. One could even revisit the notion of paying financial institutions for good-quality reporting, which goes back to *The Cash Connection* report published in 1984 but has been peremptorily dismissed ever since, to the extent that it has been considered at all.

In short, the problem of direction – or alignment between law enforcement priorities and private-sector compliance action – is a difficult one but is amenable to multiple solutions, which are currently being tried out in various jurisdictions. What is missing is any explicit acknowledgment of this issue in the FATF Recommendations, which leads me to the third area in need of the reform.

5.2.3 *Revisiting FATF Recommendations*

The FATF Recommendations are at once over-inclusive and under-inclusive. On the one hand, as already mentioned, the FATF-mandated formula of reporting suspicious activities while criminalising knowing involvement in money laundering or terrorist financing creates a raft of unintended consequences that stem from the incentives that this scheme engenders. Despite the ensuing difficulties, the FATF Recommendations contain no provisions as to the mechanisms that countries might use to resolve the alignment challenge, such as the utilisation of public–private partnerships, GTOs or 'keep open' laws. In that respect, the Recommendations are under-inclusive in stopping one step short of requiring states to establish an anti-financial crime system that actually works.

On the other hand, they are over-inclusive in requiring the filing of SARs as opposed to any other reporting model, such as that predicated on unusual transactions or those above a certain predefined threshold. Which reporting system to implement is a matter that properly belongs within a country's discretion based on its appraisal of where the right balance lies between financial surveillance and financial privacy, as well as its assessment of what information is best suited to the detection of financial crime. Suspicious activity reporting is one of a range of plausible options, but not the only one, nor necessarily the best one.

The over-inclusive and under-inclusive aspects of the FATF Recommendations are not a problem as such but have become one as a result of the influence that the Recommendations have come to exert. While the term 'recommendations' conveys the sense of non-binding standards that can be modified as appropriate, the reality of the FATF's mutual evaluation process is such that there is no room for departure from the FATF's standards unless one is willing to countenance the FATF's criticism or, in more serious cases, 'grey-listing' or 'blacklisting'. So, the FATF's Recommendations are de facto binding in their entirety, with no scope for deviation.

A sensible alternative approach could involve the identification of a set of broad objectives that any given country's legal and regulatory regime ought to contribute to, with a further assortment of suggested measures that could be drawn upon as and when necessary to achieve those objectives. This would be consistent with the FATF's ongoing reorientation towards outcomes, as opposed to legislative implementation, also known as 'technical compliance'. While these developments are welcome, it is also time to ask whether technical compliance, with its emphasis on the letter of the Recommendations, should continue to have any place at all in the FATF's scheme.

For a sense of what this reorientation towards outcomes could look like in practice, suppose that the FATF's Recommendations were replaced with the following set of six guiding principles setting out countries' overall approach to financial crime:

Proposed Guiding Principles for an Effective AML/CTF Regime

1. The overarching objectives of AML/CTF law and regulation are: (a) to facilitate the investigation and prosecution of profit-generating crime, as well as the confiscation of its proceeds; and (b) to reduce the ease and profitability of money laundering, terrorist financing and proliferation financing.
2. Consistent with those overarching objectives, countries should institute legal and regulatory regimes that enable them, to the extent feasible, to: (a) exclude the proceeds of crime from the legitimate economy; and/or (b) collect high-quality intelligence on the economic activities of suspected criminals or terrorists.
3. Competent authorities and regulated businesses should seek to maximise intelligence-gathering opportunities that serve law enforcement purposes while minimising the risk of complicity in money laundering, terrorist financing or proliferation financing.
4. A country's legal and regulatory regime should ensure that the regulated businesses' AML/CTF compliance efforts are aligned with the country's law enforcement priorities. While the tools for this are subject to each country's discretion, they could include public–private partnerships or other arrangements for the sharing of up-to-date financial crime typologies; tailored reporting requirements, such as geographic targeting orders; or the regular provision of feedback on the quality of the regulated businesses' reporting.
5. Any country can identify regulated services subject to special AML/CTF rules. This can include essential services that must be provided to the population at large, such as a basic bank account, whose provision should not in and of itself attract liability for money laundering so long as applicable reporting obligations have been met. This can also include highly specialised, high-risk services that must not be provided if a suspicion exists that the proceeds of crime are involved.
6. The nature of the reporting obligations imposed on the regulated businesses should reflect a careful consideration of the types of reporting that best support law enforcement activities in the country concerned, as well as of the privacy trade-offs involved. Possible options include threshold-based reporting; suspicious activity reporting; unusual activity reporting; or tailored reporting requirements, such as geographic targeting orders.

These principles eschew any mention of the 'integrity of the financial system', the FATF's opaque encapsulation of the endpoint that its Recommendations are meant to advance, or the 'risk-based approach', which elevates vaguely defined 'risks' at the expense of the opportunities offered by financial surveillance. These principles also impose structure and coherence on a set of measures against financial crime that has emerged organically over the past three decades – one might say, in evolution rather than through intelligent design – and, as a result, have given rise to a regime that lacks in focus.

There is no suggestion that these principles should be the only set of international standards against financial crime. Part of the value of the FATF's prescriptiveness lies in providing clear benchmarks for countries that would have taken advantage of any less precise or exacting standards. Equally, though, there is a need to distinguish between those aspects of a country's framework that can be prescribed at the international level and those that must be left to individual countries' discretion, so long as their discretion is exercised in good faith to advance the guiding principles proposed above.

5.3 GENERAL AND TARGETED EXCLUSION

Not all existing measures against financial crime are undirected in the sense of being characterised by crude regulatory incentives that may or may not produce action aligned with law enforcement priorities. One area that is marked by no such lack of direction is sanctions: in fact, sanctions can be characterised as involving manual control by governments in that they expressly identify persons – individuals or companies – to be excluded from commercial interactions, be that on the grounds of their alleged involvement in crime or other undesirable behaviour.

Sanctions are focused on the exclusion of specific persons from commercial life, rather than the exclusion or surveillance of whole classes of transactions that involve money laundering or terrorist financing. This focus on specific targets is conceptually reminiscent of several historical precedents, such as the early medieval underpinnings of the English crime of receiving stolen goods – originally to do with harbouring thieves rather than stolen property – and various forms of 'outlawry' or 'civil death', although one should take care not to push those comparisons to a point where they become hyperbolic.

In light of this fundamental difference in approach, it is useful to think of sanctions as a form of *targeted* exclusion as distinct from *general* exclusion inherent in identifying activities that may involve money laundering or terrorist financing. Targeted exclusion gives rise to a different set of challenges: instead of considering whether a particular activity is suspicious, regulated businesses need to identify their exposure to sanctioned persons. For example, for a bank this may involve establishing whether a client company is indirectly controlled by a sanctioned person or whether the recipient of a payment that a client requests is on a sanctions list. Those may sound like technical implementation challenges, but their difficulty should not be underestimated, nor should the important questions of principle that they involve be overlooked.

These can be conceptualised as the *sanctions penumbra*. While the whole purpose of targeted financial sanctions is to exclude a specific person from day-to-day commercial interactions and freeze that person's assets, for it to be effective this form of exclusion must go beyond that person himself or herself. For instance, sanctions may extend to the companies, partnerships and trusts which that person controls (and, in turn, the property they control); others who act on behalf of that person (such as family members or close associates); and, in some cases, even those who benefit from that person's behaviour (here, again, family members are the likeliest category). How far this sanctions penumbra should reach is central to sanctions law, policy and practice, implicating considerations ranging from the effectiveness of sanctions to their unintended consequences to due process. There are two particular facets to this challenge that make it especially difficult to resolve.

First of all, the task of identifying who legally owns what – let alone who de facto controls what – continues to be daunting. This is yet another manifestation of the unresolved uncertainties about the limits of financial privacy: in a world where all ownership is transparent, sanctions enforcement would be far easier. By contrast, we live in a world where the creation of companies, partnerships and trusts makes it possible to obscure ownership, even though neither of those forms of commercial arrangements originally emerged with that objective in mind. Instead, *limited visibility* into ownership, which is now enabled by companies and trusts, has developed organically as a corollary of the *limited liability* conferred by the corporate form and the origins of trusts as primarily a means of arranging one's family affairs. Whether the privacy that companies and trusts can thus afford reflects the right balance between financial privacy and other competing values is an open question.

Second, since the identification of who controls what remains highly challenging, the issue arises of the proper respective roles of the government and businesses. The resources that businesses currently use for the identification of such property are limited. They primarily include third-party software databases and beneficial ownership registers, which generally rely on self-reporting by companies concerned and involve limited, if any, verification checks. While this does not entirely exhaust the array of resources available to large-scale and sophisticated businesses, such as banks, any manual investigation of a particular customer's affairs can only be undertaken in a small number of cases, which requires appropriate prioritisation by the bank.

The government plays multiple roles in directing and supporting those sanctions compliance efforts. This includes guiding businesses as to what cases should be prioritised (e.g. by pointing out high-priority countries, categories of customers and activities); specifying the procedures and techniques that are expected of regulated businesses in carrying out sanctions compliance checks and potentially even sharing information that would help businesses identify sanctioned individuals and property. So far, governments around the world, even those of major sanctioning powers like the US or the UK, have not truly stepped up to the task of embracing these roles – all too often, they limit themselves to publishing a list of sanctioned persons without creating a legal and institutional infrastructure that would ensure its genuine enforcement.

All those challenges are exacerbated by the fact that, unlike AML/CTF regulation, sanctions apply across the board to *everyone* within the sanctioning state's jurisdiction. Furthermore, they manifest themselves across various domains of criminal justice, including money laundering and terrorist financing. This proliferation of targeted financial sanctions raises two further policy questions. First, if a state resorts to sanctions in response to a particular category of crime (e.g. drug trafficking), it needs to determine how such sanctions fit within its broader efforts within that domain of criminal justice, including its use of criminal prosecutions and non-conviction-based asset forfeiture. Secondly, such a state needs to tackle the challenges of identifying sanctioned persons and assets, including by providing the private sector with guidance and support beyond the mere publication of a sanctions list.

One category of crime that is instructive is ransomware. Like money laundering and terrorist financing, it gives rise to a variation of the choice between exclusion and surveillance: should we deny ransomware groups the opportunity to make money through crime by criminalising the payment of ransom, likely at the cost of pushing some businesses to pay in secret, or gather information about ransom payments through reporting obligations – or, perhaps, none of the above? But there is also a key difference between money laundering and terrorist financing on the one hand and ransomware on the other hand: there is no international regulation of how ransomware payments should be treated, and therefore each state is working to figure out the optimal approach for itself. So far, despite an abundance of discussions and proposals, very few states have introduced ransomware regulation. This speaks to the caution that governments exhibit in tackling the difficult issues involved in the absence of FATF-style extraneous pressure.

One step that several governments have taken is the imposition of sanctions on certain ransomware groups. The most important practical consequence of such designations is that persons within the jurisdiction of the sanctioning state cannot lawfully make ransomware payments to sanctioned groups. This creates two categories of ransomware outfits: those that can be lawfully paid and those that cannot. In turn, this two-tier ransomware hierarchy gives rise to a perfect illustration of the policy and implementation issues involved in making targeted exclusion work. At the policy level, governments need to determine when to utilise sanctions, that is what makes a particular ransomware outfit so problematic that sanctions are the best course of action. At the implementation level, governments need to consider how they can support private-sector actors – including, in this case, not only regulated businesses but *any* business that might be affected by ransomware – in ascertaining whether they are being extorted by a sanctioned group. To various degrees, similar challenges arise across all areas of criminal justice where targeted financial sanctions are used.

5.4 CONCLUDING REMARKS

The current operation of financial crime rules is ripe with difficult questions, and the temptation of easy solutions looms large. Those solutions often come in the guise of arguing that the entire regulatory regime is based on false premises and should have been discarded – except that we are too far advanced on our misguided path for the multibillion-dollar 'compliance-industrial complex'[2] to be dismantled. So, the argument goes, we remain committed to a largely futile endeavour and the best we can do is spend less money on it: as the saying goes, 'making stupid cheap'.

This book has sought to demonstrate that this is not a fair reflection of reality. For all its imperfections, the existing financial crime regime has emerged as a response to the real and serious problems inherent in having no financial crime rules at all. A time traveller would not have to venture too far back into history to arrive in a world where one could deposit a briefcase brimming with cash into a bank account with no questions asked; not even the most rudimentary controls were in place to prevent the purchase of real estate by organised crime groups; and frail French grandmothers would take the train to Zurich for no other reason than taking advantage of the tax avoidance opportunities on offer. The current regime has evolved incrementally to address those and other related issues through the pursuit of what are, in essence, two objectives: the exclusion of criminal actors from the legitimate economy and their surveillance.

There is an important difference between those two objectives. Financial surveillance is instrumental in that it is not an end in itself, but a means of achieving law enforcement outcomes such as criminal convictions and confiscation of criminally obtained property. By contrast, exclusion can either be instrumental, if aimed at the disruption of criminal operations by denying criminals access to the services they need, or an end in itself if conceived of as a means of precluding regulated businesses' complicity in crime. It might be tempting to dismiss the latter position as a puritanical, moralistic pursuit, but to do so would risk overlooking the broader context. Our notions of proper business conduct are expressive of overall social morality, and in this sense financial crime rules are a symptom of societal shifts in attitudes. They manifest a vision of society where businesses, including flagship enterprises, are not allowed to profit from a criminal clientele. The merits of that vision could itself form the subject of studies in ethics and economics, but it would be far too cavalier to reject it as inherently flawed. Tellingly, even among the most critical scholars of financial crime, the consensus is that it is scandalous for big business to profit from crime.

This way of thinking about the objectives of financial crime rules also has implications for the study of their effectiveness. Three leading scholars in this area once

[2] The term was coined in Tereza Østbø Kuldova, *Compliance-Industrial Complex: The Operating System of a Pre-Crime Society* (Palgrave, 2022).

asked whether the effectiveness of the regime could be evaluated without better data – their answer being 'no'.[3] That is probably right, but one might also wonder whether it could be evaluated *with* better data: and, if so, what that data could be. In relation to both exclusion and surveillance, there are ways of ascertaining that the AML/CTF regime does *not* work: be it a complete lack of the required reporting (as was the case in the US for the first fifteen years or so following the adoption of the Bank Secrecy Act) or an abundance of cases involving the wilful complicity of major financial institutions in money laundering (as was the case in Switzerland between the 1970s and 1990s).

It is far harder to think of the kinds of data that could ever prove the regime *does* work, or even give us a good sense of the value for money it provides. Financial intelligence is only one enabling component of successful law enforcement outcomes. It is therefore difficult to judge the effectiveness of the financial surveillance of criminals. For example, neither the number of SARs nor whether they trigger an investigation is a good indicator of their quality. Likewise, a financial investigation could be done well yet not lead to a law enforcement outcome. And, of course, successful exclusion of criminal actors from the legitimate economy is impossible to quantify because one cannot prove a negative: are criminal actors truly excluded from the economy, or merely undetected?

This does not mean that no evaluation of effectiveness should ever be attempted, but simply that any truly rigorous, scientific assessment will remain elusive. Some version of the FATF's current methodology, which relies as much on gathering the views of governmental and law enforcement stakeholders as it does on quantitative data, is a necessary evil. As discussed earlier, however, the FATF's Recommendations and mutual evaluation alike would benefit from a clearer articulation of the objectives of the regime in line with the guiding principles proposed above, instead of vague references to the integrity of the international financial system.

It is helpful to place our inability to measure the effectiveness of the financial crime regime in its proper context. Criminal justice is always riven by existential uncertainties about what we achieve by doing the things that we generally feel are right. Suppose we agree that, as postulated in the first of the guiding principles proposed above, one of the overarching objectives of financial crime regulation is to facilitate the prosecution of serious crime and the confiscation of its proceeds. But ultimately all we can ever do is shift the burden of explanation further down the line: after all, what is the point of criminal punishment and confiscation? Similarly, if we drill down to the very basics of criminal law, we are left with no choice but to question its fundamental assumption of free will. If our behaviour is ultimately a product of how our brains are wired and of the circumstances we ended up in, then the whole notion of criminal responsibility is built on illusory foundations.

[3] Michael Levi, Peter Reuter and Terence Halliday, 'Can the AML System Be Evaluated without Better Data?' (2018) 69(2) *Crime, Law and Social Change* 307.

One might be on solid intellectual ground in arguing that it is, but that is utterly irrelevant to the question of how we – living as though we have free will – structure our day-to-day interactions.

More pragmatically, everyone would agree that reducing the rates of crime would be a good thing, but financial crime controls and other criminal justice measures are *not* adopted in single-minded pursuit of crime reduction. They give expression to a wider range of moral instincts and intuitions, including a visceral sense that crime should not go unpunished, nor should one profit from it. Or, put simply, we try to do what feels inherently right as a response to crime. This is not to deny the role of rationality or evidence-based analysis, but to highlight its limitations.

That is also true of the financial crime regime. Suppose someone asked you whether, on the whole, it would be a bad thing if legitimate businesses profited from crime. The answer would likely be a resounding 'yes'. Suppose, further, that someone asked you whether law enforcement agencies should gather financial intelligence in respect of money laundering, terrorist financing, ransomware payments or sanctions evasion. Here, too, the question answers itself. These are plausible and intuitive responses but, as this book demonstrates, they are also more than that: they are also a rational reaction to the problems that emerged in the absence of any rules giving expression to those intuitions about business and crime.

The real issue, therefore, is not whether we should continue to develop our financial crime regime and invest into it. Nor, in broad terms, is there anything wrong with the twin pillars of exclusion and surveillance that it rests upon. The question remains of how existing rules and practices can be re-calibrated to better support those objectives with fewer unintended consequences. As this book has outlined, there are a few options, all of which involve some trade-offs. While there is therefore no straightforward solution to the problems involved, there is a coherent and pragmatic framework for thinking about the choices that need to be made by those working in this crucial area of law, policy and practice.

Annex: List of Interviews

All of the interviews were conducted on a no-attribution basis unless indicated otherwise.

1. Interview with a US lawyer specialising in AML/CTF (A), 14 November 2023.
2. Interview with a Canadian law enforcement expert, 27 November 2023.
3. Interview with a US lawyer specialising in AML/CTF (B), 27 November 2023.
4. Interview with a US academic lawyer specialising in AML/CTF, 1 December 2023.
5. Interview with Bruce Zagaris, 4 December 2023 (on the record).
6. Interview with Prof Mark Pieth, 15 January 2024 (on the record).
7. Interview with a Swiss banking expert, 17 January 2024.
8. Interview with two international AML/CTF experts, 18 January 2024.
9. Interview with a UK AML/CTF expert, 30 January 2024.
10. Interview with a Swiss sanctions expert, 5 June 2024.
11. Interview with an Australian AML/CTF expert (A), 14 June 2024.
12. Interview with two UK law enforcement experts, 28 June 2024.
13. Interview with an Australian AML/CTF expert (B), 1 July 2024.
14. Interview with Dr Katie Benson, 1 July 2024 (on the record).

Index

www.ingramcontent.com/pod-product-compliance
Lightning Source LLC
LaVergne TN
LVHW020234210926
848481LV00016B/1851
* 9 7 8 1 0 0 9 6 0 9 8 2 1 *